First World War
and Army of Occupation
War Diary
France, Belgium and Germany

24 DIVISION
73 Infantry Brigade
Duke of Cambridge's Own (Middlesex Regiment)
13th Battalion
21 August 1915 - 29 November 1919

WO95/2219/1

The Naval & Military Press Ltd
www.nmarchive.com
Published in association with The National Archives

Published by

The Naval & Military Press Ltd

Unit 10 Ridgewood Industrial Park,

Uckfield, East Sussex,

TN22 5QE England

Tel: +44 (0) 1825 749494

www.naval-military-press.com

www.nmarchive.com

This diary has been reprinted in facsimile from the original. Any imperfections are inevitably reproduced and the quality may fall short of modern type and cartographic standards.

© Crown Copyright
Images reproduced by permission of The National Archives, London, England, 2015.

Contents

Document type	Place/Title	Date From	Date To
Heading	WO95/2219/1		
Heading	13th Bn Middx Regt Aug 1915-Nov 1919		
Heading	13th Battn. The Middlesex Regiment. August And September (21.8.15 To 30.9.15) 1915		
War Diary	Pirbright	21/08/1915	21/08/1915
War Diary	Chobham Common	24/08/1915	24/08/1915
War Diary	Pirbright	31/08/1915	01/09/1915
War Diary	Bologne	02/09/1915	03/09/1915
War Diary	Maresquel		
War Diary	Crequy	03/09/1915	03/09/1915
War Diary	Torcy	06/09/1915	06/09/1915
War Diary	Crequy	21/09/1915	21/09/1915
War Diary	Laires	22/09/1915	22/09/1915
War Diary	Lecleme	23/09/1915	24/09/1915
War Diary	Beuvry	25/09/1915	25/09/1915
War Diary	Vermelle	25/09/1915	30/09/1915
War Diary	Lambres	30/09/1915	30/09/1915
War Diary	Vermelles	26/09/1915	28/09/1915
War Diary	Fontes	29/09/1915	29/09/1915
War Diary	Rombly	30/09/1915	30/09/1915
Miscellaneous	Enclosures. 13th Middlesex Regt.		
War Diary	Havre	01/09/1915	01/09/1915
War Diary	Hesden	02/09/1915	02/09/1915
Miscellaneous	Casualties Sept 1st Nov 30.1915 Appendix C		
Miscellaneous			
Heading	24th Division 13th. Middx Vol. I Nov 15		
War Diary	Lambres	01/10/1915	02/10/1915
War Diary	Herzeele	03/10/1915	06/10/1915
War Diary	Proven	07/10/1915	11/10/1915
War Diary	Reninghelst	12/10/1915	14/10/1915
War Diary	St Eloi (Left Centre Sector)	14/10/1915	14/10/1915
War Diary	Reninghelst	19/10/1915	19/10/1915
War Diary	St Eloi (Right Centre Sector)	22/10/1915	23/10/1915
War Diary	Reninghelst	27/10/1915	27/10/1915
War Diary	Reninghelst	29/09/1915	03/11/1915
War Diary	St Eloi	05/11/1915	08/11/1915
War Diary	Reninghelst	12/11/1915	13/11/1915
War Diary	St Eloi	15/11/1915	19/11/1915
War Diary	Reninghelst	20/11/1915	20/11/1915
War Diary	Eecke	21/11/1915	22/11/1915
War Diary	Ochtezeele	23/11/1915	23/11/1915
War Diary	Hellebourcq	24/11/1915	25/11/1915
War Diary	Zouafques & Wolphus		
War Diary	Wolphus	26/11/1915	27/11/1915
War Diary	Hellebourcq	28/11/1915	29/11/1915
Heading	Summary Of Casualties For November 1915		
Heading	24th Div 13th Middx Vol: 2 December 1915		
War Diary	Hellebroucq	01/12/1915	31/12/1915
Heading	13th Battalion Middlesex Regiment. January 1916.		
Heading	24th. Div 13 Middx Vol 3 Jan'16.		

Type	Location	From	To
War Diary	Hellebroucq	01/01/1916	01/01/1916
War Diary	St Omer	04/01/1916	05/01/1916
War Diary	Hellebroucq	06/01/1916	07/01/1916
War Diary	Poperinghe	07/01/1916	07/01/1916
War Diary	G 24.C. 6.6. Map 2.8.	08/01/1916	14/01/1916
War Diary	Sanctuary Wood I 18.d. & J 13.C.	15/01/1916	16/01/1916
War Diary	Sanctuary Wood	16/01/1916	18/01/1916
War Diary	Belgian Dugouts H.23.B.	18/01/1916	18/01/1916
War Diary	H 23 b.	19/01/1916	21/01/1916
War Diary	Sanctuary Wood	22/01/1916	26/01/1916
War Diary	Belgian Dugouts	27/01/1916	30/01/1916
War Diary	Camp B	31/01/1916	31/01/1916
Miscellaneous Diagram etc			
Miscellaneous Heading	13th Battalion Middlesex Regiment. February 1916.		
War Diary	Camp. B. G11 C 5.2.	01/02/1916	05/02/1916
War Diary	H Trenches I 12. A & C.	07/02/1916	10/02/1916
War Diary	H Trenches	11/02/1916	11/02/1916
War Diary	Ypres I 7.d.	12/02/1916	17/02/1916
War Diary	H Trenches	17/02/1916	19/02/1916
War Diary	Ypres	20/02/1916	24/02/1916
War Diary	Camp A G11.C.4.3.	25/02/1916	29/02/1916
Miscellaneous Heading	13th Battalion Middlesex Regiment. March 1916.		
War Diary	Camp A. G 11.C.	29/02/1916	02/03/1916
War Diary	Sanctuary Wood Trenches	03/03/1916	07/03/1916
War Diary	Belgian Chateau	08/03/1916	16/03/1916
War Diary	Camp A G11.C.	16/03/1916	18/03/1916
War Diary	X17.A.3.1.	19/03/1916	25/03/1916
War Diary	T2b.c.8.9.	26/03/1916	30/03/1916
War Diary	Kortepyp	31/03/1916	31/03/1916
War Diary	Trenches 136-140 Opposite Messines	31/03/1916	31/03/1916
Miscellaneous Heading	13th Battalion Middlesex Regiment. April 1916		
Miscellaneous	A Form. Messages And Signals.	05/04/1916	05/04/1916
War Diary	Trenches 136-141. Opposite Messines	01/04/1916	07/04/1916
War Diary	Red Lodge T. 18d.7.4	07/04/1916	12/04/1916
War Diary	Trenches 136-141.	13/04/1916	19/04/1916
War Diary	Kortepyp Camp T 26.G.	19/04/1916	30/04/1916
War Diary	Trenches 136-141.	29/04/1916	30/04/1916
Map Heading	13th Battalion Middlesex Regiment. May 1916		
War Diary	Red Lodge	30/04/1916	07/05/1916
War Diary	Messines Trenches T135-140	07/05/1916	13/05/1916
War Diary	Kortepyp Camp	13/05/1916	19/05/1916
War Diary	Messines Trenches	26/05/1916	31/05/1916
War Diary	Red Lodge	27/05/1916	31/05/1916
Miscellaneous Heading	13th Battalion Middlesex Regiment. June 1916		
War Diary	Messines Trenches	03/06/1916	12/06/1916
War Diary	Kortepyp Camp	16/06/1916	16/06/1916
War Diary	Wakefield Huts Locre M29a Sheet 28	17/06/1916	17/06/1916
War Diary	Spanlroekmole Trenches E1-F5	19/06/1916	28/06/1916
War Diary	Kemmel Shelters N19d. Sheet 28		
Miscellaneous			

Type	Description	From	To
Map	Sketch Map IV		
Heading	13th Battn. The Middlesex Regiment. July 1916		
War Diary	Kemmel Shelters	01/07/1916	05/07/1916
War Diary	Wytschaete Trenches G4-J3 Map N 24	06/07/1916	09/07/1916
War Diary	Badojoy Huts. Locre	09/07/1916	09/07/1916
War Diary	Dranoutre M 35-36	11/07/1916	18/07/1916
War Diary	Fletre Q 34	19/07/1916	24/07/1916
War Diary	Mothens-Vidame	25/07/1916	31/07/1916
Heading	13th Battalion Middlesex Regiment. August 1916.		
Miscellaneous	13rd 2B.	08/09/1916	08/09/1916
War Diary	Happy Valley	02/08/1916	08/08/1916
War Diary	Trenches B.A.1 Etc	17/08/1916	17/08/1916
War Diary	Arrow Head Copse	18/08/1916	20/08/1916
War Diary	Craters	21/08/1916	22/08/1916
War Diary	Sandpits	23/08/1916	31/08/1916
Miscellaneous			
Heading	13th Battalion Middlesex Regiment. September 1916		
War Diary	Pommier Redoubt	01/09/1916	11/09/1916
War Diary	Mouflers	11/09/1916	19/09/1916
War Diary	Bruay	20/09/1916	30/09/1916
Heading	13th Battalion. Middlesex Regiment. October 1916		
War Diary		01/10/1916	31/10/1916
Heading	13th Battalion Middlesex Regiment. November 1916		
Heading	War Diary 13th Middlesex Regt For The Month Of November 1916		
War Diary		01/11/1916	30/11/1916
Miscellaneous	Summary Of Casualties During The Month.		
Heading	13th Battalion Middlesex Regiment. December 1916		
Heading	Confidential War Diary Of 13th Middlesex Regiment For The Month Of December 1916		
War Diary		01/12/1916	30/12/1916
Miscellaneous	Summary Of Casualties During The Month.		
Heading	War Diary Of 13th Bn. The Middlesex Regiment For The Month Of January 1917.		
War Diary		01/01/1917	31/01/1917
Miscellaneous	Summary Of Casualties During The Month.		
Heading	13th Bn. The Middlesex Regiment War Diary For The Month Of February 1917.		
War Diary		01/02/1917	28/02/1917
Miscellaneous	Summary Of Casualties During The Month.		
Heading	War Diary For The Month Of March 1917 Of 13th Battalion The Middlesex Regiment		
War Diary		01/03/1917	31/03/1917
Miscellaneous	Summary Of Casualties During The Month.		
Heading	13th Battn. Middlesex Regiment 73rd Infantry Brigade 24th Division April 1917		
Heading	13th Middlesex Regt. For The Month Of April 1917		
War Diary		31/03/1917	30/04/1917
Miscellaneous	Summary Of Casualties During The Month.		
Heading	War Diary Of 13th Battalion Middlesex Regiment For Month Of May 1917		
War Diary		01/05/1917	31/05/1917
Miscellaneous	Summary Of Casualties During The Month.		
Heading	War Diary Of 13th Battalion Middlesex Regt. For Month Of June 1917		
War Diary		01/06/1917	30/06/1917

Miscellaneous	Summary Of Casualties During The Month.		
War Diary	War Diary Of 13th Battalion Middlesex Regiment For Month Of July 1917		
War Diary		01/07/1917	31/07/1917
Miscellaneous	Summary Of Casualties During The Month.		
Heading	13th. Battn. Middlesex Regiment For The Month Of August 1917.		
War Diary		01/08/1917	31/08/1917
Miscellaneous	Summary Of Casualties During The Month.		
Heading	13th Bn. Middlesex Regiment For The Month Of September 1917.		
War Diary		01/09/1917	30/09/1917
Miscellaneous	Summary Of Casualties During The Month.		
Heading	13th Battalion The Middlesex Regiment For The Month Of October 1917.		
War Diary		01/10/1917	31/10/1917
Miscellaneous	Summary Of Casualties During The Month		
Heading	13th. Battalion Middlesex Regiment For The Month Of November 1917		
War Diary		01/11/1917	30/11/1917
Miscellaneous	Summary Of Casualties During The Month		
Heading	13th. Battalion Middlesex Regiment For The Month Of December 1917		
War Diary	Area N.W. Of Epehy	01/12/1917	31/12/1917
Miscellaneous	Summary Of Casualties During The Month		
Heading	13th Battalion Middlesex Regiment For The Month Of January 1918		
War Diary		01/01/1918	31/01/1918
Miscellaneous	Summary Of Casualties During The Month		
Heading	13th Bn. Middlesex Regiment For The Month Of February 1918		
War Diary		01/02/1918	01/02/1918
War Diary	Hervilly	02/02/1918	15/02/1918
War Diary	In The Line	16/02/1918	28/02/1918
Heading	13th Battalion Middlesex Regiment March 1918		
Heading	13th Bn. Middlesex Regiment For The Month Of March 1918		
War Diary	Bernes	02/03/1918	21/03/1918
War Diary	Vermand	22/03/1918	31/03/1918
Miscellaneous	Summary Of Casualties During The Month.		
Heading	13th Battn. The Middlesex Regiment. April 1918		
Heading	13th. Bn. Middlesex Regiment For The Month Of April 1918.		
War Diary	Thezy Glimont	01/04/1918	03/04/1918
War Diary	Bois De Gentelles	04/04/1918	05/04/1918
War Diary	Longeau Saleux	06/04/1918	06/04/1918
War Diary	S. Valery	07/04/1918	07/04/1918
War Diary	Fressenneville	08/04/1918	17/04/1918
War Diary	Houdain	18/04/1918	30/04/1918
Miscellaneous	Casualties During April 1918 Supplementary Casualty List March 1918		
Heading	13th Bn. The Middlesex Regiment For The Month Of May 1918		
War Diary	Bully Grenay	01/05/1918	01/05/1918
War Diary	In The Line	02/05/1918	11/05/1918
War Diary	Les Brebis	12/05/1918	18/05/1918

War Diary	In The Line	19/05/1918	30/05/1918
War Diary	Les Brebis	31/05/1918	31/05/1918
Heading	War Diary For Month Of June. 13th Battalion Middlesex Regt.		
War Diary	Les Brebis	01/06/1918	02/06/1918
War Diary	In The Line	05/06/1918	17/06/1918
War Diary	Les Brebis	18/06/1918	26/06/1918
Miscellaneous	Summary Of Casualties During The Month.		
Heading	13th Bn The Middlesex Regiment For The Month Of July 1918		
War Diary	In The Field	01/07/1918	05/07/1918
War Diary	Les Brebis	06/07/1918	08/07/1918
War Diary	In The Field	11/07/1918	23/07/1918
War Diary	Les Brebis	24/07/1918	31/07/1918
Miscellaneous	Summary Of Casualties During The Month		
Heading	13th Bn Middlesex Regiment For The Month Of August 1918		
War Diary	In The Field	03/08/1918	30/08/1918
Miscellaneous	Summary Of Casualties During The Month.		
Heading	13th Middlesex Regiment War Diary.		
War Diary	In The Field	01/09/1918	30/09/1918
Miscellaneous	Summary Of Casualties During The Month.		
Heading	13th Bn Middlesex Regiment For The Month Of October 1918.		
War Diary	In The Field	01/10/1918	30/10/1918
Miscellaneous	Summary Of Casualties During October, 1918		
Heading	13th Bn Middlesex Regiment For The Month Of November 1918		
War Diary	In The Field	01/11/1918	11/11/1918
War Diary	Le Louvion	11/11/1918	30/11/1918
Miscellaneous	Summary Of Casualties During November, 1918.		
Heading	War Diary 13 Middlesex Regt		
War Diary	La Glanerie	01/12/1918	28/12/1918
Miscellaneous	Summary Of Casualties During December 1917.		
Heading	13th Bn. Middlesex Regiment For The Month Of January 1919		
War Diary	Rumes Belgium	01/01/1919	26/01/1919
Heading	War Diary 13th Bn. Middlesex Regt		
War Diary	Rumes Belgium	01/02/1919	28/02/1919
Heading	24 Division 73 Infantry Brigade 13 Battalion Middles Regiment March 1919 Missing.		
War Diary	No 2 Reception Camp. Harfleur	01/04/1919	31/05/1919
Heading	Headquarters, 98th, Infantry Brigade.	01/07/1919	01/07/1919
War Diary	No 2 Reception Camp Harfleur	01/06/1919	09/06/1919
War Diary	Terdeghem	12/06/1919	30/06/1919
Heading	24 Division 73 Infantry Brigade 13 Battalion Middlesex Regiment July 1919 Missing.		
War Diary	Terdeghem	01/08/1919	31/08/1919
Miscellaneous	War Office (S.D.2), London. S.W. 1.	03/10/1919	03/10/1919
War Diary	Terdeghem	03/09/1919	30/09/1919
Miscellaneous	War Office (S.D.2). London. S.W.1.	01/11/1919	01/11/1919
War Diary	Terdeghem	02/10/1919	02/10/1919
War Diary	France	05/10/1919	31/10/1919
War Diary	Terdeghem	01/11/1919	14/11/1919
War Diary	No 4 Rest Camp Bouldene	15/11/1919	29/11/1919

WO 95
22 19/1

24TH DIVISION
73RD INFY BDE

13TH BN MIDDX REGT
AUG ~~SEP~~ 1915-NOV 1919

24TH DIVISION
73RD INFY BDE

73rd Inf.Bde.
24th Div.

Battn. disembarked Boulogne from England 2.9.15.

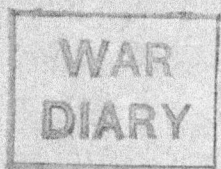

13th BATTN. THE MIDDLESEX REGIMENT.

AUGUST AND SEPTEMBER

(21.8.15 to 30.9.15)

1 9 1 5

Nov 1919

Attached:

Appendices A, B, C & D.

WAR DIARY
or
INTELLIGENCE SUMMARY

13ᵃ Batt. MIDDLESEX REGT.

Army Form C. 2118

Instructions regarding War Diaries and Intelligence Summaries are contained in F.S. Regs., Part II. and the Staff Manual respectively. Title Pages will be prepared in manuscript.

(Erase heading not required.)

Place	Date	Hour	Summary of Events and Information	Remarks and references to Appendices
PIRBRIGHT	21/8/15		The 2ⁿᵈ Division received orders for active service, overseas, and the 13ᵗʰ Middlesex Regt. was notified that it would probably embark about the 29 August.	
CHOBHAM COMMON	24/8/15		H.M. King George V. with H.M. Queen Mary and H.R.H. Princess Mary, inspected the 2ⁿᵈ Division while working in trenches, and passed along the trenches held by the 13ᵗʰ Middlesex.	
PIRBRIGHT	31/8/15	2.0 am	On the morning of the 31ˢᵗ at 2.0 am the advance party of the Battalion marched to WOKING and entrained. There for SOUTHAMPTON DOCKS.	For detail of this party see Appendix A.
	1/9/15		The Battalion entrained at BROOKWOOD STATION, in 2 trains at 6.57 pm and 6.20 pm in pouring rain; and proceeded to FOLKESTONE via GUILDFORD and REDHILL and FOLKESTONE Harbour was reached soon after 9.45 pm and in the pouring rain embarked in S.S. Duchess of Argyll. BOULOGNE was reached about midnight, disembarking the Battalion marched to a Rest Camp about 1½ miles out of the Town, where it remained for the day.	For detail of officers who sailed see Appendix B.
BOULOGNE	2/9/15			
	3/9/15		The Battalion paraded at 4.15 am, and marched to the Railway station and entrained in one train at 5.0 am and proceeded to MARESQUEL arriving shortly before 8.0 am. Here it was joined by the advance party and transport. It marched in pouring rain via BEAURAINVILLE (where it halted for breakfast), LOISON, OFFIN, HESMOND, LEBIEZ, ROYON, TORCY to CREQUY, which was reached about 3.30 pm and the men were billeted in the various farms and sheds of the village. 2 companies of the 7ᵗʰ Northants being also in the village. Battalion HQrs were established in an empty house "La Villa Marguerite".	
MARESQUEL				
CREQUY	3ʳᵈ Sept to 21ˢᵗ		The 2ⁿᵈ Division Headquarters were fixed at ROYON, and the 73ʳᵈ I. Brigade at TORCY. During this time the Battalion remained in billets, and during which time the 73ʳᵈ Brigade and sometimes the 2ⁿᵈ Division were frequently concentrated for manoeuvres and marches.	

Army Form C. 2118

WAR DIARY
or
INTELLIGENCE SUMMARY
(Erase heading not required.)

13th Middlesex Regt.

Place	Date	Hour	Summary of Events and Information	Remarks and references to Appendices
TORCY	6 Sept		Lieut-General Haking Commanding the 11th Corps met the Officers at TORCY and informed them that the Division had come under his command in the XI Corps.	
CREQUY	21st Sept		Sudden orders to march were received, and at 8.0pm the Division moved off — The Battalion forming the Advance Guard. The march was CREQUY was fairly hilly; (the night was moonlight). The route was CREQUY (where the Division concentrated) through BRUGES - ZUGY - BEAUMETZ-lès-AIRES to LAIRES, which was reached about 1.0am; the remainder of the night	
LAIRES	22nd Sept		was spent in various farms and barns. The march was resumed in the evening of the 22nd at 8.0pm; the Battalion forming the rear guard, the march was hard (about 14 miles) although there was a bright moon. The route was LAIRES - FEBVIN - PALFART - WESTREHEM - AUCHY-au-BOIS, - St HILAIRE - BOURECQ, - LILLERS to	
LECLEME	23rd Sept		L'ECLEME at 3.0am, where the Battalion were again billeted in farms and barns. The Battalion remained in billets for the rest of the day, and	
	24th Sept		Orders were received that the Division would again march in the evening, and at 6.30pm the march was resumed, the 7th Northants leading; the route taken was L'ECLEME - GONNEHEM - CHOCQUES - and through the outskirts of BETHUNE to	
BEUVRY	25th Sept		BEUVRY which was reached soon after 11.0pm, and the Battalion billeted. Disturbed by a heavy firing the next morning from our big guns; the Battalion received orders to march about 10 am and marched E along the VERMELLE ROAD, meeting	

WAR DIARY or INTELLIGENCE SUMMARY

Army Form C. 2118

Place	Date	Hour	Summary of Events and Information	Remarks and references to Appendices
VERMELLES	25th Sept		Stragglers of wounded (mostly Scotch Regiments) and some German prisoners. On arrival about 12 noon W. of SAILLY-LA-BOURSE the Battalion was diverted to the left, and formed up W of a small stream W of VERMELLE, where it was joined by the 71st and 72nd Infantry Brigades. (The remainder of the 73rd Infantry Brigade having proceeded). Soon after 4.0 pm instructions were received to move up E of VERMELLE, which was done in gathering darkness. The Battalion assembled near the railway at the W end of a long communication trench (BARTS ALLEY) leading from the original fire trenches, some 3/4 mile to the front. Here the Battalion for the first time came under fire (shells & rifle fire). About 10.0 pm the [crossed out] Battalion advanced (in artillery formation) over the open and occupied the trenches (Old British support line) which were in many places full of water, up to the men's knees. Fosse No 8 de BETHUNE, and the HOHENZOLLERN REDOUBT were to the left front and HULLUCH QUARRIES to their front and LOOS to the right front. Shell fire and frequent bursts of rifle fire continued all night. About 3.0 am orders instructions from G.O. C 73rd Infantry	
	26th Sept		Brigade. Col. Oliver, the adjutant and 2 companies A. & D., proceeded across the open to the left front towards the "Slag Heap" of No 8 FOSSE; 1 platoon of B Coy accompanied the Brigadier General as escort; from this time this party of the Battalion were continuously under heavy shell and rifle fire, repeated attacks being made by the Germans on the trenches they held, and by skillful use of machine guns and counter attacks by bombers they successfully held their own; although suffering several casualties from the enemy's fire, and feeling severely the want of food and water.	

Place	Date	Hour	Summary of Events and Information	Remarks and references to Appendices
VERMELLES	26th to 30th		Owing to the hurried departure from BEUVRY on the morning of Saturday the 25th, the Battalion had marched before rations that day went received, owing to the isolated position of the men on the front trenches, it was impossible to place any supplies, except by night, on the Sunday and Monday nights. A small quantity of water, biscuit, and ammunition was sent from the companies in support trenches to those in front, but those men would have suffered much more severely if it had not been for the kindness of the 2nd Queens Regt who generously shared with them what rations they had. The trenches occupied by these 2 companies were German Support trenches South West of the HOHENZOLLERN REDOUBT to the west of two German communication trenches (Big and Little Willie) leading from that Redoubt to the German support trenches; a Coy (Capt Hill) was on the left facing the Slag heap and occupied a portion of the trench going to the left joining up with the 2nd Queens facing FOSSE No 8). D Coy was on the right joining up with the 2nd Queens on the left of the line under the position communication trench on the SW side of the Slag heap HAINE'S Church. (The C.O. lived with this company). Heavy fighting on the left of the Battalion very precarious, but it held on to its ground until relieved on the morning of the 29th. when the party numbering about 170 all ranks marched back to BEUVRY, and thence dry town to LILLERS the remainder of the Battalion	
LAMBRES	30th		and marched to LAMBRES where they rejoined the 30th (in billets) about 11.0 am on Thursday	

WAR DIARY or INTELLIGENCE SUMMARY

Army Form C. 2118

Place	Date	Hour	Summary of Events and Information	Remarks and references to Appendices
VERMELLES	26/9/15		After the two companies had gone to the advanced trenches on the Sunday morning (26th) the other companies (B & C) were entered to occupy the length of trenches previously held by the Battalion. About 2.0pm on Sunday afternoon most of them were moved to the trenches a 100 yards or so in front, owing to shell fire, which had found out the exact range of the occupied trenches; a similar further change had to be made on the Monday afternoon owing to the same cause. A heavy attack 5.9pm cures on made about 5.0pm by the Germans on the left, but was repulsed by men of various regts (R. Scots – Black Watch – Argyll & Sutherlands – Gordons) assisted by Northants and Middlesex who were moved down to meet the attack. Throughout Monday night this attack was constantly repeated, but in every case were successfully met.	
	27/9/15		About 8.0am the Battalion was relieved and received orders to withdraw – which it did by BART'S ALLEY. After a short rest, it marched through VERMELLES to SAILLY-LABOURSE, where it was visited by Major General Sir J Ramsay Commanding 2nd Division; who warmly congratulated the Battalion on the work it had done. Brigadier General Bagot Commanding the 73rd Infantry Brigade also visited the Battalion. A draft of 40 NCOs and men had arrived at the bivouacs. About 5.0pm orders were received that the Battalion would move in the evening; at 8.30pm when the Battalion paraded to move off – it mustered 686 of all ranks – in round numbers. It marched to the NOEUX-LES-MINES about 3 miles, and was entrained about 12.0 midnight and	
	28/9/15	8.0am	arrived at BERGUETTE STATION about 2.0 AM. Wandering about in the dark it reached	

Army Form C. 2118

WAR DIARY
or
INTELLIGENCE SUMMARY
(Erase heading not required.)

13 M(D)DLESEX Regt   Vol...

Place	Date	Hour	Summary of Events and Information	Remarks and references to Appendices
FONTES	29/9/15	5.0 AM	1/2 billets about 5.0am at FONTES and by 6.0pm were settled down in billets.	
		4.0 pm	About 4.0pm was moved from FONTES a distance of some 2 miles to a little village – ROMBLY – where it was joined by the Transport, which had travelled by road.	
ROMBLY	30/9/15	10. am	The Battalion moved at 10 am to LAMBRES a distance of some 3½ miles, where it was billeted. Here Lt. Olivant and some 70 men rejoined, and the Battalion was enabled for the first time to render a casualty return.	

FIRST CASUALTY RETURN from Sept 25th – 29th

	Killed		Wounded		Missing	
	OFFICERS.	Other Ranks.	O.	O.R.	O.	O.R.
	—	13.	7	77	3	70

Names of officers wounded :- Major J. H.R. Cox.
Capt. A.C. Frost.
Lieut C.K. Allen
2nd Lieut W.L. Wong (slight)
S. Smith
R. Worthington
J.A. Bailey.

Sick in hospital. Capt. F.O. Dickit.

Missing   Capt. C.E. Hill   (since reported believed killed)
Capt. B. Wells   (since reported wounded in England.)
Lieut C.E. Harman (— · — · — and prisoner of war)

DRAFTS.

A draft of 40 NCOs & men arrived on the 28th from the 15th Battn Middlesex Regt. They appear to be of good physique and efficiency.

E.P. Hoover, Colonel

13th Middlesex Regt.

Enclosures.

War Diary for September 1915
~~October 1915~~
~~November 1915~~

Appendix A. Advance party's journey on leaving England.

Appendix B. Roll of Officers who embarked with the Battalion.

Appendix C. Summary of casualties for 1st three months

Appendix D. Summary of gallant deeds especially noticed at Vermelles. Sept 25th – 28th 1915.

WAR DIARY
on APPENDIX A
INTELLIGENCE SUMMARY

Army Form C. 2118

4th Fusiliers Regt
13th Middlesex Regt

Place	Date	Hour	Summary of Events and Information	Remarks and references to Appendices
Account of the advance party from the time it left PIRBRIGHT until it joined the Battalion again.			The advance party consisted of the Machine Gunners, Transport and details, and was under the command of Major E.J. SHARPE. Lieutenants C.B.R. KING (M.G.O.) and E.J. TYDEMAN (Transport officer) accompanied the party; also Sergt Major ANDREWS (newly appointed Sergt Major) and 105 other ranks, 78 horses and mules, and 19 waggons. On arrival at SOUTHAMPTON DOCKS, this party embarked in S.S. Matheran with mounted portions of the 104th and 129th Field Corps R.E. and transport of 7th Fusiliers. The Matheran	
HAVRE.	1st Sept		sailed at 4.0pm and duly arrived at HAVRE about 3.0am on the 1st September. It disembarked a little before noon, and marched in pouring rain to Camp No 5 about 3 miles from the Dock. After a soaking night in camp, this party proceeded at 5.0am to Point 1. (Railway Station) and found by the Transport of the 12th R. Fusiliers left HAVRE, and proceeded via ROUEN, BUCHY, ABBEVILLE to HESDIN, where it detrained at 2.0am on the 2nd Sept, and in	
HESDIN	2nd Sept		pouring rain starting at 4.45am, it reached MARESQUEL about 8.0am, just as the Battalion had arrived, and reported Headquarters.	

E. Olson Colonel
Comdg 13th Middx Regt.

WAR DIARY
or APPENDIX B.
INTELLIGENCE SUMMARY

13th Middlesex Regt   Army Form C. 2118

(Erase heading not required.)

Place	Date	Hour	Summary of Events and Information	Remarks and references to Appendices

List of Officers & Battalion Strength when sailed with the Battalion.

The following Officers accompanied the Battalion.

Colonel. L. J. Oliver.

Major J. H. R. Cox. (O.C. D Coy)

Captains C. E. Hall (O.C. A Coy); A. E. Fraser (O.C. C Coy); L. H. Dawson (O.C. B Coy); B. Wells,
P. T. Chevallier, R. O. Fearon, and B. A. James.

Lieutenants Manning, C. E. Anton, C. Butler, E. C. Matthews, C. K. Allen, and C. E. Harman.

2nd Lieutenants W. L. King, S. F. Holdsworth, A. W. Spence, P. Worthington, E. S. Crehshut, F. A. Bailey,
G. E. Romit and M. E. King.

Captain and Adjutant J. O. Dicker

Lieutenant and Quartermaster J. Spittle.

Lieutenant R. H. Fulton. R.A.M.C. attached.

The Strength of the Battalion embarking at FOLKESTONE was:-

Officers 27.   Other Ranks 846.   Total 873.
       (3)   (106)

Advance party
Appendix A.

(109)
982 Strength of Battalion
      including ultimate
      party
L J Oliver Colonel
Commdg 13th Middx Regt

Appendix C.

Casualties Sept 1st – Nov 30th 1915

	Killed		Missing Believed Killed		Died of Wounds		Wounded		Wounded & Missing		Missing		Wounded Prisoner of War		Total		Drafts Joined	
	O.	OR.	O.	OR.	O.	OR.	O.	OR.	O.	OR.	O.	OR.	O.	OR.	O.	OR.	O.	OR.
September	-	13	1	10	-	1	7	119	-	1	-	12	1	2	9	159	-	40
October	-	6	-	-	-	1	1	25	-	-	-	-	-	1	-	32	6	180
November	-	3	-	1	-	4	1	16	-	-	-	-	-	-	1	23	10	20
Total	-	22	1	11	-	6	9	160	-	1	-	12	1	2	10	214	16	240
Transferred to England Sick															4	49		
Total															15	263	16	240

Robert Colonel
Commg 13th Middx Regt S.

Names of officers
transferred to England
Sick.—
Lt.Col. C.B.R. King Sept 23rd
Capt. F.O. Dicker Sept 28
2nd QMr J Spittle Oct 7th
Lt. C.H. Butler Oct 18th

Army Form C. 2118

1st Intelligence/May 9
APPENDIX D.

WAR DIARY
or
INTELLIGENCE SUMMARY

(Erase heading not required.)

Place	Date	Hour	Summary of Events and Information	Remarks and references to Appendices
			During the operations 25th – 29th September 1915 there were many cases which were brought to notice – of gallant behaviour on the part of officers and men of the Battalion amongst which the following may be mentioned. Capt C. E. Hill held on with his Company "A" in a difficult situation and continually when our bombers had been driven back along "Slag alley" Fosse 8 at Bethune he led a mixed party of bombers with Sergt Fogg who after severe fighting assisted by the machine gun fire of Lt Norton drove the Germans before them finally causing them to quit the trench and run for the Slag Heap. Capt Hill in pursuing these men took the surrender of three Germans, who was himself hit when standing in front of them – presumably from a bullet from Fosse 8. Lieut P. Worthington even with D Coy and showed complete disregard of danger and an admirable example during the action, until he was severely wounded. Sergt Prince showed great resolve in meeting a German bombing attack and threw back the enemy's bombs for their getting home close to our trenches. Thereby delaying the enemy's advance until fresh bombs could be brought up, and saving a difficult situation.	

Army Form C. 2118

WAR DIARY
or
INTELLIGENCE SUMMARY

13th Middlesex APPENDIX 1 (continued)

(Erase heading not required.)

Place	Date	Hour	Summary of Events and Information	Remarks and references to Appendices
			During the afternoon of Monday 27th September, in front of the 10th Argyll and Sutherland Highlanders passed across the firing line held by A and I Companies and suffered very heavy casualties about 500 yards in front of our line. One of their NCOs called for volunteers to bring in wounded who were lying out and in spite of heavy fire – and of about 20 wounded men, some in Colonel Mackenzie's, a night, and about 20 wounded men were severely wounded in doing so. – No 4761 Pte S Francis of the following were recommended for the D.C.M.	
			No 1350 Coy Sergt Majr Blinco.	
			No 970 Coy Sergt Majr Llewellyn (wounded) for taking up ammunition under heavy fire. Awarded D.C.M.	
			No 1160 Sergt J. J. Triggs	
			No 4672 L/Cpl F.G. Ford	
			No 8062 Pte Monk	
			No 4532 Pte G. Graham	
			No 10347 Pte J. Cooper (wounded) awarded D.C.M.	
			Other cases of great worth may be cited – No 4368 Pte Jeffs who also took in the machine gun of the 10th Argyll and Sutherland Highlanders, and also brought in Pte Francis who was mortally wounded.	

Army Form C. 2118

13th Middlesex Regt.
Appendix D (continued)

WAR DIARY
or
INTELLIGENCE SUMMARY
(Erase heading not required.)

Place	Date	Hour	Summary of Events and Information	Remarks and references to Appendices

208005 Pte Walker brought in a wounded Highlander, 205-880 Pte Martin (wounded) made 5 trips. 20-1111 L/Cpl A Bunn did good work and prompt work in extricating Major Cox and Capt Frost when they were buried by a shell, and has since shown the greatest devotion to duty in all cases as Orderly in charge of stretcher bearers. Sergt Kennedy has also done very good work under difficult conditions in charge of stretcher bearers. 4834 Pte G V Brown, No 1204 L/Cpl H A Drage (wounded), No Pte Easton (wounded) were also mentioned by their Company officers for gallant behaviour.

T Oliver, Colonel
Commanding 13th Middx Regt.

73
13² hidæ 2 hidæ vol: I 73/34

12/7809

34 to Nvaun

Oct to
August to Nov. 15

WAR DIARY or INTELLIGENCE SUMMARY

Army Form C. 2118

13th Middlesex Regt

October 1915

Place	Date	Hour	Summary of Events and Information	Remarks and references to Appendices
LAMBRES	1st Oct	10.am	The Transport was despatched in advance to meet trains at HERZEELE. A draft of 20 other ranks joined from 15 Batt. Middlesex Regt.	
LAMBRES	2nd Oct	12.Noon	The Battalion marched at noon and entrained some 3 miles to BERGUETTE STATION; and entrained at 2.0pm, and proceeded via HAZEBROUCK to GODEWAERSVELDE STATION, which it reached about 4.0pm, and then marched N.W. halting just East of STEENVOORDE; passing through the town it reached its destination HERZEELE about 9.30pm.	
HERZEELE	3rd Oct		Remained in billets. Divine Service at 11am.	
	4th Oct	10.am	The Battalion was inspected by General Capper (Commanding 24th Div.)	
		5.pm	A party of 6 officers and 200 other ranks proceeded in motor lorries to BRIELEN, from there they were split up in parties and taken by guides to the trenches at ST JEAN and were attached to the 1st EAST YORKS and 2nd SHERWOODS, for 48 hours tour in trenches. Casualties 1 wounded OR.	
	6th Oct	12.0 a.m.	The Battalion paraded and marched 3½ miles to the Belgium Frontier which was crossed near HOUTKERQUE - thence on the PROVEN Road and found billets in various barns (huts being also provided) some 2 miles SW of PROVEN and 2 miles N of WATOU.	
		5.0 pm	A party of 3 officers and 100 other ranks proceeded by motor lorries to BRIELEN and were attached to the 1st EAST YORKS for 48 hours tour of the trenches. Casualties OR 1 wounded.	
PROVEN	7th Oct	9.am	A draft of 160 RCOs + men arrived from the 14th Batt Middlesex Regt.	
		6.pm	The party that went on the 4th for tour of trenches returned.	
	8th Oct	6.pm	A party of 5 officers and 400 other ranks (under Major Sharpe) proceeded in motor lorries to BRIELEN, where they were split up in parties and attached to the 1st EAST YORKS, 1 WEST YORKS, and 2nd SHERWOODS for 48 hours tour of trenches. Casualties OR. Killed. 1.. Wounded 4.	
	9th Oct	11.45pm	The party that went on 6th for tour of trenches returned.	
	10th Oct	10.am	Divine service held.	
	11th Oct	3.am	The party that went on the 8th for Tour in Trenches returned.	

WAR DIARY
or
INTELLIGENCE SUMMARY

(Erase heading not required.)

Army Form C. 2118

13th Middlesex Regt.

Instructions regarding War Diaries and Intelligence Summaries are contained in F. S. Regs., Part II. and the Staff Manual respectively. Title Pages will be prepared in manuscript.

Place	Date	Hour	Summary of Events and Information	Remarks and references to Appendices
PROVEN	11th Oct	(continued) 8 am	The Battalion paraded at 8 am and marched off via PROVEN, POPERINGHE and RENINGHELST, and tented in a wood about 2 miles S.E. of the latter Town. The march was only about 11½ miles, but the roads were bad, and the men very tired. 2nd Lieutenant S. V. CASTLE joined the Battalion from the 6th Batt. Middlesex Regt	
RENINGHELST	12th Oct		2nd Lieutenants T.W. O'REILLY and W.J. BURT joined the Battalion from the 6th Middlesex Regt. Captain H. WILKINSON joined the Battalion from the 15th Batt Middlesex; Captain D.B. REED and C. MIDDLETON joined the Battalion from the 14th Batt. Middlesex.	
	13th Oct	3:15pm	An advance party of 4 Officers and N.C. Other ranks, proceeded in Motor lorries via DICKEBUSCH to VOORMEZEELE - CAFÉ BELGE, from there they marched to the 6th SOMERSET LIGHT INFANTRY'S trenches, to make arrangements for the Battalion to take over that elev.	
	14th Oct	3:15pm	Paraded at 3:15pm. The Battalion marched along the YPRES Road to VOORMEZEELE and took over trenches from the 6th SOMERSET. L.I. on the left centre Section of St ELOI. Battalion on left 9th R. Sussex; Battalion on right 7th NORTHANTS.	
St ELOI (left centre Sector)	14th Oct to 19th Oct		During first tour of duty in the trenches. Casualties were – Officers Wounded 1. Captain K.O. FEARON. O.R. Killed 1. Died of wounds 1. Wounded 8. There was nothing of any unusual occurred during this tour of duty	
RENINGHELST	19th Oct	6pm	The 1st NORTH STAFFS relieved the Battalion after dark, The Battalion marched back to a rest Camp; C Camp RENINGHELST, partly in huts and partly in tents (in a wood 1½ miles SE of RENINGHELST.	
St ELOI (right centre Section)	22nd Oct 23rd – 28th		Took over the right centre St ELOI Section of trenches from 7th Northants. The Battalion on the left was the 2nd Munsters, and on the right – 8th R.W. Kents.	

WAR DIARY or INTELLIGENCE SUMMARY

Army Form C. 2118

13th Middlesex Regt.

OCTOBER

3

Place	Date	Hour	Summary of Events and Information	Remarks and references to Appendices
ST. ELOI (RIGHT CENTRE SECTOR)	23rd	28	During this 6 days tour in the trenches, the casualties were, O.R. 2 Killed, 10 wounded. On the 26th at 9.40pm a small mine was exploded by the enemy which caused all to stand to arms; simultaneously with the explosion — the enemy opened a brisk rifle fire which was replied to by our men and by the R.E. who were present; the supporting platoons moved up quickly and in a few minutes, the enemy's fire was silenced. The last two days were ar 9 and some of the trenches were flooded.	
RENINGHELST	27th		H.M. King George V visited the Troops of RENINGHELST, the Battalion sent a party of 20 men to be present at his inspection.	
ST. ELOI	28		The Battalion was relieved afterdark by the 7th Northamptons and returned to same rest camp. 2nd Lieutenants E.J.S. Vaughan, C.B. Saunders and R.M. Rickfords joined the Battalion from the 9th Batln BUFFS.	
RENINGHELST	29th		The Battalion was inspected by Major General Bayrst Commanding the 24th Division.	

Casualties for month of October.

	Killed	Wounded	Died of wounds	Total
	O.R.	O.	O.R.	O.	O.R.	
	6	0	25	—	1	32

Lt. & Qr.Mr. J. Smith was transferred to England sick 7/10/15
Lieut C.A. Butler was transferred to England sick 18/10/15

Wolver Colonel
Commg 13th Middlesex Regt.

Army Form C. 2118

WAR DIARY
or
INTELLIGENCE SUMMARY
(Erase heading not required.)

13th Middlesex Regt
NOVEMBER 1915

Place	Date	Hour	Summary of Events and Information	Remarks and references to Appendices
RENNINGHELST	3/11/15	3.0 pm	The Battalion paraded at 3.0pm and marched to VOORMEZEELE and relieved the 7th Northants Regt in the centre right centre — ST ELOI SECTOR.	
ST ELOI			Owing to the wet weather, the trenches were in a terrible state, fallen in in many places and communication trenches blocked by landslips; work of repairing and draining was at once started; practically every man not actually on sentry go, being employed on repair work.	
	5/11/15		A most interesting aeroplane fight over the lines was seen about 12.30 pm which ended in the destruction of the German aeroplane, which fell some 2 miles NE of VOORMEZEELE behind the British Trenches.	
	6/11/15		Capt C. MIDDLETON was wounded in a bombing accident at the Army Grenade School.	
	8/11/15		The Battalion was relieved by 7th Northants after dark, and returned to rest camp at RENNINGHELST. The casualties during the tour of duty was:— Killed:— OFFICERS nil.. O.R. 3. Wounded:— O. nil. O.R. 7. Died of Wounds O.R. 1.	
RENNINGHELST	12/11/15		The weather was very bad, and the camp was ankle deep in mud.	
	13/11/15		On the afternoon of Saturday the 13th on arriving from the Battalion marched to the same trenches and at dusk relieved the 7th Northants.	
ST ELOI	15/11/15		Our artillery opened a heavy bombardment between 5—7.0 pm. The Battalion was relieved at dusk, and marched back to some rest camp. During this spell of duty, it was very cold. There being severe frosts nearly nightly. The casualties were — Killed. O.R. nil. Wounded O.R. 9. Died of wounds. O.R. 3. A good many men (about 16) had Died from Trench feet of duty — communication trenches had been unbelievably bad, suffered from trench feet. During this tour of duty, it was very bad. floods, parapets fell down, and most of the trenches were under water, and the condition of the parapets very bad.	

1875 Wt. W593/826 1,000,000 4/15 J.B.C. & A. A.D.S.S./Forms/C. 2118.

WAR DIARY or INTELLIGENCE SUMMARY

(Erase heading not required.)

Army Form C. 2118

13th MIDDLESEX REGT.

NOVEMBER 1915

Place	Date	Hour	Summary of Events and Information	Remarks and references to Appendices
RENINGHELST	20/11/15	2.0 p.m.	The 10th R. Welsh Fusiliers took over camp C occupied by the Battalion at 2.0 p.m.	
		5.0 p.m.	A lorry with heavy baggage left early in the morning — and at 5.0 p.m. most of the Division concentrated at RENINGHELST and marched. The roads were dreadfully muddy but improved after 2 or 3 miles, and a hard frost further made the going easier. The route was — RENINGHELST – WESTOUTRE (where shortly afterwards the frontier was crossed) – BOESCHEPE – GODEWAERSVELDE – EECKE, a distance of about 11 miles; here the Battalion was billeted in outlying farms, where it remained for Sunday and on the night 9 day it marched at 10 a.m., leaving the Brigade.	
EECKE.	22/11/15	10.0 a.m.	The route was St SYLVESTRE CAPPEL – CASSEL – WEMAERS-CAPPEL – to OCHTEZEELE where it billeted for the night (a distance of about 10 miles). The march was a good one, the roads being hard and good, it being a frosty morning.	
OCHTEZEELE	23/11/15	2.0 p.m.		
	23/11/15	9.30 a.m.	The Battalion marched off at 9.30 a.m., owing to a thaw the roads were not so good, and the Battalion was in rear. The route taken was – OCHTEZEELE – LEDERZEELE – WULVERDINGHE – WATTEN – to HELLEBROUCQ which was reached about 4.0 p.m., a distance of about 12½ miles. 73rd Brigade Headquarters was established at EPERLECQUES. Lieutenant F. L. WIENHOLT and 2nd Lieutenant H. C. AUSTIN joined the Battalion from the 4th Battn. MIDDLESEX REGT. and 2nd Lieutenant C. J. BUTT joined from the 5th Battn., where he had been attached. One officer and 6 men proceeded on leave to England (8 days), this was the first leave granted the Battalion since its arrival in France.	
HELLEBROUCQ	24/11/15	4.0 p.m.		
	25/11/15	9.20 a.m.	The Battalion was moved from its billets to make room for the 72nd Brigade headquarters, and marched at 9.20 a.m. the route being – HELLEBROUCQ – GANSPETTE – EST MONT – OUEST MONT – NORDAUSQUES – to ZOUAFQUES and WOLPHUS on the CALAIS – STOMER Road. A distance of about 6½ miles, here it was billeted in outlying farms.	
ZOUAFQUES WOLPHUS				

WAR DIARY or INTELLIGENCE SUMMARY

Army Form C. 2118

13th MIDDLESEX REGT.

NOVEMBER 1915.

Place	Date	Hour	Summary of Events and Information	Remarks and references to Appendices
WOLPHUS	26/11/15		The Battalion remained in billets during the morning. There was a snow storm which was the first of the season.	
	27/11/15		The Battalion marched at 9.15 am and returned (by the same way which it had marched out) to HELLEBOURCQ. Battalion Headquarters was established at the Chateau d'HELLEBOURCQ.	
HELLEBOURCQ	28/11/15 29/11/15		DIVINE SERVICE was held opposite Battalion Headquarters. Ordinary training was carried on according to programme of training. Arrangements were made at Battalion Headquarters for Baths, the laundry being utilized, where it was possible to keep a continuous supply of hot water, and men bathing all day.	Appendix C
	2/11/15		Under authority granted by his Majesty the King, the Field Marshal Commanding in Chief has awarded the following decorations:— Distinguished Conduct Medals. Coy Sergt Major E. C. Llewellyn 970 13th Middlesex Regt for conspicuous gallantry on September 27th near Fosse 8, when with the greatest coolness and courage he brought ammunition to the firing line at a critical period, under heavy fire and continued to do so after being wounded. He gave a fine example of bravery and devotion to duty. 10347 Pte J. W. Cooper 13th Middlesex Regt for conspicuous gallantry on September 27th 1915. West of Fosse 8. On three separate occasions he went out under a heavy heavy fire, and brought in wounded men of the Argyll and Sutherland Highlanders. On the last occasion he was himself seriously wounded. He gave a fine example of bravery and devotion to duty.	

WAR DIARY
or
INTELLIGENCE SUMMARY

Army Form C. 2118

13? Middlesex Regt.
November 1915

Place	Date	Hour	Summary of Events and Information	Remarks and references to Appendices
			Summary of casualties for November 1915	
			KILLED. WOUNDED Died of wounds	
			Officers Other Ranks Officers Other Ranks Officers Other Ranks	Not included in Wounded. Total is 23—
			— 3 — 16. — 4	

R. Oliver Colvil

13 Etudes
vol. 2

Decembre
1955

131
——
798

13th Middlesex Regt
Army Form C. 2118

DECEMBER 1915

WAR DIARY or INTELLIGENCE SUMMARY
(Erase heading not required.)

Instructions regarding War Diaries and Intelligence Summaries are contained in F.S. Regs., Part II. and the Staff Manual respectively. Title Pages will be prepared in manuscript.

Place	Date	Hour	Summary of Events and Information	Remarks and references to Appendices
HELLEBROUCK	1/12/15		There was a Brigade Route march about 9½ miles, via EPERLECQUES - MOULLE - SERQUES - WATTEN - GANSPETTE. The Brigadier General Commanding expressed his satisfaction at the marked improvement and smart discipline on the march.	
	2/12/15		A draft of 17 other ranks joined the Battalion 11 from Hospital & 6 from the 11th Middlesex Regt	
	3/12/15		Brigt. General Carpet Commanding 24th Division visited the Battalion and delivered a lecture to Officers and NCO's at 10.30 a.m. The first Round of the inter-company football competition took place resulting in A coy v C coy 12 "Shorwed" Timatus lost 1-7. B coy v 19th coy ASC lost 0-3. C coy v C coy 9th R Sussex won 7-1. D coy v C coy Munsters lost 2-6.	
	5/12/15		Divine service was held at 10.30 a.m.	
	8/12/15		There was a Brigade Route march about 9¾ miles via MOULLE - MORINGHEM - INGHINGHEM - HOULLE. In the second round of the inter company football competition C coy lost by 0-2 to the 24th Divl Signal Coy R.E. The B & C 73rd Infantry Brigade visited the Battalion and delivered a lecture to Officers and NCOs.	
	10/12/15		General Sir Herbert Plumer visited the Divl area sent Commanding the 2nd Army, visited the Divl area, and reviewed the 73rd Brigade on a route march.	
	11/12/15		Divine service was held at 11.30 a.m. Lieut & QM C.S Burstow joined from the 15th Bn Middlesex Regt	
	12/12/15			
	14/12/15		There was a Brigade Route march about 11 miles via EST MONT - LA CALIFORNIA - WIRDAUSQUES - NORTLEULINGHEM - EPERLECQUES Cross Roads - EPERLECQUES. C coy won the Brigade inter-company Shooting competition. A draft of 45 OR arrived from the 2nd Entrenching Battalion. About 22 of these men were invalided at once to Hospital, at Lumbres. The Battalion wore (Im) 15th Battalion Middlesex Regt	
	19/12/15		Divine Service was held at 10. a.m.	
	22/12/15		A party consisting of Lt L.J. Nivot the Batt M.G.O and 1 officer per coy proceeded by motor to make tour of trenches assigned to the 73rd Brigade	

Army Form C. 2118

WAR DIARY
or
INTELLIGENCE SUMMARY
(Erase heading not required.)

DECEMBER 1915

Place	Date	Hour	Summary of Events and Information	Remarks and references to Appendices
HELLEBROUCQ	24/12/15		Col L.J. Clint and party returned from trenches.	
	25/12/15		Divine service was held at 9.0 a.m. Orders were received cancelling the move to the rear area.	
	31/12/15		Major General Capper Commanding 24th Division inspected the 72nd Infantry Brigade and expressed to the Brigadier and the C.O.s of Battalions his satisfaction at the great improvement in bearing and discipline of the men during the period of training at HOULLE. The Brigadier also specially noticed the good appearance of the Battalion and excellent turn out.	

L.J. Clint. Colonel

73rd Brigade.
24th Division.

13th BATTALION

MIDDLESEX REGIMENT.

January 1916.

Z³/24

13 Middx
Tot 3
Tam ?16

24ᵗʰ Div

Army Form C. 2118

WAR DIARY or INTELLIGENCE SUMMARY
(Erase heading not required.)

13th Middlesex Reg.t
January 1916.

Place	Date	Hour	Summary of Events and Information	Remarks and references to Appendices
HELLEBROUCQ	1st		A draft of 30 men of the Middlesex Regt from the 2nd Entrenching Battalion arrived. At the end of December Lieut. S.W.L. King was appointed Assistant Instructor of the Divisional Grenade School.	
ST OMER	4th 5th		2nd Lieut. G.B. Castle died on No 10 General Hospital ST OMER of an epidemic Cerebro Spinal Meningitis and was buried at ST OMER on the 5th inst. Capt. R. Wilkinson and a platoon of D company attended the funeral. His loss to the Battalion as he was a capable and hard working officer and looked well after the interests of his men was a great loss.	
HELLEBROUCQ	6th		There was a Brigade Route march through POPERINGHE FOREST. The Battalion packed and sent on the Transport in the afternoon to ST OMER, and at 8.30 PM left HELLEBROUCQ and marched via HAZEBROUCQ - MOULLE -	
		11.45 PM	MOULLE - TILQUES - ST MARTIN to ST OMER Railway Station arriving at 11.45 PM. The night was extremely dark and the wind cold and gusty. The Transport was already on the Train, and the Battalion entrained at midnight (6th - 7th). The Train left at 1.10 am and passing HAZEBROUCQ (2.30 am) reached POPERINGHE about 3.15 am	
POPERINGHE	7th	2.30 am 3.15 am 4.0 am	where the trucks containing the Transport were taken off the Train, which then shunted back to ST QUENTIN siding, where the Battalion detrained about 4.0 am. It then marched about 6½ miles over very muddy roads through POPERINGHE, then along the POPERINGHE - YPRES Road for about 3 miles, then by very muddy byeroads to a camp about 1½ miles N.E. of RENINGHELST (G.24.C. G.G. Map 28) which was reached about 8.30 am. Cookers and Transport formed great difficulty in marching along the narrow muddy roads, often nearly up to their axles in muck, and did not reach the camp till 2.0 pm.	G.24.C. 6.6. Map 28
	8th 9th - 10th 11th		Days spent in draining and improving the camp. Major General Copert visited the camp. Lieut. General Fanshawe Commanding the V Corps visited the camp.	

WAR DIARY
or
INTELLIGENCE SUMMARY

(Erase heading not required.)

4th Middlesex Regt. Army Form C. 2118

January 1916.

Place	Date	Hour	Summary of Events and Information	Remarks and references to Appendices
G.24.c.6.6. MAP 28	13th	1.0 pm	The specialists (machine gunners, signallers, and grenadiers) left at 1.0 pm for the trenches and took over from the 8th Bn Queens in the right section of the HOOGE Right sector at Sanctuary Wood.	All map references are of Sheet 28 of the B Series.
	14th		Major F.J. Sharpe "2nd in Command" left for England for Home Service. The Battalion left the rest camp at 10.0 am for the trenches (A Company and left behind at the camp), a halt was made for 3 hours at Belgian Chateau." (H.23.a.9.5, Map 28), on reaching the trenches it went through KRUISSTRAAT and then to the YPRES asylum, where much chemical high gun boots, the march was then continued through YPRES and the MENIN GATE and along the MENIN Rd, turning to the right at I.10.c.9.3. to GORDON HOUSE, and hence in small parties with guides to the trenches in Sanctuary Wood. C Company was in the firing line, B Company in Support and D Company in reserve, Battalion Headquarters were at I.18.c.6.2. in ZOUAVE WOOD. The 8th Queens, were relieved by 11.0 pm; The 2nd Leinsters were on the left, and the 8th Durham L.I. were on the right. 1.O.R was wounded during the relief. There was a great deal of rifle fire during the right.	Belgium not France. for reference to trenches mentioned see Sketch Map I
SANCTUARY WOOD I.18.d. & J.13.c.	15th		Attitude of the enemy quiet, but artillery was active. Work was done in improving the parapets and drains in C1, and the machine gun emplacement and bombing post in the Appendix, also drainage behind C1R and B.S.S. A Snipers loophole was treated opening and shutting in German line at J.13.a.1.1, but did no damage, and 1	
	16th		The enemy sent 12 Heavy shells over near R.S6., whizzbang and C1 retaliation was given by 12 rounds from our 18 pdrs, which	

Army Form C. 2118

WAR DIARY or INTELLIGENCE SUMMARY
(Erase heading not required.)

13th Battn Middlesex Regt
January 1916

Place	Date	Hour	Summary of Events and Information	Remarks and references to Appendices
SANCTUARY WOOD	16th		The day was quiet, work done – improving parapets and Traverses in C1. C1R. and BS8. After dusk there were a considerable number of stray bullets between Battalion Headquarters and Yeomanry Post. The night was quiet. In the evening there was an unfortunate Bombing accident in the Appendix resulting in 1 OR being killed and 3 OR wounded.	All map references are of Sheet 28. of B Series. Belgium & France
	17th		The day was comparatively quiet. The Enemy sent 1 trench mortar bomb over C1 at 11.45 am. work done – improving parapets in C1 and BS8, communication trench opened up in R52, much work is still required there. 2nd Lieut. T. W. O'Reilly Commanding C Company was wounded in the evening by a bullet in the thigh at Yeomanry Post. The enemy threw up a great many very lights in E2 (He Yup) during the night, evidently trying to locate our Bombing posts. At about 8.0pm 2 red lights went up in front of BD, which were answered by 2 red lights opposite B8 then at 8.15pm 2 red lights went up in front of B4 and were answered by 2 red lights opposite C1, then double green lights in front of junction of C1 and BS8 followed by 2 double lights one green and one red on right. Nothing unusual happened, the night was quiet.	For reference of Trenches mentioned see Sketch.
	18th		The day was quiet, work done on improving communication trench in R52. The 9th Royal Sussex relieved the Battalion in the evening the relief being complete by 10.0pm. The Battalion moved back to BELGIAN DUGOUTS, in reserve. H.23.b.	
BELGIAN DUGOUTS H.23.B.				

WAR DIARY
or
INTELLIGENCE SUMMARY
(Erase heading not required.)

Army Form C. 2118

13th Middlesex Regt.
January 1916

Place	Date	Hour	Summary of Events and Information	Remarks and references to Appendices
H 23 6.	19th		Casualties during 4 days tour in trenches. Wounded Officers: 1. (2nd Lt. W. O'Reilly). O.R. 5. Accidentally wounded 3.O.R. Accidentally Killed 1. O.R. Died of Wounds 1.O.R. Working parties were furnished for R.E.s in trenches, 400 men in all, 1.O.R. was slightly wounded.	all map references are of Sheet 28. "B" since in Belgium & France.
	20th		400 men were sent RE RE working parties to the trenches, 1.O.R. was wounded Sing?	
	21st		A Company marched up from the Rest camp and joined The Battalion, B Company marched out and even? back to rest camp. 300 men were sent on RE working parties to the trenches. 1 OR was wounded.	
	22nd		In the evening the Battalion relieved the 9th Royal Sussex in the trenches. The relief was complete by 10.30 p.m. Work done in C1 & B5 rebuilding traverses. The night was quiet.	Where Trenches are mentioned for reference see Sketch map of trenches
SANCTUARY WOOD	23rd		At about 1.15 a.m. the enemy sent several trench mortar bombs which fell 50 yds short of B5. They did no damage, the enemy was noisy but quite weak. The enemy also fired occasional rifle grenades at the Appendix, these fell short, no damage was done. An enemy working parties were heard opposite C2. At 2.0am what appeared to be a train was heard half left of C1, also the noise of unloading iron rails or girders was heard, from 11.30am to 12.30pm the enemy had an intense bombardment on C3 and 4. 2 shells fell (one hitting a tree) near the Appendix. they did no damage. The others, after this, comparatively quiet. Work was continued in rebuilding parapets in C1 and B8 and putting in inverted A5. In B58 parapets were rebuilt. In R52 drains were cut and after being reclared. The night was comparatively quiet. At 12.10 am an enemy working party was observed opposite C2 working with shovels in front of the German parapet. Our Bombing post in centre of C2	

WAR DIARY or **INTELLIGENCE SUMMARY**
Army Form C. 2118

13th Middlesex Regt.

January 1916.

Place	Date	Hour	Summary of Events and Information	Remarks and references to Appendices
SANCTUARY WOOD	24th		Fired on 17. The enemy replied with rifles and machine gun fire. Work done was on edge of wood in front of C1R. wiring in front of B58. One fire bay elevated into two in B58. Traverses were made higher and thicker and parapets rebuilt in C1 and B8. Fire bays were rebuilt in RS2. The night was quiet.	Map references are on Sheet 28 S.W. Series, Belgium & France
	25th		During the afternoon our M.G. Hantgens fired 22 rounds at J 13.C.4.8 (which is believed to be a strong point built of reinforced concrete). They obtained 3 direct hits, but they did not appear to have any effect on the work; in the evening an attempt was made to draw the fire of the machine gun in this work (the enemy being no sniping from this point), at 4.15 pm it had the effect of starting considerable sniping from this point. The enemy we examined in front of C1R from 5.30 – 9.15pm 1 Rifle grenade fell short of C1. The night was quiet. Work done at 9.15pm grenades imposed in B58. The wire was examined in front of C1R, there are three rows in all, its further was found to be in good condition throughout. A small amount of parapets improved, the wire immediately in front of C1.	Any reference to Trenches See sketch map I
	26th	7.30pm	About 1.0am a green rocket was sent up from the German line opposite C3 which was answered by a green rocket well to the right opposite. The day was comparatively quiet. The 9th Royal Sussex Regt relieved the Battalion. The relief being completed by 10.30 pm. The Battalion went back to Belgian Dugouts (see Battalion in Brigade reserve). Casualties during 4 days tour in trenches Killed 1 O.R. Died of wounds 1 O.R. Wounded 8 O.R. Suffering from Shell Shock 1 O.R. accidentally wounded 2 O.R.	

Army Form C. 2118

13th Middlesex Regt

WAR DIARY
or
INTELLIGENCE SUMMARY
(Erase heading not required.)

January 1916

VI

Place	Date	Hour	Summary of Events and Information	Remarks and references to Appendices
BELGIAN DUGOUTS	27th		350 men were sent on R.E. working parties to the Trenches. 1 O.R. was killed. Capt D.B. Reed took over the Command of C Coy vice 2nd Lieut. T.W. O'Reilly — wounded.	All map references are of Sheet 28 "B Series" Belgium & France.
	28		400 men were sent on R.E. working parties to the Trenches. 1 O.R. was wounded. Colonel L.J. Oliver having been granted leave from Jan 30th to Feb 7th 1916, 2 Major R.E. Oxspring-Palmer 2nd Leinster Regt took over command of the Battalion during his absence.	
	29th		400 men were sent on R.E. working parties to the Trenches. The 5th Battn "The Buffs" relieved the Battalion at Belgian Dugouts (B.14 & 7.0.) at 5.0 p.m., the companies marched independently to Camp B. Kit inspections held, and Camps generally cleaned up.	
Camp B	30.			
	31st		During the time the Battalion was in the Trenches the Company at the rest camp were used for working parties every night. On the 24th Jan 1 O.R. was killed. 1 O.R. wounded. Extract from London Gazette of 31/12/15: Duke of Cambridge's Own Middlesex Regt. 2nd Lieut. W.J. Burt, 5th Batn Middlesex Regt attached 13th Battn Middlesex Regt to be Lieutenant with seniority as from 1–12–15 " The following drafts arrived during the month of January. 1/1/16 30 O.R. from 15th Batn Middlesex Regt 15/1/16 30 O.R. from 2nd Entrenching Battalion 23/1/16 14 O.R. from 24th Infantry Base (men from Hospital) 26/1/16 38 O.R. from 2nd Entrenching Battalion ————— 112 O.R.	

WAR DIARY
or
INTELLIGENCE SUMMARY

(Erase heading not required.)

Army Form C. 2118

13th Middlesex Regt.

January 1916.

VII

Place	Date	Hour	Summary of Events and Information	Remarks and references to Appendices
			Summary of Casualties for Month.	

Killed		Accidentally Killed		Died of Wounds		Died		Wounded		Accidentally Wounded		Wounded "at Duty"		Suffering from Shell Shock		TOTAL		Transferred to ENGLAND SICK		GRAND TOTAL	
O	OR	O	OR	O	OR	O	OR	O	OR	O	OR	O	OR	O	OR	O	OR	O	OR	O	OR
-	3	-	1	-	2	1	17	-	5	-	2	-	1	0	31	-	16	2	49

The majority of casualties were at night time, when there were a considerable number of stray bullets about, during the day time there was very little rifle fire indeed.

Names of Officers in Casualty list.

Died   Lieut C.B. Coote.   Jan 14th 1916
Wounded 2nd Lieut T.W. O'Reilly. Jan 18th 1916

R. Dyke-Palmer Major
Cmdg 13th Middlesex Regt

WAR DIARY or **INTELLIGENCE SUMMARY**

13th Middlesex Regt.
January 1916.
Appendix E

Army Form C. 2118

Place	Date	Hour	Summary of Events and Information	Remarks and references to Appendices
	15/1/16.		A Roll of Officers serving with the Battalion on going into the trenches **HEADQUARTERS.** O.C. Colonel L.G. OLIVER. ADJUTANT. Capt. P.T. CHEVALLIER. BOMBING OFFICER. Capt. D.B. REED Transport Officer Lieut E.J. TYDEMAN. Signalling & Intelligence Officer Lieut S.H. TWINING. Machine Gun Officer. Lieut C.E. NORTON. 2nd Lieut E.S.COCKSHUT. Q.M. & Hon Lieut & RQMC BURDON. M.O. Lieut R.A.H. FULTON. R.A.M.C. **A. Company.** Captain B.A. JAMES. 2nd Lieut G.J. ROMER. 2nd Lieut E.S. VAUGHAN. 2nd Lieut E.W. EVERS. **B. Company.** Capt I.H. DAWSON Lieut W.L. KING.✱ Lieut F.I. WIGINTON 2nd Lieut M.E. KING. 2nd Lieut R.M. RICHFORD) 2nd Lieut S.G. SAUNDERS. **C. Company.** 2nd Lieut P.W. O'REILLY Lieut E.C. MATTHEWS. Lieut W.J. BURT. 2nd Lieut S.J. MOLESWORTH 2nd Lieut C.F. BUTT. **D. Company.** Capt K. WILKINSON 2nd Lieut A.W. SPENCE. 2nd Lieut C.B. SAUNDERS 2nd Lieut A.N. HINGLEY 2nd Lieut H.C. AUSTIN. ✱ This officer is Assistant Instructor at the 24th Divl. GRENADE SCHOOL. R.White Palmer Major. Cmdg 13th Middlesex Regt.	

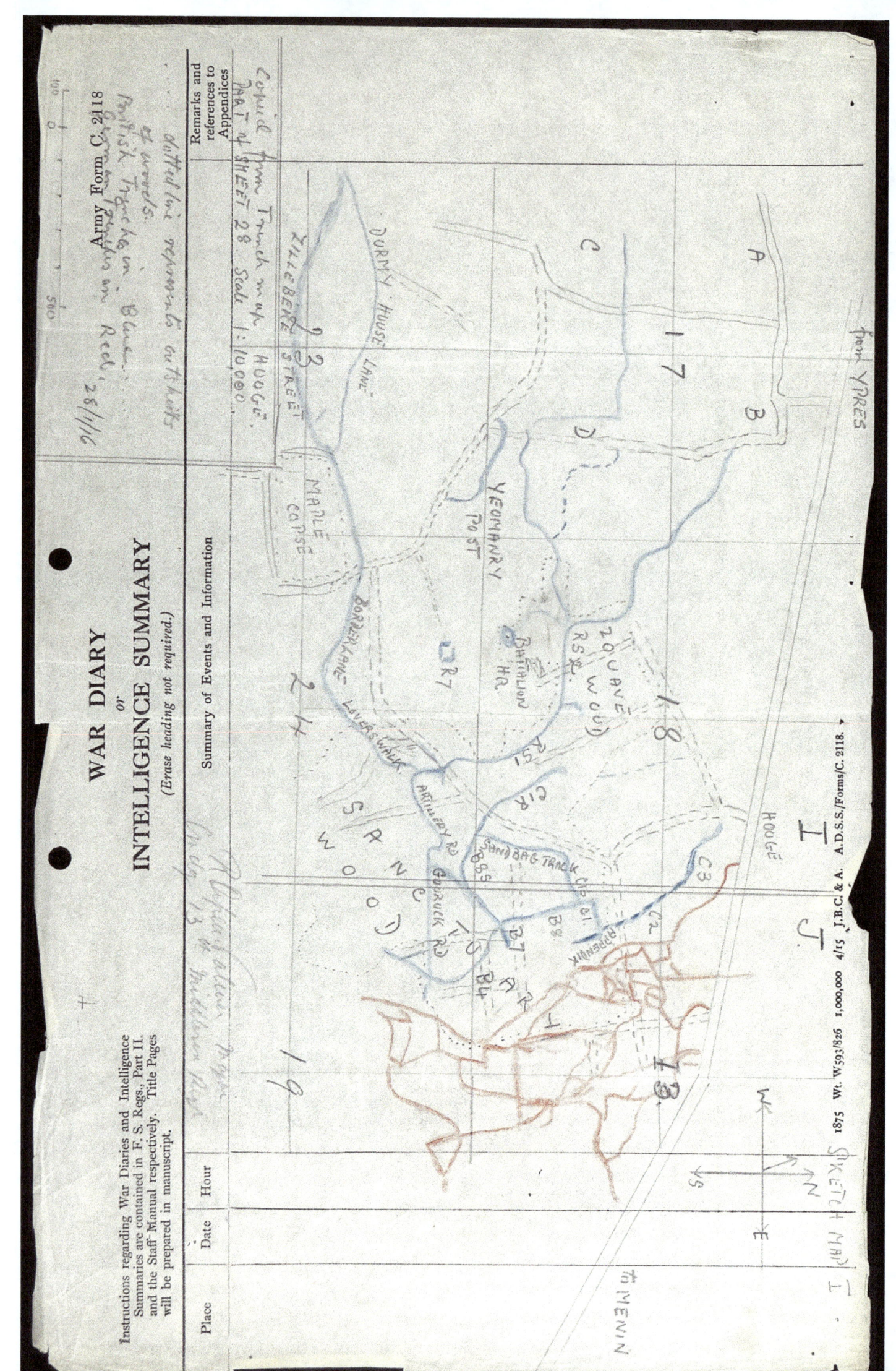

73rd Brigade.
24th Division.

13th BATTALION

MIDDLESEX REGIMENT.

February 1916.

WAR DIARY or INTELLIGENCE SUMMARY

(Erase heading not required.)

13th Middlesex Regt

February 1916

Army Form C. 2118

Place	Date	Hour	Summary of Events and Information	Remarks and references to Appendices
CAMP.B. G.11.C.5.2.	1st to 7th		The Battalion was in a rest camp; ordinary training was carried out. The Battalion had baths at the Divisional Baths at POPERINGHE.	All map references are of Sheet 28. A series Belgium & France.
	5th		There was a practice "Stand to" which was carried out well. Brigadier-General R.G. Jelf commanded the 73rd Infantry Brigade consequent on all our drafts since January 1st 1916 after the "Stand to".	
"H" Trenches I.12. a & c.	7th		The Battalion relieved the 9th Battn East Surrey Regt in the H trenches (I.12. a & c.) the relief being completed by 10.30 p.m. Casualties during relief 2.O.R. Killed. 1.O.R. wounded.	All references to trenches see Sheet Map I
	8th		A small enemy working party was dispersed by rifle fire opposite H17 at 3.0 am. During the whole day there was a heavy bombardment of our trenches. Between 10–11 am there was brisk but ineffective shelling of Muddy Lane and Y Wood. Ear? Lane was shelled from 10–11.30 am and knocked in, in three places. 4.0 Whizzbangs were fired at firing line and Y Wood from 10 am–1.0 pm and heavy shelled with 4.2 and a few 5".9 the latter being mainly directed at S16. F6 and communication trenches whilst firing line was whizz-banged. From 2–4.0 pm fairly heavy shelling as above. From 4.30–5.0 pm and 7–9.0 pm heavy shelling. The Menin Road was shelled intermittently all day from Hell fire Corner to Menin Gate. Casualties 2. O.R. Killed.	
	9th		The day was fairly quiet, at times the enemy's artillery was active. In the evening a good deal of work was done to parapets in front line and building up of muddy Lane. The Breastworks and X19 were improved. Casualties 1. OR Killed. 1 officer 2nd Lieut. S.G. Saunders wounded. A draft of 2. OR reported from 2nd Entrenching Battn.	
	10th		There was some shelling of Y wood F6. and X19. No damage done. In the early morning 12 rifle grenades were fired at the enemy's trench opposite H15. the enemy replied with rapid rifle fire. Casualties. 1. OR Wounded. 2 Dutys. Colonel L.J. Oliver returned from leave.	

WAR DIARY
or
INTELLIGENCE SUMMARY
(Erase heading not required.)

Army Form C. 2118

13th Middlesex Regt.

February 1916

Place	Date	Hour	Summary of Events and Information	Remarks and references to Appendices
"H" Trenches	11th		Machine guns were active all night. Major Orpham-Palmer left to rejoin his Battalion. During the day the enemy shelled West Lane. Brastrum's & Wurst 36, and around the Menin cellars. Sapping was reported to be heard under H16 the mining officer was informed. The 9th Royal Sussex Regt relieved the Battalion in the evening. Casualties 1 O.R. killed. 2 O.R. wounded. During the time the Battalion was in the trenches the 1st North Staffs were on the left until the night of the 8/9th when they were relieved by the 2nd Leinsters; the 1st R. Fusiliers were on the right. The Total casualties during tour were 5 O.R. Killed. 1 O.R. Died of wounds. 1 O.R. Wounded (S+B) 1 O.R wounded at duty. Trenches The Battalion went back into Brigade Support, 2 companies on Camp F, and 2 companies (B+D) in YPRES, 1 company at the ECHNK near the Cavalry barracks, the other 2 companies at the Railway station, all living in the cellars and other in the Convent near the cellars of a house opposite the Battalion HQ was established in the cellars of a house opposite the Barracks.	All map references are off Sheet 28 & Series Belgium & France, all references to trenches see Sketch Map II
YPRES I.7.d.	12th		Major P. Wood reported for duty as 2nd in Command from the 2nd London Regt. 2nd Lieut W.J.O'Meara reported for duty from the 4th Middlesex Regt. at 5.30 pm orders were received to "Stand to", the Battalion "Stood to" until 7.0pm when orders were received to "Stand down". This was due to the enemy having heavily bombarded the H Trenches and Hooge Trenches, also a heavy bombardment and an attempted attack which failed near at Pilkem.	
	13th		Working parties were sent up to the trenches in the evening. 2 Platoons garrisoned the X1 line all night	
	14th		2nd Lieut O. Fowlkes-Winks reported for duty from the 14th Middlesex Regt. This officer was originally posted to the Battalion and served with the Battalion when in England. Orders were received at 5.45pm to "Stand to" and the 2 companies at Camp F	

Army Form C. 2118

WAR DIARY or INTELLIGENCE SUMMARY
(Erase heading not required.)

13th Middlesex Regt
February 1916

Place	Date	Hour	Summary of Events and Information	Remarks and references to Appendices
YPRES J.7.d.	14th		were ordered to move and join the Battalion. The orders for "Stand to" were due to the fact that the enemy heavily bombarded the Divisional sector from 2.30 – 5.30 am and sprung two mines at H16 and H19. The enemy attempted to leave their trenches but the 9th R. Sussex started cheering and the enemy returning to his trenches. The Crater of JH6 was enormous, one complete platoon being buried alive. YPRES was heavily shelled, particularly in the evening at the same time the enemy attacked "The Bluff", a working party of 100 men from the Battalion went up to work on the craters and repair trenches, the wiring party suffered no casualties. 2 Platoons of X1 all night, 1 of H.30 am orders were received to "Stand down". L. C. E. Royston took up 2 machine gun sections to reinforce the 9th R Sussex during the early morning while getting rations up to his men he was wounded by a sniper. 16th 2nd Lieut J. L. Allingham reported for duty from 4th Middlesex Regt	All map references of A Series, Belgium + France. All references to trenches see Batch Map II
	15th		according to special instructions issued by the Brigade, the Battalion did not relieve the 9th Royal Sussex until after midnight 15th/16th. The night was quiet. The enemy shelled Y wood with whizzbangs and shrapnel intermittently throughout the night. Enemy machine guns were fairly active all night. The day was comparatively quiet. Work was carried on reconstructing H13, 14, 15 + 16 a telephone station was fixed up in H19. X1A was improved and drained. Casualties. 3 O.R. Killed.	
	16th		Enemy machine guns were less active during the night. Bombing posts were improved in the right crater and french tunnels put down, reconstruction of H13, 14, 15 + 16 was continued, support trenches in rear of H16, 17, + 18 were drained and improved. Sandbagging was continued on the Breastworks. The morning was quiet, enemy snipers were active opposite H16. A german wearing a brown uniform with a flag round cap with a white band was observed looking out the German parapet opposite H17, he was shot. At 3.15 pm the enemy shelled H16 with H.O – H.2 HE and made a direct	
	17th			

WAR DIARY or INTELLIGENCE SUMMARY

Army Form C. 2118

13th Middlesex Regt

February 1916

Place	Date	Hour	Summary of Events and Information	Remarks and references to Appendices
"H" Trenches	17th		H19 on the machine gun emplacement in H16 killing 4 men and wounding 4; the hour of the Lewis gun was damaged but the gun was unharmed; as soon as the enemy scored the direct hit they ceased fire. Retaliation by our artillery was very effective. Casualties 5 OR killed, 8 OR wounded. Work done – continued reconstruction as previous day.	All map references are of Sheet 28 A Series. Belgium & France. All references to Trenches see Sketch map LI
	18th		At 3.35 am what appeared to be a Taube passed directly over H17 towards the German lines. About the same time 3 Stokes shells were sent up by the enemy, which fell behind this lines. The morning was quiet, except for snipers who were active opposite H16. At 3.30pm the enemy shelled H19 then H16 + H17 and then lifted on to S18 with some 30 H.E. and whizz bangs. They did no damage, and retaliation was effective. Enemy machine guns were very active all night. The enemy erected a steel loophole on far side Lip of the right crater; 2 rifle grenades were fired at this, which caused snipers to cease from it for some time. Casualties 1 OR killed. Work done reconstructing S18, new support line, listening up and French Crowning crater at H18.	
	19th		The night was comparatively quiet, except for machine guns, the enemy shelled H16, 17, 18, 19 and S18 at 2.30pm with some 20 shells chiefly whizz-bangs, no damage was done. Sniping was less active. The 9th R. Sussex relieved the Battalion the relief being complete at 11.15pm. The Battalion marched to Brigade Support trench on leaving YPRES and Comm Tr. on YPRES-ZILLEBEKE road. A + B Companies in Ecol and Comm Tr in Camp E, Major J.R.H. Cox reported for duty from the 14th Middlesex, this officer originally served with the Battalion	
YPRES	20th		and was wounded at Loos. Casualties during Tour. 7 OR killed. 4 OR died of wounds. 1 O, 11 OR wounded. 10 OR wounded(?) duty. 2nd Lieut G. Horsfield and a draft of 25 OR reported for duty from the 14 Middlesex Regt. this officer served with the Battalion while in England.	

Army Form C. 2118

WAR DIARY
or
INTELLIGENCE SUMMARY
(Erase heading not required.)

13th Middlesex Regt
V
February 1916.

Place	Date	Hour	Summary of Events and Information	Remarks and references to Appendices
YPRES. Camp A. G.11.C.4.3.	20th-24th 24th 25th-29th		300 men were sent on R.E. working parties every night there was considerable sniping during these days. The 8th Bedfords, 16th Infantry Brigade 6th Division, relieved the Battalion in the evening. The Battalion went back to rest at Camp A. The Battalion had Baths at Poperinghe. Ordinary training was carried out. A working party of 150 was sent by train to work in trenches on the 27th.	All map references are off Sheet 28. A. Senis Belgium France

Casualties during the month of February

	Killed.	Accidentally Killed	Died of wounds	Died.	Wounded.	Wounded at Duty	In Tot.	Transferred to England Sick	Total
	O. OR.	O. OR.	O. OR.	O. OR.	O. OR.	O. OR.	O. OR.	O. OR.	O. OR.
	- 12.	- -	- 5.	- 1.	x2. 16.	- 2.	2. 36.	- 8.	2. 42.

x 2nd Lieut. S.G. Saunders 9/2/16
† 2nd Lieut. C.E. Norton 15/2/16

Drafts arrived during month.

	Officers	Other Ranks
	6.	27.

‡ 12/2/16   2nd Lieut. W.J. O'Meara from 4th Middlesex Regt
  12/2/16   Major P. Wood from 2nd London Regt
  16/2/16   2nd Lieut. L. Allingham from 4th Middlesex Regt
  19/2/16   Major F.R.H. Cox from 4th Middlesex Regt with a Battalion of 1/nos.
  20/2/16   2nd Lieut. A. Henshurst from 14th Middlesex Regt
  14/2/16   2nd Lieut. O. Foulkes-Winks from 14th Middlesex Regt

H. Oliver Colonel
Commdg 13th Middlesex Regt

WAR DIARY or INTELLIGENCE SUMMARY

13th Middlesex Regt

Army Form C. 2118

Appendix F. February 1916

A Casualty and Draft Summary

December 1915, January & February 1916
2nd Three months. Together with 1st three months totals.

	KILLED		ACCIDENT-ALLY KILLED		DIED of WOUNDS		DIED		WOUNDED		ACCIDENT-ALLY WOUNDED		WOUNDED AT DUTY		Suffering from Shell Shock		MISSING		MISSING Believed (KILLED)		WOUNDED & MISSING		MISSING Believed to be Prisoner of War		WOUNDED PRISONER of War		TOTAL		Transferred to Expeditionary Sick		DRAFTS JOINED	
	O	OR	O	OR	O	OR	O	OR	O	OR	O	OR	O	OR	O	OR	O	OR	O	OR	O	OR	O	OR	O	OR	O	OR	O	OR	O	OR
DECEMBER 1915	-	-	-	-	-	-	-	1	-	1	-	-	-	-	-	-	-	-	-	-	-	-	-	-	-	-	-	1	-	16	-	62
JANUARY 1916	-	3	-	1	-	2	-	1	1	16	-	5	-	2	-	-	-	-	-	-	-	-	-	-	-	2	30	-	16	-	112
FEBRUARY 1916	-	12	-	-	-	5	-	1	2	16	-	-	-	2	-	-	-	-	-	-	-	-	-	-	2	36	-	8	6	27
TOTAL	-	15	-	1	-	7	1	2	3	32	-	5	-	4	-	1	-	-	-	-	-	-	-	-	4	67	-	40	7	201
1st Three months (Sept/Oct/Nov 1915)	1	20	-	-	-	11	-	-	9	155	-	-	-	-	-	-	-	13	-	10	-	-	-	1	11	212	-	49	16	240
GRAND TOTAL for 6 months	1	35	-	1	-	18	1	2	12	187	-	5	-	4	-	1	-	13	-	10	-	-	-	1	15	279	4	89	23	441

× This has been revised since Appendix J was written.

72rd Brigade.
24th Division.

13th BATTALION

MIDDLESEX REGIMENT.

March 1916.

WAR DIARY or INTELLIGENCE SUMMARY

Army Form C. 2118

13th MIDDLESEX REGT

MARCH 1916. I

73/24

Place	Date	Hour	Summary of Events and Information	Remarks and references to Appendices
CAMP A. G.H.Q.	29/2/16		Major J.H.R. Cox was admitted to hospital. Captains F.H. Dawson and B.A. James were admitted to hospital. 2nd Lieut C.F.S. Vaughan took over temporary command of B Coy. Captain Dawson, and 2nd Lieut C.F.S. Vaughan took over temporary command of A Coy.	ALL MAP References are of SHEET 28 B Series Belgium & France.
	29/2/16 1.15/3/16		The Brigade was Brigade in Reserve for the manning which were to take place at "The Bluff". The Battalion was prepared to move at one hour's notice from 12 noon.	
	2/3/16.		The Bluff was successfully retaken, the Brigade was not called upon, the orders to Stand down were issued at 12.0 noon.	ALL References to Trenches see SKETCH MAP I.
SANCTUARY WOOD TRENCHES	3/3/16		The Battalion went by Tram to YPRES and relieved the 8th R.W. Kent's in the Trenches in Sanctuary wood, the 9th E. Surrey's being on its left and the 4th E. York's (60th Division) on the right. The Relief took a considerable time owing to the darkness of the night. 11th Snowed heavily all night.	
	4/3/16		The day was quiet. The 9th E. Surreys went on fairly actively to the clearances of the night, but Sniping was not complete till 12.30 am. The snipers were fairly active during the day. Casualties 2.O.R. killed. 1.O.R. wounded.	
	5/3/16		It snowed off and on during the day. The night was quiet. The 2nd Transports relieved the 9th E. Surreys on the left.	
	6/3/16		Sniping was less active, the enemy appeared to be very energetic in digging in front of his night was quiet, the snipers had knocked in some trenches and on must saps which he had installed during the day. Casualties 1.O.R. killed. 1.O.R. wounded. There was some snow during the night. the night was very quiet. Sniping considerable went on during the night from the left of C.6.	
	7/3/16		was less active. The new Sap opposite C.2 is 295 yds from the left of C.6.1. The night was quiet. and 600 yds from M.C. emplacements on left of C.1.R. Snowed hard all day. 9th R. Sussex A very quiet day, hardly a bullet. Casualties 1.O.R. wounded. 9th R. Sussex	
BELGIAN CHATEAU	8/3/16 to 11th		Relieved the Battalion in the evening, relief being complete at 1.30 am. Casualties 1.O.R. wounded. The Battalion was in Brigade Reserve at Belgian Chateau. During this time working parties were furnished each night Consisting of mens of the Battalion attended a demonstration of FLAMMENWERFER, that was given 2000 mtr range, representing the Division and 50 officers and men of the Battalion attended a demonstration of a	

Army Form C. 2118

13th Middlesex Regt.

MARCH 1916.   II

WAR DIARY
or
INTELLIGENCE SUMMARY
(Erase heading not required.)

Instructions regarding War Diaries and Intelligence Summaries are contained in F. S. Regs., Part II. and the Staff Manual respectively. Title Pages will be prepared in manuscript.

Place	Date	Hour	Summary of Events and Information	Remarks and references to Appendices
BELGIAN CHATEAU	11th		unfortunately the apparatus was out of order and therefore no demonstration was possible. The Battalion relieved the 9th R. Sussex in the Trenches in the evening. at the same time BH. Trench was taken over from the 12th R. Fusiliers (17th Brigade) by C. Company. The 7th Northamptons were in the left. Relief complete 12.45 am. Lieut W. F.	All map references, part of Sheet 28, Belgium & France.
	12th		Capt. K. Wilkinson was severely wounded in the head by a sniper. Lieut W. F. Burg took over temporary command of D Company. 2nd Lieut F. F. Nichols reported for duty from the 14th Battn Middlesex Regt. and joined D Company. The 2nd Leinsters relieved the 7th Northamptons on the left.	Aptd. to Tembs See Sketch MAP. I
	13th		A draft of 22 OR arrived from the 24th (B) Dpt. Regt. Pte J. H. R. Cox was struck off the strength of the Battalion on Transfer to England sick.	
	14th		At 12 noon the enemy commenced a bombardment on our support and Communication Trenches, this increased in violence between 2.0pm and gradually cleared about 3.0pm. The Communication Trenches and B.S.B. were considerably knocked about. Casualties 4 OR killed. 18 OR wounded. 2nd Lieuts E.J.S. Vaughan Commanding A Coy and 2nd Lt E. W. Evers did excellent work under most trying circumstances.	
	15th		2nd Lt H. E. KING was killed by an enemy sniper at dusk.	
	16th		The support line and Communication Trenches again came in for a short but intense bombardment from 2.15 - 3.15pm; but just at the rapid action of 2nd Lieut E.J.S. Vaughan, who withdrew his Company to C.T., there would have been severe casualties, but away to the withdrawal its casualties were small 1 Officer (2nd Lieut E. W. Evers (slight shrapnel wound in head) and 4 OR wounded. The 8th R. W. Kents relieved the Battalion in the evening relief complete 2.0 am. Total Casualties during month, 3 Officers 42 OR Killed and wounded. These were the heaviest casualties the Battalion has suffered since the Battle of LOOS.	

1875 W. W593/826 1,000,000 4/15 T.B.&C. &A. A.D.S.S./Forms/C. 2118.

WAR DIARY
INTELLIGENCE SUMMARY

13th Batt. MIDDLESEX Regt

MARCH 1916.

Place	Date	Hour	Summary of Events and Information	Remarks and references to Appendices
CAMP A G.II.C.	16/17		The Battalion returned to Camp A.	
	18th		The Battalion left camp at 12.30pm and marched to RENINGHELST, where it joined the 7th Northamptonshire Regt. The column headed by 73rd I.B. Headquarters then marched via WESTOUTRE – BERTHEN to METEREN. The Battalion left the column at SHEAKEN and proceeded to billets in farms in the vicinity of X.11 and X.17 (Sheet 28) Battalion Headquarters being established at X.17. A.3.1. arriving at billets at 6.30pm; the billets were taken over from the 1st Canadian Mounted Rifles	
X.17.A.3.1.	19-21st		3rd Canadian Division who marched the same day to Camp A. G.II.C. The Battalion had baths, and ordinary training was carried out. Capt B.A. JAMES returned from Hospital and took over command of A Coy vice 2nd Lieut E.F.S. VAUGHAN. 2nd Lieut E.F.S. VAUGHAN took over command of D Coy vice Lieut W.J. BURT. Lieut W.J. BURT took over command of B Company vice Lieut F.L. Wightman proceeding on leave:—	
	22nd	21.50	2nd Lieut A.W. Spence was admitted to hospital	
	25th	9.00am	The Battalion left its billets at 9.00am and marched along the BAILLEUL-LILLE Road – Bailleul Rd thro' junction to NEUVE EGLISE (B1 6 & 7 and Sheet 36) thence to MARTEPUYP HUTS T.26.C.8.9 when it relieved the 15th (48th Highlanders) Canadian Regt 1st Canadian Division at 12 noon. The Battalion then became "Battalion in Divisional Reserve." Ordinary training was carried out.	
T.26.C.8.9.	26/30		2nd Lieut C.H.C.B. BLACK reported for duty from 14th Batt. Middlesex Regt.	
	27-		Col. L.G. Oliver left for England on leave, being recalled to report at the War office. Major C.E. Cunningham 13th Pioneers KELAT=I=GHILZIE REGT. Indian Army also	
	30		24th Division O.S.U.3. took over the command of the Battalion.	

WAR DIARY or INTELLIGENCE SUMMARY

Army Form C. 2118

13th Middlesex Regt.

MARCH 1916.

Place	Date	Hour	Summary of Events and Information	Remarks and references to Appendices
KORTEPYP.	31st		The Battalion relieved the 9th Royal Sussex Regt in the Trenches opposite MESSINES, Trenches 136 – 140. A Company holding 136 /137 & 138. D Company 139 and 140. B Company garrisoned STINKING FARM and Highland Farm. C Company Fletcher's Field. Headquarters were established at Fisher's Place and details at La Plus Douve Fm. Regimental Bombers and Scouts at Well Walk. Relief complete 11.45 p.m. Casualties 1. OR wounded.	For ref. Trenches to Trenches see Sketch map with April's War DIARY.
TRENCHES 136 – 140 opposite MESSINES.				

Casualties for March 1916.

	KILLED		DIED of WOUNDS.		WOUNDED		accidentally wounded		wounded on duty		Transferred to ENGLAND) SICK.	
	O.	OR.	O.	OR.	O.	OR.	O.	OR.	O.	OR.	O.	OR.
	0.	9.	–	6.	⊗2.	36.	–	1.	–	1.	1.	51.

x 2nd Lt M.E. KING.

⊗ Capt. K. WILKINSON
2nd Lt E.W. EVERS.

The following draft's joined during the month.

4/3/16	50 OR.	12/3/16	2nd Lt F. Nichols. 16th Middx
13/3/16	22 OR.	27/3/16	2nd Lt H.C.P. Black. –
25/3/16	35 OR.		left the above, joined with the Battalion
29/3/16	26 OR.		when 19 was in England.
	133		

Clarence Keen Major
Cmdg 13 Middlesex Regt

Army Form C. 2118

WAR DIARY
or
INTELLIGENCE SUMMARY
(Erase heading not required.)

13th MIDDLESEX REGT.
APPENDIX G.

Summary of Events and Information

Summary of Casualties while in the YPRES SALIENT.

	KILLED		Accidentally Killed		Died of Wounds		DIED		WOUNDED		Accidentally Wounded		Wounded at Duty		SHELL SHOCK		TOTAL	
	O	OR	O	OR	O	OR	O	OR	O	OR	O	OR	O	OR	O	OR	O	OR
JANUARY 1916	-	3	-	1	-	2	-	-	1	16	-	5	-	-	-	2	1	30
FEBRUARY 1916	-	12	-	-	-	5	-	1	2	16	-	1	-	2	-	-	2	36
MARCH 1916	1	9	-	-	-	5	-	-	2	35	-	1	-	1	-	-	3	51
TOTAL	1	24	-	1	-	12	-	1	5	67	-	6	-	5	-	1	6	117

71rd Brigade.
24th Division.

13th BATTALION

MIDDLESEX REGIMENT.

April 1916

"A" Form.   Army Form C. 2121.
MESSAGES AND SIGNALS.   No. of Message ....

Prefix .... Code .... m.	Words	Charge	This message is on a/c of:	Recd. at .... m
Office of Origin and Service Instructions	Sent		.... Service.	Date ....
....	At .... m.			From ....
....	To			
	By		(Signature of "Franking Officer.")	By ....

TO { Officer i/c AG's Office Base

Sender's Number.	Day of Month.	In reply to Number.	
JF 10	5		A A A

Enclosed herewith War Diaries for April (2 sheets) and 1 French map.

P.T. Chevallier Adjt.
13th Middlesex Regt

WAR DIARY or INTELLIGENCE SUMMARY

Army Form C. 2118

13th Middlesex Regt

April 1916

Place	Date	Hour	Summary of Events and Information	Remarks and references to Appendices
TRENCHES 136-141. OM MESSINES	1/6th		Battalion relieved 9th R Sussex on night of 30/1st. The disposition of the Battalion was as follows. 2 companies in front line Bombers & Scouts in Well Walk 2 Platoons in Striking Farm, 2 Platoons in Rat Alley and Highland Farm, 1 Company in Breastworks and Fletchers Field details at La Plus Douve Farm, Battalion HQ at Fisher's Place. The 2nd Leinsters were on the left and 12th R Fusiliers on the right. Nothing unusual occurred during this tour. 2nd Lieut Welden Williams was wounded.	Map ref Sheet 28 Belgium & France "N" Series for trenches see TRENCH Map 28 SW4
RED LODGE T 18d. 7.4.	night 6/7th		Relieved by 9th R Sussex Regt. The Battalion went back to RED LODGE and became Battalion in Brigade Reserve.	
TRENCHES 136-141.	7/12 night 12/13 13/18 night 18/19		The Battalion relieved the 9th R Sussex Regt in the Trenches. 2nd Leinsters on the left. The Battalion relieved the 9th R Sussex Regt on the right. Nothing unusual occurred during this tour. 12 R Fusiliers on the right. Relieved by 9th R Sussex Regt. The Battalion went back to KORTEPYP Camp.	
KORTEPYP Camp T 26.C.	19/24 night 24/25 25/30		Ordinary training was carried out. Church parade held on Easter Day. Relieved 9th R Sussex Regt in the Trenches. 2nd Leinsters on the left. 12th Fusilier on the right.[x] On the night of the 28/29 there was a false gas alarm.[+] On the night of the 29/30. The right company the enemy released gas from his trenches at 1.10 a.m. it was enclined to particularly the Battalion were. The stand to get it, thrown the left. 17 them moved on our Well Walk, Striking Farm, La Plus Douve Farm and Highland Farm. It was practically free from gas front. No cling to the low ground by the Drive. Fishers Place. Our Artillery was excellent alarm the enemy did not attempt an infantry attack. Our damages were not effective, in front of Well the enemy put up barrage, another in front of Stenburg Farm and along Walk and Hambury Farrel, and another along the road between Plus La Striking Farm — Russians Rd. There were every little shelling of the from B line Douve to MIDLAND Farm. All was quiet by 3. 30 am.	x. Hyperno Hospital on Map the Brigade on the right HQ in the presence of any gas on that was no

1875 Wt. W 593/826 1,000,000 4/15 J.B.C. & A. A.D.S.S./Forms/C. 2118.

WAR DIARY or INTELLIGENCE SUMMARY

Army Form C. 2118

XXIV 13th Middlesex Regt

Vol 6

April 1916

Place	Date	Hour	Summary of Events and Information	Remarks and references to Appendices
Trenches 136–141.	Night 29/30"		The night was very dark. The enemy fired machine guns across our not parapets in order that the Glendon snipers not be heard and also to keep down the sentries heads. Approx casualties: 9 O.R. Killed. Wounded: I.O. (2nd Lt R.M. Rickford) 26 O.R. Found: 2 Officers (2nd Lieut Weldon Williams and 2nd Lieut J. F. Remit), 40 O.R. Some 30 O.R. slightly gassed ("at duty"). The 9th Rl Sussex Regt relieved the Battalion. The Battalion went back to Red Lodge.	Map ref. Sheet 28. Belgium & France Series "B". for Trenches see Sketch Trench Maps 28 SW 4
	Night of 30/4/16		The following drafts arrived during the month:— 10.4.16.— 1. O. 67. O.R. 18.4.16.— 2. O. — 21.4.16.— — 10 O.R. 22.4.16.— 2. O. 11. O.R. — — — — 5. Os. 88. O.R. The following Officers arrived during month:— Capt C. Middleton. Lieut C.K. Allen. 2nd Lieut V. Weldon Williams. 2nd Lieuts S. Smith, 2nd Lieut H.R. Nicholson. Approx Casualties during month. Killed. Died. Died of Wounds. Wounded (including gas) Transferred to England sick or other causes. O. OR. O. OR. O. OR. O. OR. O. OR. — 11. — 1. — 2. 4. 173. 1. 36. — 10.	

Cunningham Lt Col
Comdg 13th Middlesex

WAR DIARY
or
INTELLIGENCE SUMMARY
(Erase heading not required.)

Army Form C. 2118

Instructions regarding War Diaries and Intelligence Summaries are contained in F.S. Regs., Part II. and the Staff Manual respectively. Title Pages will be prepared in manuscript.

Sketch Map II
HOOGE LEFT SECTOR
to ROULERS.

Sheet 28. I 10.11.12. 16.17.18

Place	Date	Hour	Summary of Events and Information	Remarks and references to Appendices

British trenches in Blue.
German trenches in Red.
Craters
Machine Guns

Scale 1:10,000.

73rd Brigade.
24th Division.

13th BATTALION

MIDDLESEX REGIMENT.

May 1916

24 MAY (C. 2118)
I. JONES
Vols 7.8

WAR DIARY
or
INTELLIGENCE SUMMARY
(Erase heading not required.)

13th Middlesex Regt.
May 1916

Place	Date	Hour	Summary of Events and Information	Remarks and references to Appendices
Red Lodge	April 30/1st	3:30 am	Arrived at Red Lodge after having been relieved by the 9th R. Sussex Regt. in the Messines Trenches (T 135-140). Brigade Reserve at Red Lodge. Very large number of sick owing to after effects of the gas. 'A' coy had a nil parade state, other coys. were similarly situated. Working parties were accordingly quite small. On 3rd 2/Lieut. G.J. Roma died from the effects of gas. Major Wood on leave was struck off the strength of the battalion; and 2/Lieut. J. McKeever reported for duty from 4th Cheshire Regt.	
—	Night 6/7th		Battalion relieved the 9th R. Sussex in the Messines trenches leaving 35 men still sick at the Transport. 'B' coy with 1 platoon of 'A' + 'C' coy in the front line.	
Messines Trenches T135-140	7th-12th incl.		'A' coy in support, 'D' coy in reserve. On 8th Lieut. Fulton went to hospital and Lieut. Stewart of the 73rd Field Ambulance and 2/Lieut. J.R. Adam reported for duty from the Cadet School. On the same day took his place.	
—	Night 12th/13th		The tour was a very quiet one. Casualties Killed 1 O.R. Wounded 5 O.R. The Bn. was relieved by the 9th R. Sussex Regt. and marched to Kortepyp Camp as Div. Reserve.	
Kortepyp Camp	13th-18th incl.		The ordinary schemes of Training were carried out.	

S.J.W.

Army Form C. 2118

13th Middlesex Regt.

WAR DIARY
or
INTELLIGENCE SUMMARY

May 1916

II

(Erase heading not required.)

Instructions regarding War Diaries and Intelligence Summaries are contained in F.S. Regs., Part II. and the Staff Manual respectively. Title Pages will be prepared in manuscript.

Place	Date	Hour	Summary of Events and Information	Remarks and references to Appendices
Kortepyp Camp	13th–18th incl.		On 13th 2/Lt A.N. Hingley took over command of 'B' Coy from Lieut F.C. Wigington, and the following officers reported for duty between 14th and 18th :– 2/Lieuts. Brownrigg, Rickford (rejoined), Ward, Arnold & Trower.	
	Night 18th/19th		The Bn. relieved the 9th R. Sussex Regt. in the trenches, this was the first of the 8-day tours. On 20th 2/Lieut Trampton reported for duty. Nothing of importance occurred during this tour	
Messines Trenches			Casualties were Killed – 1 Died of Wounds – 1 Wounded 10	
	Night 26th/27		The Bn. was relieved by 9th R. Sussex Regt. and proceeded to Red Lodge as Brigade Reserve.	
	27th–31st incl.		Usual short parades and working parties took place, whilst in the latter from 27th – 3rd June inclusive 1 Off. & 8 O.R. were wounded.	
Red Lodge	27th		On 27th Lieut Fulton rejoined and on 28th 2/Lieut Weldon-Williams rejoined.	
	28th		On the night of 28th 2/Lieut C.B. Saunders was wounded whilst on a working party.	
	31st		On 31st Lieut Fulton went on leave, Capt. Dalton from the 73rd Field Ambulance taking his place. During this tour 2nd Lieut R.M. Rickford took over command of 'B' coy from 2/Lieut A.N. Hingley.	

J.W. Ottawinder[?]

A.N. Hingley

1875 Wt. W593/826 1,000,000 4/15 J.B.C. & A. A.D.S.S./Forms/C.2118.

Army Form C. 2118

WAR DIARY
or
INTELLIGENCE SUMMARY
(Erase heading not required.)

13th Middlesex Regt

May 1916

III

Place	Date	Hour	Summary of Events and Information	Remarks and references to Appendices

Summary of Casualties during the month.

	KILLED		DIED of WOUNDS		WOUNDED		EVACUATED		Transferred to England		Occidental Wounds		Total.	
	OFF.	O.R.	OFF.	O.R.	OFF.	O.R.	OFF.	O.R.	OFF.	O.R.	OFF.	O.R.	OFF.	O.R.
	–	2	1*	8	1	26	1	43	1+	1	–	1	4	81

* 2nd Lieut. Guy Ranew died from effects of gas poisoning

+ Major Wood on leave struck off on. for duty at home

Increase in strength during month

5 officers
114 men.

DRAFTS	
OFF.	O.R.
9⊕	195

⊕ Officers reported for duty

6-5-16 2/Lt. J. McKeever from 4th Cheshire Regt.
8-5-16 " J.R. Adam — Cadet School
14-5-16 " Browning — 13th Middlesex Regt.
15-5-16 " R.M. Richford — rejoined from hospital
15-5-16 " L.W. Ward from Y.O.C.
16-5-16 " Arnold — 2nd Middlesex Regt.
17-5-16 " Transter — 6th "   "
20-5-16 " Frampton — 15th "   "
28-5-16 " Whaldon-Williams rejoined from hospital

73rd Brigade.
24th Division.

13th BATTALION

MIDDLESEX REGIMENT.

June 1916

WAR DIARY or INTELLIGENCE SUMMARY

Army Form C. 2118

13th Middlesex Regt.

June 1916

Place	Date	Hour	Summary of Events and Information	Remarks and references to Appendices
Messines Trenches	Night 3/4th		The Bn. relieved the 9th R. Sussex Regt. in the Messines trenches	
	5th		2/Lieuts. Dove from the 15th Mdx and de Paas from the 6th Mdx reported for duty. Between 11.30 p.m. & 12.30 a.m. on this night Lieut-Colonel Cunningham was shot through both arms and body whilst walking along "Sussex Trench" about 20 yards behind T 140, the wounds were fortunately not mortal.	
	7th		Major Howlett, Brig. Maj. 73rd Inf. Bde. took over command of the Bn. 2/Lt Hampton shell shock	
	9th		Major Greene of the 7th Dragoon Guards took over command of the Bn. with Capt. Reed acting as 2nd in command. Capt. Middleton being in command of "C" coy.	
			Apart from change in command its tour was an uneventful one.	
			Casualties were Wounded 2 Offs. 15 O.R.	
	Night 11th-12th		The Bn. was relieved by the 9th R. Sussex Regt. and marched to KORTEPYP CAMP as Divl. Reserve	
	12th		2/Lieut Hubbard reported for duty. Officers Ante-room was started and run for 4 days with great success.	
Kortepyp Camp	16th		The Bn. handed over Kortepyp Camp to the 26th Australian Regt. and marched via Bailleul to Wakefield Huts, Locre, (taking these over from Durham Light Inf., of 50th Div.	
Wakefield Huts, Locre M29a Sheet 28	17th	1 am	The Bn. stood to for 2 hours. A heavy bombardment could be heard apparently all along the line. Gas had been released by the Germans on the same sector as before. On 20th 2/Lieut Gliddon reported for duty from 1st Mdx.	

Army Form C. 2118

WAR DIARY
or
INTELLIGENCE SUMMARY

13th Middlesex Regt.

June 1916

II

(Erase heading not required.)

Instructions regarding War Diaries and Intelligence Summaries are contained in F. S. Regs., Part II. and the Staff Manual respectively. Title Pages will be prepared in manuscript.

Place	Date	Hour	Summary of Events and Information	Remarks and references to Appendices
Spanbroekmolen Trenches E1 – F5	Night 19/20		The Bn. relieved 4th E.Yorks Regt. in Spanbroekmolen Trenches (E1 – F5). This sector is very long being about 1000 yards of front with a salient known as the Bull Ring at the S. end. Distance from enemy trenches at N. end about 300 yds. Opposite Bull Ring about 40 yds. During the tour there were constant strafes by enemy 'Minnies' with considerable effect. Our snipers accounted for 4 Germans.	
	22d		In the evening a heavy minnie dropped on a Bombers dugout in E3, killing 4 men and wounding 4.	
	23d		There was a considerable strafe about 4.30 pm with Minnies, whizz-bangs & heavies. A Stokes gun + crew including an officer were blown to pieces in Windy Lane.	
	Night 26/27		There was a raid by the 4th E. Yorks on trenches opposite the Bull Ring which was not attempted successful, there was considerable retaliation but with not much effect.	
	Night 27/28		Bn. was relieved by 9th R. Sussex Regt. and went to Kennel Shelters. Casualties were Killed 9 O.R. Wounded 31 O.R.	
Kennel Shelters N19 d. Sh. 28	Early		The Bn. was at Kennel Shelters with usual working parties till July 4th. HQ and A coy however moved into Kemmel Village on the evening of July 1st.	

JMcCullough
Major

Army Form C. 2118

13th Middlesex Regt.
III
June 1916

WAR DIARY
or
INTELLIGENCE SUMMARY
(Erase heading not required.)

Instructions regarding War Diaries and Intelligence Summaries are contained in F. S. Regs., Part II. and the Staff Manual respectively. Title Pages will be prepared in manuscript.

Place	Date	Hour	Summary of Events and Information	Remarks and references to Appendices
			Summary of Casualties during the month.	

	KILLED		DIED of WOUNDS		WOUNDED		EVACUATED		Transferred to England		Accidental Wounds		Total.	
	OFF.	O.R.	OFF.	O.R.	OFF.	O.R.	OFF.	O.R.	OFF.	O.R.	OFF.	O.R.	OFF.	O.R.
	—	10	—	3	2	41	1	36	—	3*	—	7	3	100

* 2 Transferred to Base.

Drafts during the month.

DRAFTS	
OFF.	O.R.
5	101

Increase in strength during month.

2 Officers   1 O.R.

⊕ Officers reported for duty

5-6-16   2nd Lieut Dove from 15th Middlesex Regt.
5-6-16   "   "   de Paso "   6th   "   "
9-6-16   Major Greene   "   7th Dragoon Guards.
12-6-16 2nd Lieut. Hubbard on first appointment
20-6-16 "   "   Gliddon from 1st Middlesex Regt.

WAR DIARY
or
INTELLIGENCE SUMMARY

Army Form C. 2118

13th Middlesex Regt.

Sketch Map IV

(Erase heading not required.)

Instructions regarding War Diaries and Intelligence Summaries are contained in F. S. Regs., Part II. and the Staff Manual respectively. Title Pages will be prepared in manuscript.

Place	Date	Hour	Summary of Events and Information	Remarks and references to Appendices
			BRITISH LINE — Spanbroek mole — F5 — F4 — F2 — E6 — New Cut — Bull Ring — E1 — E3 — Windy Lane — Regent St — Regent St Dug outs — Piccadilly — Railway & Road — 3.5 — 2.9 — 2.3 — Frenchman's Farm — N	

1875 Wt. W593/826 1,000,000 4/15 J.B.C. & A. A.D.S.S./Forms/C. 2118.

73rd Inf.Bde.
24th Div.

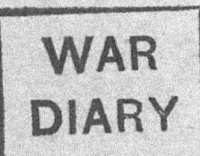

13th BATTN. THE MIDDLESEX REGIMENT.

J U L Y

1 9 1 6

WAR DIARY
13th Middlesex Regt.
INTELLIGENCE SUMMARY
July 1916

Army Form C. 2118

Place	Date	Hour	Summary of Events and Information	Remarks and references to Appendices
Kennel Shelters	Evening 1st		HQ moved to Doctor's House N 21 d 7.6 at Kennel and 'A' coy moved to the Chateau. Kennel N 21 d 3.6. The remainder of the Battalion stayed at Kennel shelters.	Rfts on Sheet 28
	2		Orders to move at an hours notice these were cancelled later.	
	evening 3		HQ moved back to Kennel shelters. 'A' coy remaining at the Chateau.	
	4/5 night		The Bn. relieved half the Northants in the Wytschaete trenches G4 – J3. 'C' coy as reserve in the Chateau. B coy + 2 platoons of 'D' in the front line. 'A' coy in support at H5 and Junveri. Town night. Remainder of 'D' coy at G5.	
Wytschaete Trenches G4 – J3 map N 24	6		The Northants took over the other half of the Northants front. There was a pretty heavy strafe with minnies and shell. One shell burst on a traverse and wounded 7 men – its legs on each side, the men were bombers. Minnies were troublesome throughout the tour, a large hole being blown in the parapet of G4. One sniper hit a German officer. 2/Lieut Weldon-Williams was accidentally killed while on a course at the Army Grenade School.	
	Night 8/9		Casualties were Killed 3 O.R. Accidentally Killed 1 Off. Wounded 29 O.R. The Bn. was relieved by the 4th Yorks Regt. and went back to Bedayon Hutts	
Bedayon Hutts, Locre	9		Locre M 29 a S.S. Capt. Allwater from 2/8th Middlesex reported for duty. 2/Lieuts S. Smith + Capt. Reed took over command of 'B' coy from Capt. Nicholson went to hospital. 2nd Lieut S. Smith.	

1875 Wt. W593/826 1,000,000 4/15 J.B.C. & A. A.D.S.S./Forms/C. 2118.

WAR DIARY

13th Middlesex Regt.

July 1916

Army Form C. 2118

Part II

(Instructions regarding War Diaries and Intelligence Summaries are contained in F.S. Regs., Part II. and the Staff Manual respectively. Title Pages will be prepared in manuscript.)

INTELLIGENCE SUMMARY

(Erase heading not required.)

Place	Date	Hour	Summary of Events and Information	Remarks and references to Appendices
Dranoutre M35-36	11	Evening	The Bn. moved to Dranoutre in billets & tents M35d & M36c. In the afternoon & early evening the village was shelled with 10 heavy H.E. but 4 were duds.	Map Ref. Sheet 28
	12		No casualties or damage resulted. Maj. Ollendorff, Capts. Smithett & Reeves from 2/7 Middlesex reported for duty.	
	18		The village was again shelled. Shells dropping quite near its Dressing Station.	
Flêtre Q34	19		The Bn. moved into very good billets just outside Flêtre area in Q34 Map 27. 2/Lt. Nicholson reported from hospital.	Map Ref. Sheet 27
	20		We were notified that in the evening of 20th 2/Lieut. Folkes-Winkes who had transferred to the T.M. Battery had been killed by a shell while going through Neuve Eglise in relief.	
	21		At a meeting of D.H. at Brigade commanders it was disclosed that the Division would shortly be moving southwards.	Map Ref.
Méteren – Vidame	24	3pm	Battalion moved off from billets entraining at Godeswaersvelde stn. at 4.50pm. 2/Lieut. Sidney Smith reported from hospital.	Amiens Sheet 17
	25	3.10am	Detrained at Saleux and marched into crowded billets at Molliens-Vidame	
	31	4.30	Bn. marched to Hangest-sur-Somme entrained there, detraining at Vacquemont	

Army Form C. 2118

WAR DIARY 13th Middlesex Regt.
INTELLIGENCE SUMMARY July 1917

(Erase heading not required.)

Place	Date	Hour	Summary of Events and Information	Remarks and references to Appendices
	31		at 2 p.m. and marched with a very hot sun into Corbie	Annex 9Jul-17
			Summary of Casualties during the month	

KILLED		ACCIDENTALLY KILLED		WOUNDED		TOTAL	
OFF.	O.R.	OFF.	O.R.	OFF.	O.R.	OFF.	O.R.
1	3	-	1	1	29	2	32

Drafts during month

4 officers

Major Oldendorff from 2/7 Middlesex
Capt. Reeves   " 2/7   "
  "   Smith   " 2/7   "
  "   Winter   " 2/8   "

73rd Brigde
24th Division.

13th BATTALION

MIDDLESEX REGIMENT.

August 1916.

To
/3rd I.B.

Herewith War Diary of this Battalion for the month of August, 1916.

8.9.16

J. Green, Major
COMMANDING
13th BN. MIDDLESEX REGT.

Army Form C. 2118

WAR DIARY
or
INTELLIGENCE SUMMARY

(Erase heading not required.)

13th MIDDLESEX REGT.
AUGUST 1916
73 Vol 10
Vol I

Instructions regarding War Diaries and Intelligence Summaries are contained in F. S. Regs., Part II. and the Staff Manual respectively. Title Pages will be prepared in manuscript.

Place	Date	Hour	Summary of Events and Information	Remarks and references to Appendices
HAPPY VALLEY	Aug 2.		Moved off at 4.30 a.m by road, reaching Sailly le Sec 7.30 a.m. Rested by River for day, moved off 6.30 p.m. to HAPPY VALLEY reaching there at 10.30 p.m. Camped there.	
	8		Training each day 5.30 – 9.0 a.m., then nothing. 2 p.m. marched across ridge to camp in valley on other side in bivouacs. Practised attacking GUILLEMONT trenches till July 17th.	
TRENCHES B.A.I ele & ARROW HEAD COPSE	17		Battalion moved up into trenches B.A.I. ele and ARROW HEAD COPSE. QUEENS were to have gone over this night but did not do so. Enemy counter barrage very heavy during night. ⟨?⟩ MOLESWORTH wounded	
	18		LIEUT. BURT first wounded by our shells then killed while going down to dressing station. 2nd LIEUT. B.PASS wounded in shoulder by our shells. CAPT. MIDDLETON & REEVES & LIEUT. PARKES buried in TEALE TRENCH and were dug out. CAPT. MIDDLETON REEVES sent to hospital.	
		2.45 pm.	Battalion attacked GUILLEMONT trenches but was held up just outside them by M.G.S from strong point on right and then shelled heavily while lying in the open. CAPTS REED, JAMES, VAUGHAN killed. 2/LIEUTS ADAM, BURCH, BLACK killed. LIEUTS. ALLEN, KING, TROWER, NICHOLSON, & SMITH wounded. About 340 O.R. casualties.	
	19		Bn. moved to BRICQUETTERIE for night. Battalion moved to CRATERS at A.S. a.8.3.	
	20		Battalion lay at CRATERS, nothing to report.	

WAR DIARY or INTELLIGENCE SUMMARY

13TH MIDDLESEX REGT.
AUGUST 1916

Place	Date	Hour	Summary of Events and Information	Remarks and references to Appendices
CRATERS	August 21		Battalion still at CRATERS, addressed by Brigadier at 2 P.M. Brigade in reserve to Division. Ready at 15 minutes notice to support either 71st or 72nd Brigade attacking on left of TRONES-GUILLEMONT ROAD from 4.30 P.M. onwards.	
	22		Relieved at CRATERS by 12th RIFLE BRIGADE at 11:45 a.m. Marched to SANDPITS CAMP arriving 4 P.M.	
SANDPITS	23		Still lying at SANDPITS, training & light parades only	
	24		Battalion relieved at SANDPITS camp and marched to bivouac E.13.7.4. taking over from 5th DIV. Weather very bad	
	25, 26		Still lying in bivouac at E.13.7.4. General training carried out	
	27		Still at E.13.7.4. Addressed by Gen: CAPPER. Ordinary training.	
	28 & 29		Training at E.13.7.4. Weather awful.	
	30		Left E.13.7.4. at 1 P.M. in pouring rain. Marched via DERNANCOURT – MEAULT to MAMETZ where two were served out guides of 4th SUFFOLKS met platoons who marched independently to GREEN DUMP and eventually completed relief of TEA TRENCH, WORCESTER TRENCH – PONT STREET & ORCHARD TRENCH at 7.30 A.M.	
	31		Trenches knee deep in mud. 7 blocked by troops. At 8.30 A.M enemy bombardment commenced on all trenches - increasing up to 2 P.M. when attack was launched driving "B" Coy out of TEA TRENCH and "A" Coy back up WORCESTER TRENCH to MACDOUGAL CT and PONT ST. Enemy advanced to ORCHARD TRENCH where they were stopped by 2/LT. GREEN with about 12 men of "D" Coy and a L.G. This party forced to retire did so in good order holding up enemy small cup forts could be brought up. "A" Coy with detachments from PONT ST. & CARLTON TRENCH also remnants of "B" & 1 platoon "D" C. Coy took stand at ___	

WAR DIARY
or
INTELLIGENCE SUMMARY

(Erase heading not required.)

Army Form C. 2118

13th Middlesex Regt.
August 1916
—III—

Summary of Casualties during the Month.

	KILLED		ACCIDENTALLY KILLED		WOUNDED		ACCIDENTALLY WOUNDED		MISSING		TOTAL	
	OFF	O.R.	OFF	O.R.	OFF	O.R.	OFF	O.R.	OFF	O.R.	OFF	O.R.
	9	88	-	1	17	321	-	7	-	146	26	563

Drafts during Month.

OFFICERS	O. RANKS
11	330
	274

2/Lieut: P. Young from 6th Middlesex Regt.   2/Lieut. P.L. Hudson from 1st Middlesex Regt.
  "   O.P.S. Grubb   "   5th   "   "   "   L. Pearson   "   "   "
  "   J.C. Tuckey   "   5th   "   "   "   L. Seaton   "   15th   "
Lieut. C.R. Studdaford from 14th Middlesex Regt. "   H.O. Davis   "   "   "
2/Lieut. A.C. Jenkins   "   "   "   "
  "   N. Blackall   "   "   "   "
  "   J.J. Bishop   "   "   "   "

73rd Brigade
24th Division.

13th BATTALION

MIDDLESEX REGIMENT.

September 1916

WAR DIARY or INTELLIGENCE SUMMARY

Army Form C. 2118

13th MIDDLESEX REGT.
SEPTEMBER 1916
I

Place	Date	Hour	Summary of Events and Information	Remarks and references to Appendices
PONNIER REDOUBT	Sept.1	Morning	"A" "B" Coys, sent to GREEN DUMP. "D" Coy withdrawn from PONT STREET and sent to GREEN DUMP. Battalion relieved by 3rd Rifle Brigade and withdrawn to PONNIER REDOUBT. 2/Lieut F.L. ROGERS and A.E. MEGSON joined the Battalion here about 4 p.m. and Capt J. NORCUTT and 2/Lieut M.S. McGAHEY at about 7p.m. the same day.	
	Sept.1 to Sept 5 inc:		Battalion provided parties for carrying ammunition, assisting at Dressing Station and detonating bombs for the 17th BRIGADE and finally the 72nd Brigade	
"	2		Captain C. ALLISTON and 2/Lieut. O.P.S. GREEN left the Battalion Sick. 2/Lieut N.E.D. CARTLEDGE and S. LIVINGSTONE joined the Battalion at the Transport Line. Two lewis gun teams sent up the line to report to 72nd Brigade	
	5		Battalion moved at 4.30 P.M. via. MAMETZ - FRICOURT. TRANSPORT LINES - MEAULTE - VIVIER MILL to DURNANCOURT. Tea was served at the Transport Lines and DURNANCOURT was reached about 9.30 P.M.	
	6		Left DURNANCOURT at 6.45 a.m. and entrained at EDGE HILL siding for LONGPRÉS. EDGE HILL dep. 9.50 A.M. LONGPRÉS arr. 1.15 P.M. Battalion detrained and marched via CONDÉ FOLIE to L'ETOILE to MOUFLERS 16 miles.	
	7		Easy day - General cleaning down. Transport which had come by road arrived in the afternoon.	
	8		Address to the whole Battalion by MAJOR GENERAL T.E. CAPPER. Ordinary training.	
	9		8 A.M. at MOUFLERS. Ordinary training. Address by C.O. to officers at 3.30 P.M.	
	10		Sunday Church Parade 9.0 A.M. Route march 10.15 A.M. 2/Lieut S. LIVINGSTONE proceeded to 4th ARMY Infantry School. No parades in the afternoon.	
	11		Still at MOUFLERS. Ordinary training. Bombing, Signalling and trench digging. Battery near L'ETOILE in afternoon. Lieut. E.S.D. Baulton from 27th MIDDLESEX joined the Battalion	

WAR DIARY or INTELLIGENCE SUMMARY

Army Form C. 2118

13th MIDDLESEX REGT
September 1916
II

Place	Date	Hour	Summary of Events and Information	Remarks and references to Appendices
MOUFLERS	11		Major C. B. "B" Coy. 2/Lieut. A. N. HINGLEY rejoined from hospital (wounded). Capt. HANNAY of 12th NORTH STAFFS took charge of reinforcement camp and was attached to "A" Company.	
"	12		Ordinary training. Transport visit at AILLY-LE-HAUT-CLOCHER. A working party of 200 for unloading ammunition left MOUFLERS at 5.30 p.m. returning about 12.30 a.m.	
"	13		Wet day. Lectures etc under cover. 2/Lieut N.E.D. CARTLEDGE proceeded to LE TOUQUET to undergo a Lewis Gun course.	
"	14		Ordinary training	
"	15		Battalion route march VAUCHELLES - LES - DOMART - BUCHAMPS - SURCAMPS and MOUFLERS. Capt. PITCHEVALIER left for ENGLAND on leave. Bus received from DIVN. Hd. Qrs to be ready to move at a short notice.	
"	16		Lieut E.B.D. BRUNTON appd. Acting Adjt. Ordinary training	
"	17		Sunday. Church Parade Into bay football matches in afternoon. 1.30 p.m. Major L.M. DAWSON reported and appointed SECOND IN COMMAND.	
"	18		Wet day. Outdoor training cancelled by Brigade Ords. Instructions received for Battalion to entrain at LONGPRÉS at 5.30 a.m. September 19th 1916. Capt. HANNAY NORTH STAFFS: Camp Cmdt. MOUFLERS Reinforcement Camp attached to 13th Middlesex on the breaking up of Camp, until further orders.	
"	19		Battalion left MOUFLERS at 2.30 a.m. in full marching order, arriving at LONGPRÉS about 4 a.m. Weather very wet. Ma arrived from COLERNE Train left LONGPRÉS 6.50 a.m. proceeding via DOULLENS and ST POL arrived FOUQUEVIL at about 2 p.m. Detrained and marched to BRUAY and billeted there arriving about 5 p.m.	
BRUAY	20		BRUAY - Settling down into billets. Inspections etc. Just Norths. 2/Lieut A.E. NEGSON appointed to act as I.O. until further orders.	
"	21		Ordinary training in Trench warfare, Bayonet fighting Gas helmet drill ac. Part consisting of Major J. GREENE Lewis Gun Officer and Coy Company Commanders proceeded up the line file made tour of trenches Bus M.Gs attached them up at Loos proceeding the C. 5 took them to Loos Crossing N 11a 37 Sheet 36B). The following Officers reported for duty today	

1875 Wt. W5593/826 1,000,000 4/15 J.B.C. & A. A.D.S.S./Forms/C. 2118.

WAR DIARY or INTELLIGENCE SUMMARY

Army Form C. 2118

13th MIDDLESEX REGT
September 1916.
III

Place	Date	Hour	Summary of Events and Information	Remarks and references to Appendices
BRUAY	21		2/Lieuts. L C VOGAN, S.J.H. DILE, H.O.WILLIAMS, R HARRISON, C.A.PERRY, H.C.PRICE, C.W.WALLIS joined.	
	22		2/Lieut. N.E.D CARTLEDGE rejoined Battalion from Lewis Gun Course at LE TOUQUET. Party consisting of the Second in Command, Bombing Officer, Signalling Officer and one Officer per Company proceeded to HALLYCOURT from Chieux by bus to CARENCY to make a tour of trenches to be taken over. — Battalion left BRUAY at about 7.25 and proceeding via HOUDAIN & ESTREE reached GUOY-SERVINS about 12 noon. Battalion Headquarters at Q35d 5.3. (Sheet 36B) Brigade Head quarters at VILLERS AU-BOIS. Ref. x 19a.5.4 (Sheet 36B)	
	23		Fine Day. — Battalion left GUOY-SERVINS at 6 minute intervals starting at 8.15 a.m. in following order. — "D" Coy, Signalling "Observers" "H" Coy, "C" Coy, "D" Coy Party taken GOUY SERVINS level crossing W18 a 5.7 (36 B Sheet) — road into CARENCY running parallel to left railway running due East from level crossing through CARENCY village and into trench at x 16 c Q 3. (Sheet 36B) to HOSPITAL CORNER x 16. d 5. h (Sheet 36B) from thence SE along the road to entrance to CABARET trench at Pont G. down CABARET HERSATZ trench to KINGS CROSS (sp. 1. h.) Battalion Headquarters. Brigade taken over from SOUCHEZ RIVER Sa.n.m 7 to Pt. 316.a 1. 6. Battalion left over the left half of this front viz from SOUCHEZ RIVER to pt 38 a. 8. 7 and was known as Left Battalion which included LEINSTERS on the right, SUSSEX and NORTHANTS in reserve. In Battalion front "B" Coy provided LEFT PICQUET and CENTRE PICQUET, "C" Coy the RIGHT PICQUET. "D" Coy the RIGHT SECTOR & "A" Coy in support in the QUARRY. Comparatively quiet day except for 6 or 7 Minenwerfers & rifle grenades exchanged. 2/Lieut C.W.WALLIS left for Bayonet Fighting Course 7.2x14. 2/Lieut J.J.BISHOP came up from transport to replace him.	2nd Lt. C.A. PERRY
	24		Gas alert still on. — 4.16 a.m. a raid by our troops on our right. Dispositions unchanged. 2/Lt. C.A. PERRY admitted to hospital.	
	25		Gas alert still on. Ordinary holding of the line. 2/Lieut P. YOUNG up to ENGLAND, 2/Lieut N.E.D CARTLEDGE "D" Coy took his place, for Battalion Lewis Gun Officer.	
	26		2/Lieut J.J.BISHOP attached 129 Turnering Coy until further notice.	
	27 28		Brigadier General paid a Gas/Enemy Tour a camouflet on night. More Minenns. Turners still. — Brigadier General J.E. CAPPER paid a visit in morning. Capt. J. NORROY proceeded to transport Lines and 2nd Lt. Q.F.BUTT took command of "B" Company.	

1875. Wt. W593/826 1,000,000 4/15 J.B.C. & A. A.D.S.S./Forms/C. 2118.

WAR DIARY
or
INTELLIGENCE SUMMARY

(Erase heading not required.)

Army Form C. 2118

13th Middlesex Regt.
September 1916
IV

Place	Date	Hour	Summary of Events and Information	Remarks and references to Appendices
	29		Junction Post. 2/Lt. H.F. FRAMPTON & 2/Lt. J. BURGESS joined Battalion.	
	30		" 2/Lt. L.C. VOGAN granted leave to ENGLAND. 2/Lt. S. WEBB joined Battalion.	
			" Brigadier General – Brigade Major paid a visit.	

Summary of Casualties during the Month.

	KILLED		ACCIDENTALLY KILLED		WOUNDED		ACCIDENTALLY WOUNDED		MISSING		TOTAL	
	OFF	OR	OFF	OR	OFF	OR	OFF	OR	OFF	OR	OFF	OR
	-	3	-	-	-	15	-	-	-	-	-	18

Drafts during Month.

OFFICERS	O. RANKS
18	98

Major L. Dawson rejoined from England.
Capt. J. Morgan from 14th Middlesex Regt.
Lieut. E. Bog. Brockton from 27th Middlesex Regt.
2/Lieut. A.E. Mepard from 5th Middlesex Regt.
" F.J. Rodgers " "
" M.S. McCarthy " "
" T.B.P. Cartledge from 28th "
" S. Livingstone " 27th "
" L.G. Vogan on first commission from 18th Bedfordshire Regt.
" S.F. Pile " " " 28th London Regt.
" H.O. Williams " " " 28th "

2nd Lieut. R. Harrison from 6th Middlesex Regt.
" " C.H. Perry " 6th "
" " H.C. Price " 6th "
" " C. Wardle " 6th "
" " J. Burgess on first appointment 2 R.S.
" " H.F. Frampton from 4th I.S.B.
" " E. Webb from 16th Middlesex Regt.

O.C. 13th Middlesex Regt.

73rd Brigade
24th Division.

12th BATTALION

MIDDLESEX REGIMENT.

October 1916

Army Form C. 2118.

VOL 12

WAR DIARY
or
INTELLIGENCE SUMMARY.
(Erase heading not required.)

13 Middlesex.
Period Oct 1st to Oct 31st/16 inc.

Place	Date	Hour	Summary of Events and Information	Remarks and references to Appendices
	Oct 1		Battalion relieved in the LEFT sub-section of the CARENCY sector by the 9th Royal Sussex Regt. - Relief completed about 2 P.M. - Battalion proceeded via ERSATZ ALLEY - CABARET ROAD - HOSPITAL CORNER and CARENCY to VILLERS-AU-BOIS to billets - Major J GREEN granted rank of Lt/Col. -	
	Oct 2 to Oct 9		Battalion in billets at VILLERS-AU-BOIS. Ordinary training resumed & carrying parties provided. Battalion HQ at X.19.A.4.1. - 2nd Lt BUTT reported to C.R.E. for duty (2) 2nd Lt IIOVE took command of B Coy (2/10) Major E.H. CRICK and 2nd Lieut KEENE, both from the 6th/MX joined the battalion (3/10) 2nd Lieuts McCluskey, Rogers and Stratton proceeded to DIV SCHOOL at MAISNIL BOUCHÉ for course of instruction. (4/10) Lt/Col GREEN left for C.O. Conference near BOULOGNE (7/10).	

Army Form C. 2118.

WAR DIARY
or
INTELLIGENCE SUMMARY.
(Erase heading not required.)

Place	Date	Hour	Summary of Events and Information	Remarks and references to Appendices
Oct	2		Church Parade 9.30am in concert hall VILLERS-AU-BOIS on Sunday Oct 8/16. - 2nd-Lt VOGAN rejoined from leave (9/10).	
Oct	9	(Ctd)		
Oct	10		Battalion relieved by the 3rd Rifle Brigade & proceeded via CAMBLAIN L'ABBÉE to ESTRÉE-CAUCHIE where R.B.s billets - Relief completed about 6 P.M. Battalion Hq at W.2.d. 1, 2. - 2nd-Lt PRICE proceeded to Trench Warfare Course at PERNES. -	
Oct	11		Battalion in billets at ESTRÉE-CAUCHIE. - Working parts of 10th & 50 men still attached to T.M. Bty in the line & relieved from here. - Ordinary training resumed. - Baths - Practice trench raid carried out on trenches dug in V.10.b near HERLIN-LE-VERT (14/10) - Officers reconnoitring Oruen sector (15.1607/10).- 2nd-Lieut WEBB proceeded to 1st Army School of Sniping at LINGHEM (11/10) 2nd-Lt Brownrigg proceeded to attend course of instruction for musketry instructors at M.G. School. -	
Oct	17			

WAR DIARY
or
INTELLIGENCE SUMMARY.
(Erase heading not required.)

Army Form C. 2118.

Place	Date	Hour	Summary of Events and Information	Remarks and references to Appendices
			3	
Oct 16	11		LT/COL I. GREENE rejoined from C.O's Conference (16/10) Capt. T.H. SCHOOLING from 5th Int. took command of C Coy.	
Oct	17		2nd Lt ROGERS rejoined from course.	
Oct	18		Battalion relieved the 9th East Surrey Regt in the left out-section of the BERTHONVAL SECTOR. Batt moved up via VILLERS-AU-BOIS - CROSS COUNTRY TRACK - BOYAU 123 & WORTLEY AVENUE. Relief complete about 5 P.M. - Batt Hd Qrs at LIVERPOOL DUMP - Disposition 4 Coys in front line & 2 Coys of 9th Royal Sussex in support. -	
Oct 16	19		Tour in trenches - The battalion suffered no casualties whatever during tour. - 2nd Lts Mickeley & Shatter rejoined from course (20/10) - 2nd Lts Berry & Price rejoined from course (22/10). 2nd Lt PILE proceeded on a course of instruction (23/10) 2nd Lt PARKES proceeded to England on leave. (24/10.) Small fighting patrol sent out by our left Coy. - No enemy encountered. - 2nd Lt HARRISON admitted Hospital.	
Oct	26			

Army Form C. 2118.

WAR DIARY
or
INTELLIGENCE SUMMARY.
(Erase heading not required.)

Place	Date	Hour	Summary of Events and Information	Remarks and references to Appendices
			4	
Oct	27		Battalion relieved by 13th Canadians - Relief complete about 1/30 P.M. - Our A+B coys & Hqrs proceeded via ERSATZ ALLEY - CABARET ROAD - HOSPITAL CORNER and CARENCY to CAMBLAIN L'ABBÉ & billetted there for one night - C+D coys proceeded via the same route to VILLERS-AU-BOIS billetted there for one night. Batt Hq at W22.a.5.5.	
Oct	28		Battalion mrhed by road via GRANDS SERVINS - COUPIGNY- and HERSIN to NOEUX-LES-MINES & billetted there for one night.- Batt Hq at K.24.R.9.6. - 2nd Lt VOGAN returned from course (27/10). -	
Oct	29		Battalion proceeded via Petit-SAINS - BULLY GRENAY & GRENAY CHURCH to MAROC NORTH & relieved the 19th Welsh Rgt in Brigade Reserve.- Batt Hq at M2.d.7.9½. Relief complete about 3.30 a.m. Battalion Batt Rgan admitted to hospital (29/10).	
Oct to Oct	30 31		Battalion providing working parties daily.- Practically every available man employed in this way. -	

Army Form C. 2118.

WAR DIARY
or
INTELLIGENCE SUMMARY.
(Erase heading not required.)

Instructions regarding War Diaries and Intelligence Summaries are contained in F. S. Regs. Part II. and the Staff Manual respectively. Title pages will be prepared in manuscript.

Place	Date	Hour	Summary of Events and Information	Remarks and references to Appendices

5

SUMMARY of CASUALTIES during the Month

	KILLED		ACCIDENTALLY KILLED		WOUNDED		ACCIDENTALLY WOUNDED		MISSING		TOTAL	
	O	OR	O	OR	O	OR	O	OR	O	OR	O	OR
Maj E.H.CRICK from 6TH MX.	-	-	-	-	-	2#	-	1	-	-	-	3
2/Lt R. KEENE " 6TH "												
Capt I.H. SCHOOLING " 5TH "												

\# Includes one self inflicted.

Drafts during Month.

OFFICERS	OTHER RANKS
3	20

Major J.J. KEENE granted temp'y rank of L/Col with permission to wear badges of that rank. — Date from which this apfst takes place will be notified later.
(Authy - 1st Div A/4767/10/29.9.16)

Lieut. E.B.D. BRUNTON reported to 17th MX. 5.10.16 —
Admitted to hospital :— Major E.H.CRICK 10.10.16. 2n/Lt R. HARRISON 18.10.16.
2n/Lt H.F. FRAMPTON 12.10.16. 2n/Lt F.I. ROGERS. 30.10.16.

L.H. Dawson Major
Comdg 17th Middx Regt.

73rd Brigade.
24th Division

13th BATTALION

MIDDLESEX REGIMENT.

November 1916

Army Form C. 2118.

WAR DIARY
or
INTELLIGENCE SUMMARY.
(Erase heading not required.)

Vol 13

War Diary

13rd Middlesex Regt.

For the month of
November 1916

Army Form C. 2118.

WAR DIARY
or
INTELLIGENCE SUMMARY.
(Erase heading not required.)

13TH Middlesex Regt

Place	Date	Hour	Summary of Events and Information	Remarks and references to Appendices
Mar	1916			
	1st to 6th		Battalion in Brigade reserve at NORTH MAROC. Battn Hq at M.2.b.7.9½. 2nd Lt. Browning rejoined from course (4th). 2nd Lt Pile rejoined from course (3rd). 2nd Lt R.S.D. granted leave to ENGLAND (3rd). Lt Col J. Greene resumed command of the Battalion (3rd).	
	6th		Battalion relieved the 9th Royal Sussex Regt in the left subsection LOOS sector. Battn Hq at HATCHETTS, at G.35.d.5¼.5. Disposition. 2 Coys in the front line and two in immediate support in the ENCLOSURE M.5.1.9.8.	
	6th to 12th		In the line. No casualties. 2/Lt W.I. O'Meara granted leave to ENGLAND (9th). 2/Lt Perry Price Williams proceeded on course (12th). Lt/Col J. Greene proceeded to Commanding Officers Conference CINDETTE (12th). Major Dawson in command.	
	12th		Battalion relieved by the 9th Royal Sussex Regt.	

WAR DIARY
or
INTELLIGENCE SUMMARY.
(Erase heading not required.)

Army Form C. 2118.

Place	Date	Hour	Summary of Events and Information	Remarks and references to Appendices
Nov.	12th		and proceeded to MAROC as battalion in support. Batt Hq at M.3.a.9.4½ - disposition - Batt Hq & 2 coys in MAROC, 1 coy in DUKE ST and 1 coy garrisoning TRAVERS KEEP, ST JAMES KEEP & Q.G.1.	
	12th to 18th		In support - Working parties. 2Lt. F.H. More from 3rd Batt "The Queens" joined the battalion (14/11). 2/Lt. F.I. Rogers transferred to England - sick (14/11). Battalion relieved the 9th Royal Sussex Regt in the left subsection 106 sector. Batt Hq at HATCHETTS - dispositions as before -	
	18th		Dispositions as before.	
	18th to 24th		In the line. 4 men presented with medal ribbons by the Army Commander at divisional hqrs. (19/11). Lt/Col Grand returned from C.O.s conference resumed command of the battalion (19/11). 2/Lt Butt & 2/Lt Pile granted leave to ENGLAND (19/11). 2/Lt Butt struck off strength - (19/11). 2/Lt Pile granted leave to ENGLAND (29/11). Major Dawson in command	
			4/Col Greene admitted hospital (24/11).	

WAR DIARY or INTELLIGENCE SUMMARY

Army Form C. 2118.

Place	Date	Hour	Summary of Events and Information	Remarks and references to Appendices
Nov	24.11.		2/Lt. Ho Davis assumed duties of Officer I/C Snipers & Scouts (24/11). Only 5 casualties during tour. Battalion was relieved by the 9th Royal Sussex Regt. & became the Battalion in reserve. Dispositions - Batt. HQ & 2 Coys in NORTH MAROC - Huts in LES BREBIS & 2 Coys in LES BREBIS - Batt HQ at Hus No 519 LES BREBIS.	
	24.11. to 30.11.		In reserve - Training according to Programme - Inspections, musketry, Bayonet fighting, Bombing, Range practice, Gas Helmet drill etc. 2/Lt. KEENE proceeded on Course (25/11). 2/Lt. C.J. Arnold discharged hospital & rejoined the Battalion (24/11). 2/Lt. T.J. Bishop appd R.T.O. Loos tramways (25/11). 2/Lt. Browning proceeded to Base Depot for Tour of duty as instructor (29/11).	
	30.11.		Battalion relieved the 9th Royal Sussex Regt. Batt. lg at LOOS section - Batt. lg at HATCHETTS in the Left subsection.	

Army Form C. 2118.

WAR DIARY
or
INTELLIGENCE SUMMARY.
(Erase heading not required.)

Summary of Events and Information

Summary of Casualties during the Month

KILLED		ACCIDENTALLY KILLED		WOUNDED		ACCIDENTALLY WOUNDED		MISSING		TOTAL	
OFF	OR	OFF	OR	OFF	OR	OFF	OR	OFF	OR	OFF	OR
-	1	-	-	-	8	-	4	-	-	-	13

Drafts during Month.

OFFICERS	O. RANKS
1	14

Place	Date	Hour		Remarks and references to Appendices

73rd Brigade.
24th Division

13th BATTALION

MIDDLESEX REGIMENT.

December 1916

Army Form C. 2118.

WAR DIARY
or
INTELLIGENCE SUMMARY.

(Erase heading not required.)

T332

Vol /4

Confidential

Army Corps of
Intelligence Regiment
for the month of
December 1916.

WAR DIARY or INTELLIGENCE SUMMARY

Army Form C. 2118.

13th Battalion Middlesex Regt

Month of December 1916

Place	Date	Hour	Summary of Events and Information	Remarks and references to Appendices
DECEMBER 1916 1st to 6th inc.			In the line. Left subsection LOOS SECTOR - 7 casualties. Lieut. Qt. Brimt. RAMC. acting M.O. vice Capt R.H. Fulton R.A.M.C. admitted hospital 30/11/16. 2/Lt. C.J. Arnold appointed a/Quartermaster 30/11/16 - 6/Lt. P.M. Rickford proceeded to special duty under 24th Div. 3/12/16. 2/Lt. F.J. Stratten assumed command of A coy. 3/12/16.	
6th.			Battalion was relieved in the left subsection LOOS sector by the 9th Royal Sussex Rgt. and became the Battalion in Brigade Reserve with Batt. HQ and 2 coys in hutted in MAROC and 1 coy in DUKE ST and 1 coy in TRAVERS KEEP, ST. JAMES KEEP & O.G.1. Batt HQ at M.3.a.9 4 5 -	
6th to 12th inc.			In Brigade Reserve - 2 casualties. Draft of 60 men reported from A1 at G.B.D. 7/12/16.	
12th.			Battalion relieved the 9th Royal Sussex Rgt. in	

… Army Form C. 2118.

WAR DIARY
or
INTELLIGENCE SUMMARY.
(Erase heading not required.)

Place	Date	Hour	Summary of Events and Information	Remarks and references to Appendices
1916	DECEMBER			
	12th to 18th incl.		the left subsection has been. Batt H.Q. at HATCHETTS. On the line – 3 casualties. 2/Lt. H.C. Price wounded 13/12/16. Major (Acting Lieut/Colonel.) J. Greene appointed to permanent command of 13th Bn. Middlesex Regt. with effect from 9/12/16.	
	18th		Battalion relieved by the 9th Royal Sussex Regt. and became the Battalion in Divisional Reserve with Batt H.Q and two Cos in hutts at Les Brebis and two Cos in NORTH MAROC. Batt HQ at house 519 Les Brebis.	
	18th to 24th incl.		In Divisional reserve. Wiring practice, musketry, Officers Lt. KENDALL and F.D. YATES joined battalion from 6th Bn Middlesex Regt. 21/12/16. Draft 17 2/5 arrived. Proceeded to 24th Divisional Training Camp at ALLOUAGNE 19/12/16.	
	24th		Battalion relieved the 9th Royal Sussex Regt. in	

Army Form C. 2118.

WAR DIARY
or
INTELLIGENCE SUMMARY.
(Erase heading not required.)

Instructions regarding War Diaries and Intelligence Summaries are contained in F. S. Regs., Part II. and the Staff Manual respectively. Title pages will be prepared in manuscript.

Place	Date	Hour	Summary of Events and Information	Remarks and references to Appendices
	1916 DECEMBER.			
	24th to 30th inc.		The left subsector LOOS Sector Battalion Ho at Hatchetts - 3 casualties. In the line.	
	30th.		Battalion relieved by the 9th Royal Sussex Regt & became the Battalion in Brigade Reserve with Batt Ho & 2 coys at MAROC and 1 coy in DUKE ST & another in TRAVERS KEEP, ST JAMES KEEP and D.G.1. Batt Ho at M.3.9.90-45. Working & carrying parties.	

Army Form C. 2118.

WAR DIARY
or
INTELLIGENCE SUMMARY.
(Erase heading not required.)

Instructions regarding War Diaries and Intelligence Summaries are contained in F.S. Regs., Part II. and the Staff Manual respectively. Title pages will be prepared in manuscript.

Place	Date	Hour	Summary of Events and Information	Remarks and references to Appendices

Summary of Casualties during the Month.

KILLED		ACCIDENTALLY KILLED		WOUNDED		ACCIDENTALLY WOUNDED		MISSING		TOTAL	
OFF	OR	OFF	OR	OFF	OR	OFF	OR	OFF	OR	OFF	OR
-	2	-	-	1	12	-	1	-	-	1	15

Drafts during Month

OFFICERS	O RANKS
2	296

J. Greene Lt. Col.
15th Middlesex Regt.

Army Form C. 2118.

WAR DIARY
or
INTELLIGENCE SUMMARY.
(Erase heading not required.)

War Diary of
13th Bn. The Middlesex Regiment
for the month of
January 1914

9 Oct 15

Army Form C. 2118.

WAR DIARY
or
INTELLIGENCE SUMMARY.
(Erase heading not required.)

Jany 1917   13 Batt Middlesex Regt

Place	Date	Hour	Summary of Events and Information	Remarks and references to Appendices
1917				
	Jan 1st to 4th inc.		In Brigade Reserve at Maroc. 2/Lieut P.G. HUTSON proceeded for duty to Divisional Headquarters. 2/Lieut R. KEENE accidentally wounded. 2/Lieuts W.R.T. SKINNER and H.B. RANGER joined the Battalion from 6th Mx Regt. (2-1-17). Major L.H. DAWSON proceeded to England to attend 2nd Senior Officers Course at Aldershott (4-1-17).	
	Jany 5th		Battalion relieved the 9th Royal Sussex Regt in the left subsection. Bn sector. Battn HQ at HATCHETTS.	
	Jany 5th to 10th inc.		In the line. 8 casualties. Major J.H. COOKE 4th Battalion Shropshire Light Infantry attached (5th to 8th).	
	Jany 11th		Battalion relieved by the 9th Royal Sussex Regt and became the Battalion in Divisional Reserve with HQ and 2 Coys in les Brebis and 2 Coys in NORTH MAROC. Battn HQ at Rue de Brebis.	
	Jany 11th to 16th inc.		In divisional reserve. Capt P.T. CHEVALLIER and Major J.H. ELLWOOD mentioned in dispatches in London	

WAR DIARY
or
INTELLIGENCE SUMMARY.

Army Form C. 2118.

Place	Date	Hour	Summary of Events and Information	Remarks and references to Appendices
	Jany 17th		Gazette of Jan 4/17 and Sgt H. KING awarded distinguished Conduct Medal and Sgt Loder Lugette (1-1-17). Capt R.M. RICHFORD rejoined from special duty with 24th DIV. (16-1-17).	
	Jany 17th to 22nd incl		Battalion relieved the 9th Royal Sussex Regt in the HATCHETTS - LOOS SECTOR - Batt H.Q. at HATCHETTS - left Subsector. Casualties. 1 Officer 13 O.R. Capt N. McMICKING., Black Watch attached to Battalion H.Q. from 17th to 23rd inclusive. B.V. WADLOW joined Baton from 5th Bn mx Regt (18-1-17). Capt R.M. RICHFORD assumed duties of 2nd-in-Command (19-1-17).	
	Jany 21st		The Battalion carried out a successful raid on enemy trenches at 9.30 a.m. blowing up many dugouts containing Germans & one machine gun emplacement with mobile charges, killing 6 of the enemy in his trench & bringing back 3 prisoners - Our casualties were 1 Officer (2/Lieut H.O. WILLIAMS) missing believed killed and	

WAR DIARY
or
INTELLIGENCE SUMMARY.
(Erase heading not required.)

Army Form C. 2118.

Place	Date	Hour	Summary of Events and Information	Remarks and references to Appendices
			3 Other ranks wounded and one OR killed. The names of the officers who took part are:- Lieut- PARKES D.W. (O.C. Raid). " WILLIAMS H.O. " PILE S.J.H. " VOGAN L.C. Congratulating messages were received from the following:- General Sir. H.S. HORNE K.C.B. Army Commander Maj General J.E. CAPPER C.B. Commanding to Brig General B.R. MITFORD C.B. D.S.O. Temporarily commanding 24th Div.	
Jan 23rd			Battalion relieved by the 9th Royal Sussex Regt and became Battn in Brigade Reserve with Batt HK & 2 Coys in MAROC. 1 Coy in DUKE ST and 1 Coy finding garrisons in O.T. 1, TRAVERS and ST JAMES KEEPS.- Batt HQ at M.3.a.90.45.-	
Jan 23rd to 29th inc			In Brigade Reserve - Manual working parties provided	

Place	Date	Hour	Summary of Events and Information	Remarks and references to Appendices
	29th Jan		Battalion relieved the 9th Royal Sussex Regt in the left Subsection. has relie. Batt no Let HATCHETTS.	
	Jan 29th to 31st inst		In the line.	

Army Form C. 2118.

WAR DIARY
or
INTELLIGENCE SUMMARY.
(Erase heading not required.)

Instructions regarding War Diaries and Intelligence Summaries are contained in F. S. Regs., Part II. and the Staff Manual respectively. Title pages will be prepared in manuscript.

Place	Date	Hour	Summary of Events and Information	Remarks and references to Appendices
			Summary of Casualties during the Month.	

KILLED		DIED OF WOUNDS		ACCIDENTALLY KILLED		WOUNDED		ACCIDENTALLY WOUNDED		MISSING		TOTAL	
OFF	OR	OFF	OR	OFF	OR	OFF	OR	OFF	OR	OFF	OR	OFF	OR
-	5	-	2	-	-	1	19	1	-	1	-	3	26

Drafts

OFFICERS	O. RANKS
9	109

J. Greaves, Lieut Col,
Comdg 18th Middlesex Regt.

Army Form C. 2118.

WAR DIARY
or
INTELLIGENCE SUMMARY.
(Erase heading not required.)

Vol/6

Place	Date	Hour	Summary of Events and Information	Remarks and references to Appendices
Confidential			13th Bn. Yorkshire Regiment war diary for the month of February 1917.	

Army Form C. 2118.

WAR DIARY
or
INTELLIGENCE SUMMARY.
(Erase heading not required.)

13th Middlesex Regt.

Month of February 1917

Place	Date	Hour	Summary of Events and Information	Remarks and references to Appendices
1917 Feb-	1st to 4th inc		In the line - left subsection Loos Sector - Casualties 13. 2/Lieut A.B. Ingram wounded in action (1·2·17) 7818 Sgt S.O. Saunders and 41821 L/Cpl H. Stewart awarded the military medal.	
Feb-	4th		Battalion relieved by the 9th Royal Sussex Regt and became Battalion in Divisional Reserve. Killed at Les Brebis- Batt Hq at house no 519.	
Feb-	4th to 10th inc		In Divisional reserve - Training as per programme. Capt R.M. Richard granted special leave to England (4·2·17 to 5·3·17) 2/Lieut E.A. Groves joined the Batt from 7th Reserve Batt Mx Regt (5·2·17). Temp Lieut R.S. Dove appointed temporary Captain (London Gazette 15·1·17) Capt J. Nagney wounded at duty (7·2·17). 2/Lieut F.H. Moore accidentally wounded (9·2·17).	
Feb-	10th		Battalion relieved in Divisional Reserve by 8th East Lancs Regt & marched via NOEUX-LES-MINES (one night) VAUDRICOURT HESDIGNEUIL - GOSNAY and LABEUVRIERE	

Army Form C. 2118.

WAR DIARY
or
INTELLIGENCE SUMMARY
(Erase heading not required.)

Instructions regarding War Diaries and Intelligence Summaries are contained in F. S. Regs., Part II. and the Staff Manual respectively. Title pages will be prepared in manuscript.

Place	Date	Hour	Summary of Events and Information	Remarks and references to Appendices
Feb.	10th (cty)		to LAPUGNOY for Divisional Rest. Batt Hd at Château at 11.16 a. 6. 0. -	
Feb	10th to 28th inc		On Divisional rest. Batt training as per programme & with special reference to open warfare. Lieut/Col J Greene granted special leave to England (13-2-17 to 14-3-17) Major C. A. Vickers Jones assumed command of the Batt vice lt/col J. Greene (13-2-17). Capt A.N. Hingley assumed duties of Second-in-command vice Major C.A. Vickers Jones (13-2-17). 2/Lieut H.T. Kendall appointed Bombing Officer (12-2-17). 2/Lieut T. Bruning transferred to Royal Flying Corps (14-2-17). 2/Lieut H.E. Marriott from H.A.C. joined the Batt - The Battalion along with the other battalions of the 73rd Inf Bde, was inspected by General Nivelle, Generalissimo of the French Army, at HESDIGNEUIL (16-2-17)- Interpreter LeRoy joined the Batt as Interpreter.	

Army Form C. 2118.

WAR DIARY
INTELLIGENCE SUMMARY.
(Erase heading not required.)

Instructions regarding War Diaries and Intelligence Summaries are contained in F. S. Regs., Part II. and the Staff Manual respectively. Title pages will be prepared in manuscript.

Place	Date	Hour	Summary of Events and Information	Remarks and references to Appendices
Fel	10th to 28th inc.		Vice Interpreter General transferred (15-2-17) - Military Cross awarded by the Field Marshal Commanding in Chief to:- Lieut. D.W. Parkes 2/Lieut. S.J.H. Pile - 2/Lieuts. H. Rogerson and T.B. Faulkner from 26th Bn (County of London) Regt. joined the Batt (25-2-17) - Capt J. Holt Schooling and 2/Lieut. H.T. Kendall admitted hospital (27-2-17).	

Army Form C. 2118.

WAR DIARY
or
INTELLIGENCE SUMMARY.

(Erase heading not required.)

Summary of Events and Information

Summary of Casualties during the Month

KILLED		DIED OF WOUNDS		ACCIDENTALLY KILLED		WOUNDED		ACCIDENTALLY WOUNDED		MISSING		TOTAL	
OFF	OR	OFF	OR	OFF	OR	OFF	OR	OFF	OR	OFF	OR	OFF	OR
1	2	1	1	1	1	2	9	1	2	1	1	3	13

Drafts

OFFICERS	O. RANKS
4	17

Williams Major
Commanding 13th Manchester Regt

Army Form C. 2118.

WAR DIARY
or
INTELLIGENCE SUMMARY.
(Erase heading not required.)

Vol 17

War Diary for the month of
March 1917
of
13th Battalion the Middlesex Regiment

Place	Date	Hour	Summary of Events and Information	Remarks and references to Appendices
Seven				

Army Form C. 2118.

WAR DIARY
or
INTELLIGENCE SUMMARY.
(Erase heading not required.)

13th Middlesex Regiment

Summary of Events and Information

Month of March 1917.

Place	Date	Hour	Summary of Events and Information	Remarks and references to Appendices
1917 March	1st to 4th		In Divisional Rest at LAPUGNOY.	
	4th		Battalion marched from LAPUGNOY to billets at HAILLICOURT staying there one night.	
	5th		Battalion relieved the 2nd Battalion of the 1st Canadian Infantry Brigade in the left subsection Souchy II Sector, marching via HERSIN - BOUVIGNY and AIX NOULETTE. Battalion headquarters at M.32.C.05.05 in Headquarters Trench.	
	5th to 10th		In the line - casualties - 6.	

Army Form C. 2118.

WAR DIARY
or
INTELLIGENCE SUMMARY.

(Erase heading not required.)

Instructions regarding War Diaries and Intelligence Summaries are contained in F. S. Regs., Part II. and the Staff Manual respectively. Title pages will be prepared in manuscript.

Place	Date	Hour	Summary of Events and Information	Remarks and references to Appendices
1917 March	10th		Battalion was relieved in the left subsection Souchez II sector by the 9th Royal Sussex Regiment and became Battalion in Brigade Reserve, manning the LORETTE SPUR DEFENCES. Battalion Headquarters at X.10.d.5.2. in ABLAIN ST NAZAIRE.	
	10th to 16th		In Brigade Reserve. Improving LORETTE DEFENCES.	
	16th		Battalion relieved the 9th Royal Sussex Regt in the left subsection Souchez II sector. Battalion Hq at M.32.c.05.05.	
	16th to 22nd		In the line - Casualties 7. Capt A.N. HINGLEY assumed command of the Battalion vice Major C.H. VICKERS JONES admitted hospital 16-3-17. Capt N.R. MATTHEWS A.A.M.C. performed the duties of	

WAR DIARY or INTELLIGENCE SUMMARY.

Army Form C. 2118.

Place	Date	Hour	Summary of Events and Information	Remarks and references to Appendices
March	1917			
			M.O. to the Battalion vice Capt R.A.H.FULTON R.A.M.C. admitted hospital 18-3-17 to 30-3-17.- 2/Lt H.P.LUSCOMBE transferred to ENGLAND sick 6-3-17.	
	22nd		Battalion relieved by the 9th Royal Sussex Regt and became the Battalion in Divisional Reserve with H.Q. and 2 Coys in HELLS in SAINS EN GOHELLE and 2 Coys in BOUVIGNY HUTS. Batt H.Q. at the Château. R.I.d.9.2↑.	
	22nd to? 31st		In divisional reserve.- Lt/Col T.GREENE rejoined from leave to England and resumed command of the battalion. 23-3-17 66 Cavalry Draft proceeded to ROUEN to report to S.O. Sundry Reinforcements 27-3-17 — 2/Lt. M.S. McGAHEY granted Special leave to ENGLAND 30-3-17 — 2/Lt J.J.BISHOP granted leave resumed	

Army Form C. 2118.

WAR DIARY
or
INTELLIGENCE SUMMARY.

(Erase heading not required.)

Instructions regarding War Diaries and Intelligence Summaries are contained in F. S. Regs., Part II and the Staff Manual respectively. Title pages will be prepared in manuscript.

Place	Date	Hour	Summary of Events and Information	Remarks and references to Appendices
1917				
March	22nd to 31st		duties of R.T.O. at AIX NOULETTE 29-3-17 — Batt Hq and 2 Coys in SAINS EN GOHELLE moved to billets in FOSSE 10. Batt Hq at R.8.b.6.8. — 29-3-17 — draft of 43. O.R. arrived from HIst- I.B. Depot. 29-3-17 — Major C.H. VICKERS JONES assumed command of the Batt vice Lt/Col J. GREENE temporarily commanding 73rd Inf. Brigade 27-3-17 — 2/Lt C.A. PERRY performed the duties of Adjutant- to the batt vice Capt P.T. CHEVALLIER performing the duties of Staff Captain at 73rd I.B. Hq. — 29-3-17 —	

Army Form C. 2118.

WAR DIARY
or
INTELLIGENCE SUMMARY.
(Erase heading not required.)

Instructions regarding War Diaries and Intelligence Summaries are contained in F. S. Regs., Part II. and the Staff Manual respectively. Title pages will be prepared in manuscript.

Place	Date	Hour	Summary of Events and Information	Remarks and references to Appendices

Summary of Casualties during the Month

KILLED		DIED OF WOUNDS		ACCIDENTALLY KILLED		WOUNDED		ACCIDENTALLY WOUNDED		MISSING		TOTAL	
OFF	OR	OFF	OR	OFF	OR	OFF	OR	OFF	OR	OFF	OR	OFF	OR
-	1	-	-	-	-	-	8	-	4	-	-	-	13

Drafts

OFFICERS	O. RANKS
1	58

Vickery, Major
Commanding 13th Middlesex Regt.

13th BATTN. MIDDLESEX REGIMENT

73rd INFANTRY BRIGADE

24th DIVISION

APRIL 1917

Army Form C. 2118.

WAR DIARY

INTELLIGENCE SUMMARY

(Erase heading not required.)

Vol 18

73rd

13th Middlesex Regt.
For the month of
April 1917

Instructions regarding War Diaries and Intelligence Summaries are contained in F. S. Regs., Part II. and the Staff Manual respectively. Title pages will be prepared in manuscript.

Place	Date	Hour	Summary of Events and Information	Remarks and references to Appendices

17th Bn. MIDDLESEX REGT.
Army Form C. 2118.
ORDERLY ROOM.

WAR DIARY
or
INTELLIGENCE SUMMARY

(Erase heading not required.)

13th Middlesex Regt.

April 1917.

Place	Date	Hour	Summary of Events and Information	Remarks and references to Appendices
	1917			
	Night of March 31st/April 1st		Advance Party proceeded to CARENCY SECTORS to take over from the 46th & 47th CANADIAN BNS. 2/Lt. A.E. MEGSON wounded in action.	
	Night of April 1st-2nd		The BN relieved the CANADIANS holding the line from BOYAU BRISSON to SOUCHEZ RIVER.	
	April 2nd		Our preliminary bombardment started at 8 a.m., bringing heavy retaliation. The trenches were in very bad condition. Capt. J.N. MORPHY ('C'Coy) & 2/Lt. B.K. WORSLEY ('D'Coy) Major L.H. DAWSON rejoined the BN from leave. Offrd. arriv'd ALDERSHOT, Major C. VICKERS-JONES moved to the Transport lines. April 4th. Capt. A.N. HINGLEY ('D'Coy) wounded at duty.	
	April 3rd		'A'&'D' Coys proceeded to CHATEAU DE LA HAIE & their place in the line was taken by the 44th & 46th CANADIAN BNS. April 8th Lt. O.W. PARKES ('B'Coy) wounded in action.	
	Night of April 8/9		At 5:30 a.m. the CANADIANS attacked from KENNEDY CRATER onwards. On the night of April 9/10 'A'&'D' Coys returned from CHATEAU DE LA HAIE & relieved the 44th & 46th CANADIAN BNS.	
	April 9th		On the night of April 11/12 the BN was relieved by the 44th, 46th & 50th CANADIAN BNS. & moved into huts at CHATEAU DE LA HAIE.	
	April 13th		The BN moved into Billets at FOSSE 10 (SAINS).	
	April 14th		At 9.30 a.m. the BN moved to AIX NOULETTE (BDE. H.Q.) for instruction.	

WAR DIARY
INTELLIGENCE SUMMARY

(Erase heading not required.)

Army Form C. 2118.

Place	Date	Hour	Summary of Events and Information	Remarks and references to Appendices
			2/	
	April 15th		advanced by ARRAS RD. TR, RATION TR, & over the open in Artillery formation under considerable shell fire, to ANGRES to form BDE RESERVE in the advance on LENS. On the night of the 14/15 'B' Coy sent a working party to the 12th Royal Fusiliers in BOIS DE RIAUMONT. Steady long-range shelling through the night round Batn. H.Q. Operation orders from Brigade received at 7 a.m. Battn advanced in small parties to front line at Eastern edge of the BOIS DE RIAUMONT. The word was told by 2 Coys of 12th Royal Fusiliers, & the general idea was for the 13th Middx to advance through these Coys, with their final objective in the suburbs of LENS. But the advance was not to be pushed in face of serious opposition; in that case the Brigades on our flanks would be more likely to be able to get through. At 9:15 a.m. a patrol of 12 men under 2nd Lt CARTLEDGE advanced from the wood, they at once came under M.G. fire from houses & trenches in CITÉ RIAUMONT. 2nd Lt CARTLEDGE wounded in arm, 7 O.R. killed or wounded.	

WAR DIARY or INTELLIGENCE SUMMARY

Army Form C. 2118.

Place	Date	Hour	Summary of Events and Information	Remarks and references to Appendices
	April 16.		3/ The Coy patrols pushed on, A Coy on Right C Coy on left & made progress in face of steady opposition. A footing was obtained in the N. end of CITÉ RIAUMONT. Our advanced posts held on until dusk, when they were ordered to withdraw to the line of the wood by G.O.C. 2nd Division, who was visiting the front line. Advanced Batln H.Q. was withdrawn at night from the western edge of the BOIS DE RIAUMONT to cellars in LIÉVIN, moving up again next day when operations were resumed. 2nd Lt YATES, an excellent officer, died in every one killed today. About 50 50 other casualties. Proportion of killed unusually high. Operations resumed, after artillery preparation. Progress was again made. But A Coy on the right found themselves up against a very strong position, little damaged by our artillery. 2nd Lt VOGAN severely wounded, casualties other ranks about 20. 2nd Lt NORTHANTS & went in to In the evening the Battn was relieved by 7th NORTHANTS & went in to Brigade Support on SOUCHEZ RIVER line. HQ at WHITE CHATEAU, LIÉVIN.	

WAR DIARY
or
INTELLIGENCE SUMMARY.

(Erase heading not required.)

Army Form C. 2118.

Place	Date	Hour	Summary of Events and Information	Remarks and references to Appendices
	April 17 & 18.		In Brigade support. Heavy shelling night of 17th/18th. Relieved evening of 18th by 8th Sherwood Foresters, 46th D wision. Battn marched to PETIT SAINS to billets.	
	April 19.		Marched to MARLES-LES-MINES.	
	April 20.		Marched to Regtl billets in FLECHIN. 13 mile march. Men did very well.	
	April 20-25.		At Rest in FLECHIN. On 23rd Battn inspected by B.G.C. 73rd Bde. Genl DUGGAN, who complimented the Battn on their recent work. Training of specialists started.	
	April 26.		Marched to AUCHEL. Lt ROBERTS, 2nd Lt PHILIPPS & DAWKINS joined from 62nd Battn.	
	April 27.		Marched to NOEUX-LES-MINES, still where 73rd Bde became Bde in Reserve to 1st Corps.	
	April 28.		Training at NOEUX. 2nd Lt VOGAN died of wounds in hospital. A great loss to the Battn.	
	April 29 & 30.		Training.	

Army Form C. 2118.

WAR DIARY
or
INTELLIGENCE SUMMARY.

(Erase heading not required.)

Instructions regarding War Diaries and Intelligence Summaries are contained in F. S. Regs., Part II. and the Staff Manual respectively. Title pages will be prepared in manuscript.

Place	Date	Hour	Summary of Events and Information	Remarks and references to Appendices
			Summary of Casualties during the Month	

KILLED		DIED OF WOUNDS		ACCIDENTALLY KILLED		WOUNDED		ACCIDENTALLY WOUNDED		MISSING		WOUNDED & MISSING		TOTAL	
O	OR	O	OR	O	OR	O	OR	O	OR	O	OR	O	OR	O	OR
3	48	1	4	-	-	3	91	-	2	-	2	-	1	4	151

Drafts

OFFICERS	O. RANKS
4	23

J. Grimm, Lieut: Col.
Commanding 13th Middlesex Regt.

2353 Wt. W2544/1454 700,000 5/15 D. D. & L. A.D.S.S. Forms/C. 2118.

Confidential

Vol 19

War Diary
of
13th Battalion Middlesex Regiment
for month of
May 1917

Army Form C. 2118.

WAR DIARY
or
INTELLIGENCE SUMMARY.

(Erase heading not required.)

13th Middlesex Regiment

May 1917

Place	Date	Hour	Summary of Events and Information	Remarks and references to Appendices
1917	May 1st		Lt Col. J. Greene to hospital. Major L.H. Dawson assumed command of the Battalion. Training continued.	
	May 2nd to May 4th		Training continued. 2nd Lieut R.S. HARRIS joined the Battalion from 5th Middlesex Regt on 4th May.	
	May 5th		Battalion marched to LAPUGNOY – a very hot march.	
	May 6th		Rested. 2nd Lt S.S. SMITH joined Battalion from 5th Middlesex Regt.	
	May 7th		Training.	
	May 8th		Battalion marched to BUSNES.	
	May 9th		Battalion marched to BUSNES.	
	May 10th		Battalion marched to PECQUEUR.	
	May 11th		Battalion inspected by Major General J. CAPPER C.B. Comdg 24th Div. Lt C.K. ALLEN and 2nd Lt E.D. GODDARD joined Battalion from 5th Middlesex.	
	May 12th		Battalion marched to STEENVOORDE area via HAZEBROUCK – a very long march (16½ miles) and an exceedingly hot day.	
	May 13		Rested.	

WAR DIARY
or
INTELLIGENCE SUMMARY

Army Form C. 2118.

13th Middlesex Regiment

May 1917

Place	Date	Hour	Summary of Events and Information	Remarks and references to Appendices
1917			(2)	
	May 14		Battalion marched in the evening to the DICKEBUSCH (Cont'd) via RENINGHELST. Battalion H.Q. and 2 Companies at Trench Warfare School. H.26.d. central. 2 Companies in DICKEBUSCH and A Coy at WALL GARDEN at North Eastern edge of village. Supplement to London Gazette dated May 15th 1917 Lt Col. J. GREENE mentioned in Despatches for the second time. The whole of the 73rd Inf. Bde. placed at the disposal of the C.E. X Corps for work.	
	May 15			
	May 16		Work continued under the C.E. X Corps	
	May 17			
	May 18		Captain A.N. HINGLEY assumed the duties of Second in Command to the Battalion with effect from 1.5.17. Work continued.	
	May 19			
	May 20		Lt.Col. J. GREENE transferred to England Sick 14-5-17. Authority given for the interned Officers to wear the badges of the ranks stated against their names, in the London Gazette —	

Major. J.H. DAWSON — Lieut. Colonel
Captain. A.N. HINGLEY — Major.
2nd Lieut. M.S. McGAHEY — Captain.

WAR DIARY
or
INTELLIGENCE SUMMARY

Army Form C. 2118.

May 1917   1/3 Middlesex Regiment

Place	Date	Hour	Summary of Events and Information	Remarks and references to Appendices
1917			(3)	
	May 21st		Work continued. C.O. 2nd in Command and Company Commanders made a general reconnaissance of the 23rd Divisional Front held by 69th Inf Bde. with Headquarters at RAILWAY DUGOUTS I.21.c.4575.	
	May 22nd		Authority granted for 2nd Lieut W.T. O'MEARA to wear the badge of rank of Lieutenant pending the publication of promotion in the London Gazette. Work continued. 2nd in Command and Company Commanders made a detailed reconnaissance of the 41st Divisional Front, held by 122nd Inf Bde. with H.Q. at BURGOMASTER FARM, I.34.c.5.	
	May 24.		Work continued.	
	May 25.		Work continued. 2nd in Command & Company Commanders made a general reconnaissance of the 47th Divisional Front, occupied by 141st Bde. with H.Q. at BEDFORD HOUSE.	
	May 26.		Work continued. Captain P.T. CHEVALLIER proceeded to 73rd Bde. H.Q. as a Staff Learner.	

Army Form C. 2118.

WAR DIARY
or
INTELLIGENCE SUMMARY.
(Erase heading not required.)

Instructions regarding War Diaries and Intelligence Summaries are contained in F. S. Regs., Part II. and the Staff Manual respectively. Title pages will be prepared in manuscript.

Place	Date	Hour	Summary of Events and Information	Remarks and references to Appendices
	May. 27.		Work continued. The Walled Garden was heavily shelled between 6am & 8am. In the afternoon A & B Coys. moved to Bivouacs at H 26 d 30.10.	
	May. 28.		Work continued. The Bn. moved in the evening to a camp at HERSKEN M.8.c. 30.40. after being relieved by the 12th Bn. ROYAL FUSILIERS. 2nd Lieut. N.H.R. JADE. was admitted to Hospital.	
	May. 29.		Rested.	
	May. 30.		Battalion bathed.	
	May. 31.		The Battalion moved into the STEENVOORDE training area, with Bde. H.Q. at K 25 c 40.15.	

Army Form C. 2118.

WAR DIARY
or
INTELLIGENCE SUMMARY.
(Erase heading not required.)

Summary of Events and Information

Summary of Casualties during the Month

KILLED		DIED		MISSING		WOUNDED		WOUNDED AT DUTY		TOTAL	
OFF	ORS	OFF	ORS	OFF	ORS	OFF	ORS	OFF	ORS	OFF	ORS
-	-	-	-	-	-	-	3	-	-	-	3

Drafts during Month

OFFICERS	O RANKS
16	338

A.N. Huxley, Major
Commanding 13th Middlesex Regt

Army Form C. 2118.

WAR DIARY
or
INTELLIGENCE SUMMARY.

Vol 20

War Diary of
13th Battalion Middlesex Regt
for month of
June 1917

Army Form C. 2118.

13th Middlesex Regt.
June 1917.

WAR DIARY
or
~~INTELLIGENCE SUMMARY.~~
(Erase heading not required.)

13th Bn. MIDDLESEX REGT.
No. M108/512 Date 30.6.17
ORDERLY ROOM

Instructions regarding War Diaries and Intelligence Summaries are contained in F. S. Regs., Part II. and the Staff Manual respectively. Title pages will be prepared in manuscript.

Place	Date	Hour	Summary of Events and Information	Remarks and references to Appendices
	June 1-4		73rd Bde Pioneer Battalion training area just north of STEENVOORDE (BOIS DE BEPUVOORDE)	
	" 2.		2/Lt S. WEBB proceeded on leave to ENGLAND.	
	4.	6.30 p.m.	Bn. moved to tents at G.26.c.4.3. (next night)	
	5.	11 p.m.	Bn. moved to Camp "P" at H.13.a.90.00. Slept in the open as the were no tents which there. (X-Y night)	
	6.	Midnight.	Bn. moved to Assembly Area (Trenches between IRON CHATEAU & CHATEAU CIGARE) Carrying party under 2/Lt E.D. GODDARD detail, etc. remained behind at "P" Camp.	
			During the day the following officers rejoined the Bn from leave.	
			2/Lt H.E. MARRIOTT.	
			2/Lt H. ROGERSON.	
			2/Lt J.B. FAULKNER.	
			They did not proceed with the Bn to the Assembly Trenches.	
			Maj A.H. HINGLEY. (Second in cmd)	
			Capt J.H. SCHOOLING. (O.C. C Cy)	

WAR DIARY
or INTELLIGENCE SUMMARY.

Army Form C. 2118.

Place	Date	Hour	Summary of Events and Information	Remarks and references to Appendices
	June 7th		Capt. M.S. McGahey (O.C. D'Coy). The above officers moved with last Assembly Trenches and returned the same night to the Transport lines. (Y-Z night's) Capt (Temp Lt-Col.) J. GREENE, Dragoon Guards, attd. 18th Middx Regt awarded D.S.O. The assembly trenches were reached abt 2 a.m. At 3.10 a.m. the 41st Divn went over the top & captured the Ridge. (1st objective). At the same time several large mines were exploded. Trenches bombarded heavily all morning & during that time the Blue (DAMM STRASSE) & Black lines (2nd & 3rd objects) were taken by the 41st Divn.	
		11.30 a.m.	The 18th Middx Regt moved forward to ECLUSE TRENCH & OLD FRENCH TRENCH.	
		1.30 p.m.	The Bn moved forward to the BLACK LINE (present front line) & jumping off line for 73rd Bde). Within a few minutes of arrival the Bn went over the top (3.10 p.m.) under an excellent barrage. DISPOSITION:— Rt Front Coy B Coy under Capt R.S. DOVE.	

WAR DIARY
or
INTELLIGENCE SUMMARY.
(Erase heading not required.)

Army Form C. 2118.

Place	Date	Hour	Summary of Events and Information	Remarks and references to Appendices
			Lt FRONT Coy A Coy under Capt F.J. STRATTEN. Rt SUPPORT " D " " 2/Lt DAWKINS. Lt " " C " " Lt ROBERTS. Mopping-up were commanded by 2/Lt C.W. WIGGS (D Coy) & 2/Lt R.W. PHILLIPS (B Coy) Our objective was known as the Green Line. She extended from the front edge of RAVINE WOOD on the right, via OLIVE TRENCH to the HOLLEBEKE RD on the left. The objective was gained without much difficulty, the Coy on the right consolidating well in front of RAVINE WOOD & VERHAEST FM. Owing to the Division on our left not coming forward with us, D Coy was left with their flank in the air, & had to perform a difficult movement to protect themselves. They were therefore unable to consolidate the left half of OLIVE TRENCH. C Coy (left Support Coy) had to be called on to assist B Coy (left Front) to form the defensive flank.	

Place	Date	Hour	Summary of Events and Information	Remarks and references to Appendices

June 8

During the first day the enemy's artillery was more active. Bn. suffered more from back-spray than from anything else. During the attack about 100 unwounded & 20 wounded were captured, mostly in the RAVINE — also 5 machine guns, trench mortar & a large quantity of material. The prisoners included 2 officers. Quiet in the morning. Patrols on right (?) front found no sign of enemy — on left OLIVE TRENCH was found to be held by enemy. Shelling in afternoon. Heavy reciprocal fire by both artilleries from 7 p.m. to 9 p.m.

June 9

Sporadic shelling, chiefly on support & reserve lines. Strong patrols in conjunction with Division on our right pushed up OLIVE TRENCH at dusk. Trench found strongly held & could not be captured without artillery preparation. 2nd I/C MAKE HAM wounded & missing after operation, after casualties about 15. D.S.P. Lit. on Batt's H.Q. (a converted German dug out), no harm done

WAR DIARY
or
INTELLIGENCE SUMMARY.
(Erase heading not required.)

Army Form C. 2118.

Place	Date	Hour	Summary of Events and Information	Remarks and references to Appendices
	June 10.		Steady shelling at intervals. Heavy bursts of fire of all calibres at 10 p.m. Batt. relieved by 2/1st KRR, & marched by platoons to DOMINION CAMP.	
	June 11. to 12			
	June 13. 15		Batt. moved in evening to MICMAC CAMP. Batt. moved in evening to new camp at H.26.d.8.4, a Batt. in Reserve to the Brigade.	
	16 to 18		Training in Camp, & working parties daily up the line.	
	June 19.		Batt. relieved 2nd LEINSTERS in the line, from RAILWAY EMBANKMENT & BATTLE WOOD to YPRES-COMINES CANAL inclusive. Much shelling during relief & 4 casualties. A Coy on Reft, C Coy on Left, B Coy on SPOIL BANK on right, D Coy in Reserve.	
	June 20 to 23.		Consolidating & strengthening neg. line under persistent heavy shelling, especially by night. 2nd Lt HARRIS wounded on June 22, & died of wounds on 24th. 2nd Lt WEBB wounded by the same shell.	

Army Form C. 2118.

WAR DIARY
or
INTELLIGENCE SUMMARY.

(Erase heading not required.)

Instructions regarding War Diaries and Intelligence Summaries are contained in F. S. Regs., Part II. and the Staff Manual respectively. Title pages will be prepared in manuscript.

Place	Date	Hour	Summary of Events and Information	Remarks and references to Appendices
	June 23-24.		Batts relieved by 9th EAST SURREYS. Very steady shelling during relief. marched to MICMAC CAMP, last Coy arriving at 6 a.m.	
	25 trg. 26. 27.		Training & resting. Entrained at RENINGHELST SIDING area. Detrained at 10 p.m. at LUMBRES, marched 4 miles to billets near NIELLE.	
	June 28-30.		Resting, refitting & training.	

Army Form C. 2118.

WAR DIARY
or
INTELLIGENCE SUMMARY.
(Erase heading not required.)

Instructions regarding War Diaries and Intelligence Summaries are contained in F. S. Regs., Part II. and the Staff Manual respectively. Title pages will be prepared in manuscript.

Place	Date	Hour	Summary of Events and Information	Remarks and references to Appendices

Summary of Casualties during the Month.

KILLED		DIED of wounds		WOUNDED		WOUNDED AT DUTY		MISSING		TOTAL	
OFF	OR	OFF	OR	OFF	OR	OFF	OR	OFF	OR	OFF	OR
-	1	-	-	-	7	-	-	-	-	1	7

Drafts during Month.

OFFICERS	O. RANKS
1	261

S. [signature]
Major,
Commanding 12th Middlesex Regt.

2353 Wt. W2544/1454 200,000 5/15 D. D. & L. A.D.S.S. Forms/C. 2118.

Army Form C. 2118.

WAR DIARY
or
INTELLIGENCE SUMMARY.
(Erase heading not required.)

War Diary
of
13th Battalion Middlesex Regiment

for month of July 1917

WAR DIARY
or
INTELLIGENCE SUMMARY.
(Erase heading not required.)

Army Form C. 2118.

M2 194

10. 8. 17.

Instructions regarding War Diaries and Intelligence Summaries are contained in F. S. Regs., Part II. and the Staff Manual respectively. Title pages will be prepared in manuscript.

Place	Date	Hour	Summary of Events and Information	Remarks and references to Appendices
	July 1		2nd Lieut N.H.R. DADE granted 21 days sick leave from No 14 Stationary Hospital.	
	2		2nd Lieut W.R.T SKINNER granted leave to England from 30/6/17 to 19/7/17. 2nd Lieut S.V.H. PILE transferred to England, sick 26/6/17.	
	4		H.B. RANGER granted leave to England from 4/7/17 to 14/7/17.	
	6		Capt (A/Major) A.N. HINDLEY proceeded to Aveluy hot to attend 4 Courses at Senior Officers School commencing 8th July and struck off strength of Battalion.	
	8		Draft of 100 O/Ranks arrived for the Battalion. Capt J.H. SCHOOLING rejoined from Lewis Gun Course at LE TOUQUET.	
	9		C.S.M T.J. CORBEY awarded the D.C.M.	
	10		24 O/Ranks arrived for the Battalion.	
	11		2nd Lieut E.D GODDARD proceeded to WANDRECOURS for duty with 2nd Div TM Battery. Battalion Sports were held this day. Major Q.H.V. JONES admitted to Hospital.	
	13		Capt F.J. STRATTON granted leave to England from 12/7/17 to 22/7/17. Draft of 100 O/Ranks arrived for the Battalion.	

Army Form C. 2118.

WAR DIARY
or
INTELLIGENCE SUMMARY.
(Erase heading not required.)

Place	Date	Hour	Summary of Events and Information	Remarks and references to Appendices
	July 14.		Draft of 22 O/Ranks arrived for the Battalion. 2nd Lt. CAPERRY appointed Assistant Adjutant to the Battalion.	
		1–17	This period was spent in general training. Operation orders for a forthcoming advance in the North were received on the 6th July.	
		18	Battalion moved to billets at RENESCURE, stopping there on night of 18th.	
		19	Battalion moved to billets at CAESTRE.	
		20	Battalion moved to billets at RENINGHELST.	
		21	2nd Lt. A.H. BAKER granted leave to England from 22nd July to 1st August.	
		23	Battalion moved to camp at DICKEBUSCH.	
		25	Battalion relieved 9th EAST SURREYS in Support Area. Bn. D Companies at LARCH WOOD and A & C Coys. at SCOTTISH WOOD. 2nd Lieut S.R. GOULBURN reported for duty from 6th Batt'n. Lt. Col. L.H. DAWSON admitted to hospital. MAJOR J.R. FREND, 2nd LEINSTER Reg't assuming temporary command of the Battalion. 2nd Lieut E.D. BODDARD posted to V/24 T.M. BATTERY and struck off strength of the Battalion.	

WAR DIARY
or
INTELLIGENCE SUMMARY.

Army Form C. 2118.

Place	Date	Hour	Summary of Events and Information	Remarks and references to Appendices
	July 31		13th Battn. Middlesex Regt. acted as Battalion in support to the 73rd Infantry Brigade in the fifth army offensive. Zero hour for the attack was at 3·50 A.M. on 31st July, 1917. B Company were in close support to 2nd Leinster Regt. on the left and D Company in close support to 7th Northamptonshire Regt. D Company was called up to support the Northants very soon after Zero and during a minor operation on the flank lost all the Company Officers, 2nd Lt. C.W. WALLIS. temporarily in command of the Company, being killed and 2nd Lieuts. J.B. FAULKNER & G.G. HOLT, both gassed. as the assaulting Battalions failed to advance beyond their first objective and also had very heavy casualties in gaining their first objective, The 13th Battn Middlesex Regt. was called upon to relieve the two front battalions on the night of 31st July. D Company also being relieved having suffered rather heavy casualties.	

Date	Hour	Summary of Events and Information	Remarks and references to Appendices
July 31		Battalion Headquarters moved up from LARCH WOOD to CANADA ST. DUG OUTS during the evening of the 31st. A.C. & B. less 1 platoon B Coy, taking over the front line and one platoon B Coy in support. D Company when relieved proceeded to Transport lines, The following Officers did not proceed with the line with the Battalion. Capt F.J. STRATTEN. " M.S. McGAHEY. Lieut A.H. ROBERTS " S. SMITH.	

Army Form C. 2118.

WAR DIARY
or
INTELLIGENCE SUMMARY.
(Erase heading not required.)

Instructions regarding War Diaries and Intelligence Summaries are contained in F. S. Regs., Part II. and the Staff Manual respectively. Title pages will be prepared in manuscript.

Place	Date	Hour	Summary of Events and Information	Remarks and references to Appendices
			Summary of Casualties during the Month.	

KILLED		DIED of WOUNDS		WOUNDED		WOUNDED AT DUTY		MISSING		TOTAL	
OFF	OR	OFF	OR	OFF	OR	OFF	OR	OFF	OR	OFF	OR
3	41	–	9	5	191	2	3	–	10	10	254

Grand total during Month.

OFFICERS	O. RANKS
10	103

Sidney Jones
Commanding 18th Middlesex Regt.

Lewis Colonel
Middlesex Regt.

Army Form C. 2118.

73/24.

Vol 22

WAR DIARY

INTELLIGENCE SUMMARY.

(Erase heading not required.)

Instructions regarding War Diaries and Intelligence Summaries are contained in F. S. Regs., Part II. and the Staff Manual respectively. Title pages will be prepared in manuscript.

Place	Date	Hour	Summary of Events and Information	Remarks and references to Appendices
Secret.			13th Batn. Middlesex Regiment for the month of August 1917.	

WAR DIARY
or
INTELLIGENCE SUMMARY.

(Erase heading not required.)

Army Form C. 2118.

13th Bn. MIDDLESEX REGT.
ORDERLY ROOM.

Place	Date	Hour	Summary of Events and Information	Remarks and references to Appendices
	August 1st 1917		On the night of 31 July/1st Aug A&C Coys moved from LARCH WOOD TUNNELS to relieve the 2nd LEINSTERS in the front line (SHREWSBURY FOREST). During the day (31/7"/'17") B&D Coys had moved into the front line to support the LEINSTERS & on the arrival of A & C Coys, D Coy moved back to our Transport lines at MICMAC CAMP, while B Coy less 1 Platoon continued to act A Coy & held the left Coy front. C Coy took over the right Coy front & relation of B Coy train in Support near the western edge of SHREWSBURY FOREST. During the last 24 hrs the Bn. had suffered heavy casualties, so that it became necessary to bring up most of the reserve officers & men from the Transport Lines. Officer casualties under this date:— 2Lt. H. ROGERSON Comdg A Coy. Killed in action. 2Lt. C.W. WALLIS " D " Killed in action. 2Lt. H.E. MARRIOTT A Coy Wounded in action. 2Lt. G.G. HOLT D Coy Wounded in action (Gas) 2Lt. J.B. FAULKNER " " Wounded in action (Gas)	

Army Form C. 2118.

WAR DIARY
or
INTELLIGENCE SUMMARY.
(Erase heading not required.)

Instructions regarding War Diaries and Intelligence Summaries are contained in F.S. Regs., Part II. and the Staff Manual respectively. Title pages will be prepared in manuscript.

Place	Date	Hour	Summary of Events and Information	Remarks and references to Appendices
	August 1st.		2LT N. BLACKALL attd 93rd L.T.M. Bty. wounded at duty.	
	August 4th.		On the night of the 4/5th D Coy came up from the Transport lines & relieved A. Coy less 1 platoon (which remained in the front line) & C Coy less one platoon, which moved up to support in place of 1 platoon of B Coy. This platoon of B went into the front line.	
	August 5th.		On Aug 5/6 during the night 16th the Bn was relieved by the 8th BUFFS, 7th & 1st I.B. Lincolns & went into the DICKEBUSCH area. There ordinary training was carried on. During this time the ground was in a very bad state owing to the rain. Enemy's shelling was heavy. MAJ. E. S. C. GRUNER 1st BN ESSEX RGT assumed temp. command of the Bn.	
	August 9th.		The following officers reported for duty from the 5th Bn MIDDLESEX Rgt & were posted as under: 2LT H. W. CATTLE to A Coy.	

WAR DIARY
INTELLIGENCE SUMMARY

Place	Date	Hour	Summary of Events and Information	Remarks and references to Appendices
	August 9th		2Lt A.R. HAYFORD to D Cy. 2Lt A.J. REPSTON " " Transferred to ENGLAND sick. 2Lt H.B. RANGER to B Cy.	
	August 10th		2Lt S.J. ASHMAN reported for duty from 5th Bn MIDDLESEX Regt & posted to D Cy. He (might with him a draft of 41 O.Rs. Night 11/12 73rd N.I.B. relieved 17th Bde. (Rect ~~from S. Forces~~), ~~Essex~~ SHREWSBURY FORESTERS in LARCH WOOD TUNNELS) B'd Coys relieved 2 Coys A 12/k ROYAL FUSILIERS while A'C Coys relieved 1 Cy of the 3rd RIFLE BDE. in CANADA ST TUNNELS (MT SORREL). Bn H.Q. at LARCH WOOD TUNNELS. The Bn was in reserve to the rest of the Bde, consequently the consisted entirely of working & carrying parties. The enemy's artillery	
	August 11th		was active than last night. Lt A.H. ROBERTS C Cy) to France to hospital 2Lt R. KEENE " ")	

Army Form C. 2118.

WAR DIARY
or
INTELLIGENCE SUMMARY.
(Erase heading not required.)

Instructions regarding War Diaries and Intelligence Summaries are contained in F.S. Regs., Part II. and the Staff Manual respectively. Title pages will be prepared in manuscript.

Place	Date	Hour	Summary of Events and Information	Remarks and references to Appendices
	August 11th		2 LT E.G. BAKER reported for duty from 4/th I.B.D. transferred to A Coy.	
	August 12th		A/R.S.M. M.W. KERRIGAN wounded in action	
			CAPT J.H. SCHOOLING to hospital	
			2 LT E.G. BAKER	
	August 13th		2 LT G. BURTON reported for duty from 5th Bn MIDDLESEX REGT transferred to C Coy.	
	August 14th		2 LT E.G. BAKER returned from hospital.	
	August 15th		On the night 15/16. 7/2 I.B. relieved 73 I.B.	
			A Coy was relieved by a Coy of 9th E. SURREYS.	
			B. C. D Coys were relieved by 8th QUEENS.	
			Bn moved to MICMAC CAMP (N.W. of DICKEBUSCH) & the ordinary training was carried on.	
	August 16th		CAPT R.H. FULTON R.A.M.C. to hospital, sick.	
			CAPT I. VAN. DANDAIQUE R.A.M.C. reported for duty as Bn M.O.	
	August 19th		Bn moved to "K" Camp DICKEBUSCH. Training.	
			The following officers sent to hospital —	

WAR DIARY
or
INTELLIGENCE SUMMARY.

Army Form C. 2118.

Place	Date	Hour	Summary of Events and Information	Remarks and references to Appendices
	August 19th		2 LT H.W. CATTLE B Cy. 2 LT G.W. DAWKINS D Cy. The following officers reported for duty from 6th Bn Middlesex Regt. Lt F.L. WIGINGTON 2 LT B. TEDMAN D Cy 2 LT A.A. FOSTER C Cy	

	August 23rd		Night 23/24 73rd I.B. relieves 17th Y.B.
			 Bn. takes over Left Sub Section from 1st R.F. (extends S. of INVERNESS COPSE)
			 Dispositions Rt Front Cy B.
			                  Centre Cy C.
			                  Lt Front Cy D.
			 Close Support Rt Front Cy A.
			 Bn H.Q. in HEDGE ST TUNNELS (E of OBSERVATORY RIDGE)
			 Enemy shelling was heavy during this &n. 6th morning 5th R.F. & TD Coys repelled an enemy Counter attack. This attack was an	

WAR DIARY
or
INTELLIGENCE SUMMARY.

(Erase heading not required.)

Army Form C. 2118.

Place	Date	Hour	Summary of Events and Information	Remarks and references to Appendices
	August 24th		on the [crossed out] part of the enemy to recapture a dugout which had been taken from him 2 nights previously.	
	August 25th		Enemy attacked division on his left (14th). Dcy see opposite the left flank of the attackers succeeded in holding their line. Lt-Col. D.H. DAWSON Hampshire REGt and Lt.	
	August 26th		2 Lt. B. TEDMAN D.cy wounded at duty.	
	August 27th		Night 27/28 72.13 relieved 73.1.13. BN relieved by 4th QUEENS & ? ? very wet muddy much the relief extremely difficult. 2 Lt E.C. ANDERSON reported for duty from 5th Bn MIDDLESEX Regt was posted to B.cy.	
	August 28th		Authority was given for following offrs to wear Pledge March as shown Maj E.S.C. GRUNE. Lt. Col. Capt. P.S. DOVE. MAJ. Lt. P. LIVINGTON. CAPT. Strand C. Cy. 2Lt. R. HARRISON assumes Cmd of B Cy. Lt. H. ROBERTS. C. Cy. Hampshire REGt LAND Lct,	

WAR DIARY
or
INTELLIGENCE—SUMMARY.

(Erase heading not required.)

Army Form C. 2118.

Place	Date	Hour	Summary of Events and Information	Remarks and references to Appendices
	August 28th		Lt. W. J. O'MEARA Transport Offr. assumes duties of Bde. T.O. & acts as Orderly officer of Capt.	
	August 29th		2Lt R. KEENE C. Coy returns from hospital.	
	August 30th		2Lt H.O. DAVIES transferred from C & D Coy. BN. moves to R Camp. DICKEBUSCH. Training.	
	August 31st		2Lt N. BLACKALL attd L.T.M. BTY to hospital.	

Signed [signature]

Army Form C. 2118.

WAR DIARY
or
INTELLIGENCE SUMMARY.

(Erase heading not required.)

Summary of Events and Information

Instructions regarding War Diaries and Intelligence Summaries are contained in F. S. Regs., Part II. and the Staff Manual respectively. Title pages will be prepared in manuscript.

Place	Date	Hour		Remarks and references to Appendices

Summary of Casualties during the Month.

KILLED		DIED OF WOUNDS		ACCIDENTALLY KILLED		WOUNDED		ACCIDENTALLY WOUNDED		MISSING		WOUNDED & MISSING		TOTAL	
O	OR	O	OR	O	OR	O	OR	O	OR	O	OR	O	OR	O	OR
1	6	-	1	-	-	-	19	-	-	-	-	-	-	1	26

Drafts

OFFICERS	O. RANKS
4	332

L H Dawson Lieut: Col.
Commanding 13th Middlesex Regt.

Army Form C. 2118.

WAR DIARY
or
INTELLIGENCE SUMMARY.
(Erase heading not required.)

Vol 23

Secret

13th Bn. Middlesex Regiment
for the month of
September 1917.

Army Form C. 2118.

12th Bn. MIDDLESEX REGT.
No. M...
Date 30.9.17
ORDER (UNMARKED) Wfd
references to Appendices

WAR DIARY
or
INTELLIGENCE SUMMARY.

(Erase heading not required.)

Instructions regarding War Diaries and Intelligence Summaries are contained in F. S. Regs., Part II. and the Staff Manual respectively. Title pages will be prepared in manuscript.

Place	Date	Hour	Summary of Events and Information	references to Appendices
	September 1st & Sept 2nd.		The Bn was in Divisional Reserve at "K" Camp, DICKEBUSCH. Training. Lt-Col. E.S.C. GRUNE took over the strength of the Bn with effect from this date.	
	Sept 3rd.		2Lt S.V. ASHMAN proceeded to 98th Corps at 2nd Army Grenade & Light Trench Mortar School, TERDINGHEM. 24th Div. took over from 25th Div. on front J19. & J.7.15 J14 C 2.9. (Ref. Maps. ZILLEBEKE Ed. 5a)	
	Night 3/4th		73rd I.B took over front from S.E. corner of BODMIN COPSE to J14 C 2.9. 13th MX was Bn in reserve & was disposed as under. A & B Coys in TOR TOP TUNNELS. C & D Coys & in RAILWAY DUGOUTS (about I20d 9.8. ZILLEBEKE East) H.Q. During this tour the Bn was chiefly used for salvage work & carrying parties.	
	Sept 4th.		2LT B. TEDMAN previously reported "wounded" reported "Killed in Action". Extract from London Gaz. effect dated Aug 4th. "Temp Capt" (A/Major) A.N. HINSLEY	

2353 Wt. W2544/1454 700,000 5/15 D. D. & L. A.D.S.S. Forms/C. 2118.

WAR DIARY
or
INTELLIGENCE SUMMARY

Army Form C. 2118.

Place	Date	Hour	Summary of Events and Information	Remarks and references to Appendices
	Sept 4th (Continued)		M.C. to be Temp. Maj. 19.11.16. + " 2LT (A/CAPT) M.S. McGAHEY MC (Spec. Res) to be Temp. Capt. 27.3.17. "Under Authority granted by His Majesty The King the Field Marshal Commanding-in-Chief awarded decorations to the undermentioned officers. THE MILITARY CROSS Capt. P.T. CHEVALIER. (former Adj't) Capt (A/Maj) R.S. DOVE. 2LT. C.J. ARNOLD.	
	Sept 5th.		2 LT. H.O. DAVIES admitted to Hospital. 2 LT. C.V. ARNOLD rejoined from 24th Divisional Reg'd Course of Instruction. LT. Q.M. S.H. HENDERSON wounded at Duty. 2 LT. A.H. BAKER rejoined from Hospital. Bn was relieved in number & proceeded to "B" Camp, MICMAC CAMP. (DICKEBUSCH AREA) A & B Coys to TOR TOP TUNNELS relieved by 2 Coys 1st N. STAFFS (72 I.B.)	
	Sept 6th.			
	Night 6/7th.		C & D " " RAILWAY DUGOUTS " 1. 2 " 9th E. SURREYS (72 I.B.)	

Army Form C. 2118.

WAR DIARY
or
INTELLIGENCE SUMMARY.
(Erase heading not required.)

Instructions regarding War Diaries and Intelligence Summaries are contained in F. S. Regs., Part II. and the Staff Manual respectively. Title pages will be prepared in manuscript.

Place	Date	Hour	Summary of Events and Information	Remarks and references to Appendices
	Sept 8th		Training.	
	Sept 9th		Training. The undermentioned Officers reported for duty & posted as stated.	
			LT. D. A. ROSHER from 24th Training Res. Bn. to C Cy.	
			2LT F. TROLLOPE " 24th " " " to D Cy.	
			2LT. A. HORSFORD " 6th Bn MDDX Rgt. to B "	
Sept 10th			Bn moved from "B" Camp, MICMAC CAMP, to "U" CAMP, DICKEBUSCH (between ETANG de DICKEBUSCH & DICKEBUSCH - CAFE' BELGE RD)	
			Capt. R.M. RICHFORD having been transferred to the Establishment of 10th Corps School was struck off the strength of the Bn. with effect from 5.9."17.	
			The undermentioned Officers reported for duty have posted as under,	
			2LT W. E. PEARCE 5th Bn MDDX Rgt. to A Cy.	
			2LT P. L. TAYLOR. 24th Training Res. Bn. to B Cy.	
			LT. W.H.D. de PASS 6th Bn. MIDDx. Rgt. to C Cy.	
			LT. D.A. ROSHER was transferred from C Cy. to D Cy.	
			2LT. G. H. DAWKINS transferred to ENGLAND, sick.	
Sept 11th			Training. LT. COL V. GREENE. D.S.O. reported for duty.	

Army Form C. 2118.

WAR DIARY
or
INTELLIGENCE SUMMARY
(Erase heading not required.)

Place	Date	Hour	Summary of Events and Information	Remarks and references to Appendices
	Sept 12th		Lt-Col. J. GREENE. D.S.O. having rejoined from ENGLAND assumed Command of the Bn.	
	Sept 13th		Training. 2Lt. C.J. ARNOLD transferred from B Cy. to D Cy. with effect from 8"9"17	
	Sept 14th		Bn marched to WESTOUTRE. N.E. area.	
	Sept 15th		Bn moved by Bus to BERGUIN area. 2Lt. C.A. PERRY rejoined from 2nd Army Central School of Instruction. 2Lt. P.J. ASHMAN rejoined from 2nd Army Grenade & L.T.M. School. Training	
	Sept 16th		Capt (T/Maj) E.S.C. GRUNE, Suffolk Rgt. made A/Lt-Col.whilst commanding a Bn. 8"9"17. Temp. Capt. R.S. DOVE M.C. to be A/Maj whilst employed as second in command 16"7"17.	
	Sept 17th		Temp. Maj. L.H. DAWSON relinquishes A/Rank of Lt-Col. on ceasing to command a Bn. 24"7"17. Authority granted to the undermentioned Officers to wear badges.	

WAR DIARY
or
INTELLIGENCE SUMMARY.
(Erase heading not required.)

Army Form C. 2118.

Place	Date	Hour	Summary of Events and Information	Remarks and references to Appendices
	Sept 17th (continued)		of rank as stated. 2 LT. R. HARRISON LIEUT. LT. R. HARRISON CAPT. Whilst commanding a Coy LT. C. R. ALLEN. CAPT.	
	Sept 18th.		Training. 2Lt. W.E. STOCKLEY joined the Bn from 6th Bn MDDX Regt & was posted to C. Coy.	
	Sept 19th.		Training.	
	Sept 20th.		Authority granted for 2Lt C.A. PERRY to wear badges of rank of LIEUT. Training.	
	Sept 21st.		Bn entrained at BAILLEUL (MAIN) Stn & proceed to BAPAUME via HAZEBROUCKE, ST. POL, & ARRAS. About 11.20 P.m. just past ACHIET-le-GRAND, 2 trucks were derailed & overturned by an improperly set point. 4 O.Rs were killed & several injured.	
	Sept 22nd.		Arrived at BAPAUME early in the morning. & marched to camp near HAPLINCOURT.	

WAR DIARY
~~INTELLIGENCE SUMMARY~~
(Erase heading not required.)

Army Form C. 2118.

Place	Date	Hour	Summary of Events and Information	Remarks and references to Appendices
	Sept 22nd (Continued)		Capt. C.K. ALLEN appointed Adjt. with effect from 1·9·17. Vice Capt. P.T. CHEVALIER. M.C.	
	Sept 23rd.		Capt. J. HOLT SCHOOLING "Dismissed His Majesty's Service" with effect from 19·9·17.	
	Sept 24th.		Bn. marched to HAUT ALLAINES, 1.15a. (Ref. Map. 57c &62c Sysia) ROCQUIGNY, MANANCOURT & MOISLAINS 2Lt F.W. MAXTED reported for duty from 5th Bn. MDDX REGT 23·9·17 & posted to A Coy.	
	Sept. 25th		Temp. Lt. W. O'MEARA (2 Lt MDDX. REGT) made A/CAPT. (adjt.) Temp. . Burnaved by bus to ROISEL. 2 Lt W.E. PEARCE admitted to Hospital.	
	Sept 26th		Training.	
	Night 26/27th		73rd I.B. relieved 102nd I.B. (34th Div.) in the line (HARGICOURT) 13th MDDX REGT relieved 20th NORTHUMBERLAND FUSILIERS in the left front-sector. Dispositions. left front Coy A.	

2353 Wt. W2544/1454 700,000 5/15 D. D. & L. A.D.S.S. Forms/C. 2118.

WAR DIARY
INTELLIGENCE SUMMARY

Army Form C. 2118.

Place	Date	Hour	Summary of Events and Information	Remarks and references to Appendices
	26/9 (continued)		Right front Coy C Left front Coy B Reserve Coy D. The enemy was ok twenty quiet. Very little artillery activity. Weather good. 1 gunner very little shelled. 2 Lt C.V.A. Gowers proceeded for duty at Divisional Coy. Stores (24th Div) (Continues quiet in the line.)	
	Sept 28th.			
	Sept. 29 – 30.			

J. Greene Lt. Col.
Comdg 13th Bn. Middlesex Regt.

Army Form C. 2118.

WAR DIARY
or
INTELLIGENCE SUMMARY.
(Erase heading not required.)

Instructions regarding War Diaries and Intelligence Summaries are contained in F. S. Regs., Part II. and the Staff Manual respectively. Title pages will be prepared in manuscript.

Place	Date	Hour	Summary of Events and Information	Remarks and references to Appendices
			Summary of Casualties during the Month.	

ACCIDENTALLY KILLED		DIED of WOUNDS		WOUNDED		ACCIDENTALLY WOUNDED		WOUNDED AT DUTY		WOUNDED MISSING		TOTAL	
OFF	O/R	OFF	O/R	OFF	O/R	OFF	O/R	OFF	O/R	OFF	O/R	OFF	O/R
–	4	–	1	1	10	–	1	1	–	–	1	2	17

Drafts during Month.

OFFICERS	O. RANKS
9	69

S. Greene, Lieut Colonel,
Commanding 13th Middlesex Regt.

WAR DIARY

INTELLIGENCE SUMMARY

Confidential

13th Battalion Middlesex Regiment

for the month of

October 1917.

Vol 24

WAR DIARY or INTELLIGENCE SUMMARY

13th MIDDLESEX RGT.

OCTOBER 1917

Army Form C. 2118.

Place	Date	Hour	Summary of Events and Information	Remarks and references to Appendices
	Oct 1st. Oct 2nd. Oct 3rd.		Bn in the line (NE of HARGICOURT. Maj. A.N. HINGLEY M.C. rejoined the Bn from 4th Lewin Officers Course, ALDERSHOT. 2.Lt A.G. ASHFORD struck off the strength of the Bn. 18.5.17	
	Oct 4th & 4/5th		73rd I.B. altered its front from a 3. to a 2 Bn front. 13th MIDDLESEX RGT extended its front to SUGAR TRENCH on the right. At the same time an inter Coy. relief took place within the Bn. Coys disposed as under, Left Front A Coy. Right Front C Coy. Left Support B Coy. Right Support D Coy.	
	Oct 5th Oct 9th		2Lt. W.E. PEARCE transferred to ENGLAND sick. Divine Service for Support Coys held at Right aid Post HARGICOURT at 10.a.a. Temp. Lt. F.L. WIGINTON (promoted to Temp. Capt. 19.8.16.	
	Oct 8th & 8/9th		Bn relieved by 9th ROYAL SUSSEX RGT, marched to Divnl Res. at HERVILLY. The night was very wet & dark. HARGICOURT was shelled	

WAR DIARY
or
INTELLIGENCE SUMMARY.

Army Form C. 2118.

Place	Date	Hour	Summary of Events and Information	Remarks and references to Appendices.
	Oct 8th		The enemy was intermittently during the relief. There was only one casualty.	
			This tour of 12 days was extremely quiet & the weather was good. In spite of the small numbers of men available for work, the trenches were improved considerably during this tour.	
	Oct 9th		Authority granted for Undermentioned Officers to wear badges of rank of LIEUT.	
			2nd Lt. J. HORSFORD. 2nd Lt. W.E. STOCKLEY 2nd Lt. E.G. BAKER	
			" P. L. TAYLOR, " P.G. HUTSON " C.A. GOWERS	
			" S. WEBB, " L.W. WARD. " A.H. BAKER	
			" J.J. BISHOP. " H.O. DAVIES. " F. TROLLOPE.	
			The above promotions were confirmed 13th Oct 1917.	
	Oct 10th		Bn. Training. 70 men were employed on working parties.	
	Oct 11th		Bn. Training 130 " " " " " "	
	Oct 12th		Bn. Training 160 " " " " " "	
			Temp. Capt. P.T. CHEVALLIER M.C. ceased to hold the appointment of Adj't (to Rgtl. Duty.) 31.8."17	
			2. Lt. R. HARRISON appointed a/Capt while acting as a Cy. 5.8."17.	

Army Form C. 2118.

WAR DIARY
or
INTELLIGENCE SUMMARY.
(Erase heading not required.)

Instructions regarding War Diaries and Intelligence Summaries are contained in F.S. Regs., Part II. and the Staff Manual respectively. Title pages will be prepared in manuscript.

Place	Date	Hour	Summary of Events and Information	Remarks and references to Appendices
	Oct 13th		Bn Training. 160 men were employed on working parties.	
	Oct 14th	10.45 a.m.	Divine Service at Generation Wkt. HERVILLY. 50 men were employed on working parties. Bn relieved 9th ROYAL SUSSEX RGT of the line. Coys disposed as under.	
			Left Front — B Coy	
			Right Front — D Coy	
			Left Support — A Coy	
			Right Support — C Coy	
	Oct 15th		2nd LT. C.J. ARNOLD M.C. admitted to hospital. LT. A. HORSFORD proceeded to III Corps School for Bombing Instrs. MAJ. R.S. DOVE M.C. granted leave to ENGLAND (to Nov 14th) The undermentioned Officers reported for Duty from 41st I.B.D.	
			2nd LT. S.J. SQUIBB posted to B Coy	
			" " W.H. THOMPSON " " D "	
	Oct 16th		The undermentioned Officer reported for Duty from 41st I.B.D. 2 LT. H.A. SHEMMONDS posted to A Coy.	

WAR DIARY
or
INTELLIGENCE SUMMARY

Army Form C. 2118.

(Erase heading not required.)

Place	Date	Hour	Summary of Events and Information	Remarks and references to Appendices
Oct 16th			The undermentioned Officers appointed hereto in Command of Coys.	
			2nd LT. S. LIVINGSTONE — A Coy	
			LT. C.A. GOWERS — B "	
			2. LT. S.R. GOULBURN — C "	
			2nd LT. S.J. ASHMAN — D "	
Oct 17th & 18th			Bn. front shortened to CARBINE TRENCH (exclusive) on the right.	
			Coys. disposed as under:-	
			Left Front — A Coy	
			Right Front — C Coy	
			Support Coy — D Coy	
			Reserve Coy — B Coy	
Oct 20th & 21st			Bn. relieved by 9th ROYAL SUSSEX REGT. & moved into Support. H.Q. & B. 9 D. Coys at TEMPLEUX QUARRIES. A & C Coys at QUARRIES, L. 10. a. (Ref. Map. 62 C 1/40000)	
Oct 21st			CAPT. E.S.C. GRUNE struck off the strength & to report to War Office.	
			Temp. CAPT. R.M. RICHFORD transferred to Establishment of X. Corps.	

WAR DIARY
or
INTELLIGENCE SUMMARY.
(Erase heading not required.)

Place	Date	Hour	Summary of Events and Information	Remarks and references to Appendices
	Oct 21st Oct 22nd		School 18 " 5 " 17. Lt-Col. J. GREENE. D.S.O. having proceeded to attend a Course for Commanding Officers at 3rd Army Inf. School, MAJ A.M. HINGLEY M.C. assumes temp. command of the Bn. From Oct 22nd to Oct 24th (both dates inclusive) practically the whole Bn. was engaged in working parties.	
	Oct 26th Oct 27th		2.LT. N. BLACKALL (attd L.T.M.B.) discharged from hospital. 2.LT. S.J. SQUIBB admitted to hospital.	
	27/28th		Bn. relieved 9th ROYAL SUSSEX RGT. in the line. Capt. Chopped as under:- Left Front B Coy. Right Front D Coy. Support C Coy. Reserve A Coy.	
	Oct 29th		Temp CAPT. R.S. DOVE M.C. to be Acting MAJ whilst 2nd in Cmd of Bn. July 16th.	

Army Form C. 2118.

WAR DIARY
or
INTELLIGENCE SUMMARY.
(Erase heading not required.)

Instructions regarding War Diaries and Intelligence Summaries are contained in F. S. Regs., Part II. and the Staff Manual respectively. Title pages will be prepared in manuscript.

Place	Date	Hour	Summary of Events and Information	Remarks and references to Appendices
	Oct 29th.		2nd Lt. L.R. HARRISON (S.R.) to be Temp. Lt. (June 25th.) Authy. granted to undermentioned Officers to wear Badges of rank of Lieut.	
	Oct 31st.		2nd Lt. W.H. THOMSON " H.A.S. SHEMMENDS. R.E. Coy. Releif Coys disposed as under. Left Front . . . A Coy. Right Front . . . C " Support . . . B " Reserve . . . D "	

Army Form C. 2118.

WAR DIARY
or
INTELLIGENCE SUMMARY.
(Erase heading not required.)

Place	Date	Hour	Summary of Events and Information	Remarks and references to Appendices

Summary of Casualties during the Month.

KILLED		ACCIDENTALLY KILLED		WOUNDED		ACCIDENTALLY WOUNDED		MISSING		TOTAL	
OFF	OR	OFF	OR	OFF	OR	OFF	OR	OFF	OR	OFF	OR
—	1	—	1	1	5	—	—	—	—	1	6

Drafts during Month.

OFFICERS	O. RANKS
4	26

R.K. Longley. Major.
Commdg. 13th Middlesex Regt.

Instructions regarding War Diaries and Intelligence Summaries are contained in F. S. Regs., Part II. and the Staff Manual respectively. Title pages will be prepared in manuscript.

Army Form C. 2118.

WAR DIARY

INTELLIGENCE SUMMARY.
(Erase heading not required.)

13th Battalion Middlesex Regiment

for the month of

November 1917

WAR DIARY
or
INTELLIGENCE SUMMARY.
(Erase heading not required.)

13th MIDDLESEX   Army Form C. 2118.
November 1917

Place	Date	Hour	Summary of Events and Information	Remarks and references to Appendices
Nov.	1st 2nd 3rd 4th		Battalion in the line (N.E. of HARGICOURT)	
	5th		Batt. relieved by 1/5 of Royal Sussex Reg't in the afternoon and marched & bivouac'd in RESERVE at HERVILLY.	
	6th		Coys available, men on working parties	
	7th		Battalion engaged in a Contact Aeroplane Scheme with 1/Batt. ROYAL FUSILIERS.	
	8th		Batt. Training 170 men on working parties	
			Batt. Training 220 men on working parties	
	9th		2nd Lieut S/14/S9166 transferred to 1/4 of R.S. 6-11-17	
			Batt. relieved the 9th ROYAL SUSSEX in the line Coys disposed as under	
			Left front B. Coy. Support A. Coy	
			Right front D. Coy. Reserve C. Coy.	
	10		2nd Lieut. A TEDMAN taken in charge of Battalion 3-11-17	
	11		2nd Lieut S/14/14 struck off establishment of Battalion 3-9-17	
	12	14/13	June- Coy relief Coys disposed as under — Left front A coy	

WAR DIARY
or
INTELLIGENCE SUMMARY.
(Erase heading not required.)

Army Form C. 2118.

Place	Date	Hour	Summary of Events and Information	Remarks and references to Appendices
	April			
			2nd Lieut R Kane attached to C Coy.	
			2nd Lieut B Tedman " " D Coy.	
			2nd Lieut E.W. Maxted " " B Coy.	
			Right front C Coy.	
			Support Coy D Coy.	
			Reserve Coy B Coy.	
	13		2nd Lieut R Kane attached to VII Corps	
			2nd Lieut B Tedman arrived from 24 Div. Training Battn	
			2nd Lieut E.W. Maxted proceeded to VII Corps Gas School HAMEL.	
			2nd Lieut F.C. ANDERSON attached R Artillery	
			2nd Lieut A.G. REDSTON to VII Corps Bombing School	
	14		Battalion relieved by 1st ROYAL SUSSEX REGT. H.Qrs and Coys	
			disposed as under.	
			H.Qtrs. L.10.a	Ref. Map. 62C.
			A and B Coys TEMPLEUX QUARRY	
			C and D Coys L.10.a	
	15		Battn in Brigade Reserve. Every available man on working	
			parties by night.	
	16		The PH gas helmet was withdrawn from use.	

WAR DIARY
or
INTELLIGENCE SUMMARY.
(Erase heading not required.)

Army Form C. 2118.

Place	Date	Hour	Summary of Events and Information	Remarks and references to Appendices
Épehy	17		Very quiet restful day weather ideal. Bath on working parties	
	18		2nd Lieut. E.G. ANDERSON hypning from attachment to 2nd Dvl Artillery	
	19		2nd Lieut F. DEWS taken from the strength of the battalion 15-11-17	
			The Battalion had both platoons at RD.16.e.1. and TEMPLEUX QUARRIES	
	20	8.30	Opening bombardment of the attack by 16 Divisions left (5°5'7)	
			no counter battery work and batteries were 6 to 8	
	21		Battalion relieved the 9. Royal SUSSEX in the line	
			Disposition on relief :-	
			Left front B Coy Support C Coy	
			Right front D Coy Reserve A Coy	
			Temp. Lieut CAPERRY & ½ Templeux	
			(Auth: The London Gazette Supplement no: 30357	
			Temp. Lieut. E.K. Allen to Temp. Capt. October 7-1916	
			(Authority. The London Gazette Nov 7th 1917)	
			Captain C.V. Otter returned from leave to England	
	22		In the line. Line very quiet practically no shelling whatever	

WAR DIARY
or
INTELLIGENCE SUMMARY

Army Form C. 2118.

Place	Date	Hour	Summary of Events and Information	Remarks and references to Appendices
	Jan 23		Another quiet day. Our patrols out all night watching for parties or signs of enemy withdrawal. 4th HINDENBURG LINE. Into Tay Relief. Coys disposed as under.	
	24		Left Front — A. Coy Right Front — C. Coy Left Support B. Right Support X	
	25		Day has been still quiet. Our patrols found the Support Coys active during night, on both Coy fronts. 2nd Lieut C.H. GOWERS to be T/Lieut and remain acted. July 1st 1917. (Authority London Gazette Supplement 20th 1917) Day quiet today. Hard work done by Both Batteries in supporting on abnormal enemy movement in back areas. Our patrols did good work in locating enemy posts.	
	26		4th O/m Officers taken on Strength of the Both. 2 3-11-17 2 Lieuts C.H. WILTSHIRE W. COLVIN and T.M.Y. WOOD. Temp Capt. C.K. Allen R be Adjutant Sept 1st (Authority the London Gazette Supplement Nov 21 17)	

WAR DIARY
INTELLIGENCE SUMMARY

Army Form C. 2118.

Place	Date	Hour	Summary of Events and Information	Remarks and references to Appendices
	27.		Bn relieved H by 9th ROYAL SUSSEX RGT. in the line & proceeded to Divisional Reserve at HERVILLY.	
			2.LT. S.R. GOULBOURN proceeded to G.H.Q. School at LE TOUQUET.	26.11.17
			Capt. C.K. ALLEN proceeded for attachment to ADV. G.H.Q.	26.11.17
			2.LT. S LIVINGSTONE admitted to Hospital	24.11.17
	28.		The n/m Officers posted to Coys as follows:	
			2.LT. C.H. WILTSHIRE A Coy.	
			" F.H.V. WOOD. B "	
			" W. COLVIN C "	
			" F.W. DEWS. D "	
			2.LT R.W. "	
			2.LT. R.W. PHILLIPS proceeded to Course of Instruction at Army Signal School DUNSTABLE	27.11.17
	30.		Bn received to leave HERVILLY at 1 PM & proceeded by route march to MOISLAINS area. At 10 a.m. this order was cancelled altr. Bn placed at 1 hr in fighting order. Shortly afterwards Bn marched with first line transport to area S.E. of ST. EMILIE. 15 R Bn in support to 164 BDE 55 S.S. Div. This Div. had been heavily attacked by the	

Army Form C. 2118.

WAR DIARY
or
INTELLIGENCE SUMMARY.

(Erase heading not required.)

Instructions regarding War Diaries and Intelligence Summaries are contained in F. S. Regs., Part II. and the Staff Manual respectively. Title pages will be prepared in manuscript.

Place	Date	Hour	Summary of Events and Information	Remarks and references to Appendices
	30.		enemy early in the morning & that succeeded in breaking through some considerable depth.	
		About 12.30 p.m	Bn moved further north to E.12.d. (Map 62c)	
		2.30 p.m	" " W.30 central (Map 57c). The Bn arrived at this area about 4.15 p.m & took over shelters alongside a railway embankment which ran due east & west. Lewis gun posts were placed on its eastern extreme & patrols sent out to get in touch with units in front & on our flanks. The Bn had no rations all day. They arrived eventually at 11 p.m.	

Army Form C. 2118.

WAR DIARY
or
INTELLIGENCE SUMMARY.
(Erase heading not required.)

Instructions regarding War Diaries and Intelligence Summaries are contained in F. S. Regs. Part II. and the Staff Manual respectively. Title pages will be prepared in manuscript.

Place	Date	Hour	Summary of Events and Information	Remarks and references to Appendices
			Summary of Casualties during the Month.	

KILLED		DIED OF WOUNDS		WOUNDED		WOUNDED AT DUTY		MISSING		TOTAL	
OFF	OR	OFF	OR	OFF	OR	OFF	OR	OFF	OR	OFF	OR
-	44	1	5	1	146	-	3	1	10	3	208

Drafts during Month

OFFICERS	O. RANKS
3	23

LIEUT. COL.
COMMANDING 13th BN. MIDDLESEX REGT.

WAR DIARY
or
INTELLIGENCE SUMMARY

Army Form C. 2118.

Vol 26

13th Battalion Middlesex Regiment
for the month of
December 1917

WAR DIARY or INTELLIGENCE SUMMARY

13th MIDDLESEX RGT.
December 1917
Army Form C. 2118.

(Erase heading not required.)

Place	Date	Hour	Summary of Events and Information	Remarks and references to Appendices
AREA N.W. OF EPÉHY. GAUCHE WOOD and VILLERS-GUISLAINS. about 2000yds N. of the railway. (Map 57c) Railway from W62 Central to W24 Central	Dec 1st		At 6.20 a.m. two parties of TANKS co-operating with cavalry could-attacked. The enemy put down a defensive barrage. After 5 or 10 minutes the barrage moved onto the railway, where it remained for about a Quarter an hour. We had no casualties. During the day the enemy shelled the valley south of the railway. There was a large number of _____ fired some guns in the valley, but considering the amount of shelling little damage was done. Our aeroplanes were very active in spite of low visibility. No enemy aeroplanes were seen. In the course of the afternoon the enemy again put down a barrage on the railway. Our casualties were slight. At 4 p.m. A Coy moved forward to RAILWAY EMBANKMENT in X19a (57c). In the evening the Bn. was relieved by the 10th K.O.Y.L.I., 21st DIV. and reached HERVILLY in the early hours of the morning.	
	Dec 2nd.		Training and watering Parties.	

Extract from LONDON GAZETTE:— 2nd Lts to be Lts from July 1st '17
2nd LT. S. J. SQUIBB
2nd LT. H. A. S. SHEMMONDS.

Army Form C. 2118.

WAR DIARY
or
INTELLIGENCE SUMMARY.
(Erase heading not required.)

Place	Date	Hour	Summary of Events and Information	Remarks and references to Appendices
	Dec 3rd		Training and working Parties	
	Dec 4th		Bn. relieved 9th Royal Sussex Regt. in the line N.E. of HARGICOURT. Coys. disposed as follows:- Left Front - B Coy. - Right Front. D Coy. Support Coy, C Coy. - Reserve Coy. A Coy	
	Dec. 5		In the line. A draft of 22 O.R.s arrived from 24th Div. Depot Bn. The w/m Officers proceeded to attend Courses of Instruction at VII Corps School 2Lt A. WADSWORTH 2Lt H.W. CATTLE. 2Lt A.G. REDSTON rejoined from VII Corps School	
	Dec 6th		In the line.	
	Dec 7th		Lt. P.L. TAYLOR proceeded to attend L.G. Course at LE TOUQUET.	
	Dec 8th		In the line. 2Lt J. RAWLE having reported for duty 8-12-17 taken with strength of the Bn. and posted to B Coy. 2Lt. B. TEDMAN proceeded to attend Course of Instruction at 3rd Army Musketry Camp	

WAR DIARY
or
INTELLIGENCE SUMMARY.
(Erase heading not required.)

Army Form C. 2118.

Place	Date	Hour	Summary of Events and Information	Remarks and references to Appendices
	Dec 8th		Lt A. HORSFORD proceeded for attachment to 180th Tunnelling Coy. 2Lt S.R. GOULBURN rejoined from Course of Instruction at G.H.Q. Lewis Gun School	
	Dec 9th		In the line.	
			Authority granted for w/m to wear badges of rank of LIEUT. 2LT N. BLACKALL. 2LT W.R.T. SKINNER.	
	Dec 10th		In the afternoon the Bn. was relieved by the 9th ROYAL SUSSEX RGT in the line and marched to Bde. Support at ~~HERVILLY~~ TEMPLEUX QUARRIES and HARGICOURT QUARRY (Vide. Ref Map 62 c.)	
	Dec 11th		In support. Working parties.	
	Dec 12th		2nd Lt. N. BLACKALL transferred to est attachment of 73rd L.T.M. Bty and struck off the strength of the Bn.	
	Dec 13th to 15th		In Bde support.	
	Dec 16th		Bn. relieved 9th ROYAL SUSSEX RGT in the line. Two Coys in front line, one in support and one in Reserve.	

WAR DIARY
INTELLIGENCE SUMMARY
(Erase heading not required.)

Army Form C. 2118.

Place	Date	Hour	Summary of Events and Information	Remarks and references to Appendices
	Dec 17th		In the line.	
			The u/m Officers proceeded to ENGLAND to report for Duty at Tank Corps Training Centre and were Struck off the strength of the Bn:-	
			Lt. W.E. STOCKLEY.	
			Lt. W.H. THOMPSON	
			CAPT. F.J. STRATTEN (O.C. 'A' Coy) granted leave to United Kingdom.	
			18.12.17 to 17.1.18. 2Lt S.R. GOULBURN ('C' Coy) in temp Cmd of 'A' Coy.	
			CAPT M.S. McGAHEY rejoined from Course of Instruction at III Army School.	
			Lt D.B. ROSHER rejoined from III Army Sniping and Observation School	
	Dec 18th		In the line.	
	Dec 19th		During the last days two the Divisional front was shortened from a three Bde to a one Bde front, the 73rd Bde being its Bde in the line. On the 19th Dec the 73rd Bde was relieved by the 17th Bde.	
			The 13th Mx Rgt were relieved as follows:-	
			Left Coy Front and Reserve Coy by 1st ROYAL FUSILIERS.	
			Right Coy Front (MALAKOFF FM) by 12th ROYAL FUSILIERS.	
			The 73rd Bde moved back to Bde in Div Support. 13th Mx at HERVILLY.	

Army Form C. 2118.

WAR DIARY
or
INTELLIGENCE SUMMARY.
(Erase heading not required.)

Instructions regarding War Diaries and Intelligence Summaries are contained in F. S. Regs., Part II, and the Staff Manual respectively. Title pages will be prepared in manuscript.

Place	Date	Hour	Summary of Events and Information	Remarks and references to Appendices
	Dec 20th		Training and working parties.	
	Dec 21st		" " " "	
	Dec 22nd		" " " "	
	Dec 23rd		Church parade 9.15 a.m.	
	Dec 24th		Training and working parties	
	Dec 25th		Voluntary Service at 11 a.m. A and B Coys had Christmas dinner at 1 p.m. C & D Coys had Christmas dinner at 1 p.m. At 6 o'clock Her Majesty a splendid concert held at 6 o'clock. Has been demonstrated in no uncertain manner their appreciation of Major HINGLEY's successful efforts to ensure them having a merry Christmas.	
	Dec 27th		Training and working parties	
	Dec 28th		The Battalion relieved the 1st Royal Fusiliers in the left sector Coys disposed as follows:— Front line A Coy. Immediate support "C" Coy. Support B Coy. Reserve D Coy.	

Army Form C. 2118.

WAR DIARY
or
INTELLIGENCE SUMMARY.
(Erase heading not required.)

Place	Date	Hour	Summary of Events and Information	Remarks and references to Appendices
Lee	29ᵗʰ		In the line Lieut E.G. BAKER proceeded to attend course of instruction at Fifth Army School, 2/Lt F.C. ANDERSON to Fifth Army S.O.S. School	
Lee	30ᵗʰ		2/Lieut R. KEENE granted leave to the UNITED KINGDOM till 13ᵗʰ JANUARY 1918	
Lee	31.		In the line	

Army Form C. 2118.

WAR DIARY
or
INTELLIGENCE SUMMARY.
(Erase heading not required.)

Summary of Casualties during the Month.

KILLED		DIED		WOUNDED		WOUNDED AT DUTY		MISSING		TOTAL	
OFF	OR	OFF	OR	OFF	OR	OFF	OR	OFF	OR	OFF	OR
-	1	-	1	1	7	-	1	-	-	1	10

Drafts during Month.

OFFICERS	O. RANKS
1	29

J. Greene Lieut Colonel
Commanding 13th Middlesex Regt.

WAR DIARY
INTELLIGENCE SUMMARY.
(Erase heading not required.)

Army Form C. 2118.

13th Battalion Manchester Regiment
for the month of
January 1918

WAR DIARY or INTELLIGENCE SUMMARY

13th MIDDLESEX

JANUARY 1918

Army Form C. 2118.

Place	Date	Hour	Summary of Events and Information	Remarks and references to Appendices
Jan	1		Battalion in the line NE of HARGICOURT. "C" Coy relieved "A" Coy in front line. Captain R.A.H. FULTON R.A.M.C. granted leave to U.K. from 1-1-18 to 30-1-18. His place taken by Capt C.H.T. ILOTT. R.A.M.C. 74th Fd Amb. 2Lt B. TEDMAN rejoined from course of instruction at 3rd Army Musketry Camp.	His place
	2		2Lts A WADSWORTH & H.W. CATTLE rejoined from Course of instruction at 7th Corps School.	
			In the line — Lt. P.L. TAYLOR admitted to hospital.	
	3		In the line —	
	4		In the line	
	5		Battalion relieved in the line by the 9th EAST SURREY REGT (72nd BRIGADE) — marched to Brigade in support at HERVILLY. Church parade 5.30 p.m. 1st S. LIVINGSTONE discharged from hospital.	
	6		A draft of 21 O.Rs arrived from 2nd Div. Training Depôt. Every available man on working parties.	
	7		" " " " Lt. P.L. TAYLOR transferred to No. 5 C.C.S. Major A.N. HINGLEY M.C. assumed temp command of the battn this day vice	

Army Form C. 2118.

WAR DIARY
or
INTELLIGENCE SUMMARY.
(Erase heading not required.)

Instructions regarding War Diaries and Intelligence Summaries are contained in F. S. Regs., Part II. and the Staff Manual respectively. Title pages will be prepared in manuscript.

Place	Date	Hour	Summary of Events and Information	Remarks and references to Appendices
	7		Lt. Col. J. GREENE D.S.O., to temp. Command of 73rd Inf. Bde in absence of Brig Genl W.J. DUGAN CMG. DSO. on leave	
	8		Capt. F.L. WIGINTON rejoined from duty at Corps Reinforcement Camp. Battalion moved to brigade in reserve at Camp A, HANCOURT. 2Lt S.J.H. PILE MC. arrived from 41st I.B.D. & posted to "A" Co.	
	9		Training & working parties. Authority granted for 2Lt S. LIVINGSTONE to wear badges of rank of LIEUT pending notification in Gazette.	
	10		Training & working parties. 2Lts. A.R.F. MUSK & B. BEATER arrived from 24 – I.T. Depôt Bath on 8.1.18 & taken on the strength accordingly. Capt M.S. McGAHEY proceeded to attend Course at 7th Corps Gas School. Lt A.H. BAKER proceeded to attend annual of instruction in methods of communication with contact patrols.	
	11		All companies tested power-respirators at Gas Chamber, VRAIGNES.	
	12		All officers & NCOs attended a lecture by the Div Gas Officer on the use of projection by the enemy. Training & working parties.	
	13		Church parade & working parties.	

Army Form C. 2118.

WAR DIARY
or
INTELLIGENCE SUMMARY.
(Erase heading not required.)

Instructions regarding War Diaries and Intelligence Summaries are contained in F. S. Regs., Part II. and the Staff Manual respectively. Title pages will be prepared in manuscript.

Place	Date	Hour	Summary of Events and Information	Remarks and references to Appendices
	14		2/Lt C.H. WILTSHIRE proceeded to attend Course at 3rd Corps School.	
	15		Lt A.H. BAKER rejoined from Course of Instruction. Working parties. Training & working parties. CAPT M.S. McGAHEY rejoined from Course of Instruction at 7th Corps Gas School.	
	16		Training & working parties. Lt-H.A.S. SHEMMONDS rejoined from Course of Sanitation. 2/Lt R. KEENE reported from duty with 3rd Corps.	
	17		Training & working parties. CAPT P.T. CHEVALLIER M.C. to be GSO. 3rd Grade, Lt-Lt.- Struck off strength accordingly. 2/Lt F.W. MAXTED proceeded to England for transfer to Tank Corps & is Struck off strength accordingly. Lt H.A.S. SHEMMONDS proceeded for employment at 2/4th Div. Bomb Store.	
	18		Training & working parties.	
	19		"	
	20		Q 4635 Sgt. F. DICKENSON 'C' Coy, & 4646 Cpl. FORSTER 'D' Coy, awarded the D.C. Medal. 2/Lts J. RAWLE & A.G. REDSTON proceeded to attend a Course of instruction at 5th Army musketry Course. 2/Lt H.W. CATTLE proceeded for duty with 258-T.Coy R.F.	

WAR DIARY or INTELLIGENCE SUMMARY

Army Form C. 2118.

Place	Date	Hour	Summary of Events and Information	Remarks and references to Appendices
	21		Battalion relieved 1st R. Fus. (17th Inf Bde) in left sub section (N.E. of HARGICOURT)	
			Halted for dinners at RONSEL. Companies disposed as under:-	
			Front line - "D" Coy, 1st Support "B" Coy, 2nd Support "A" Coy, Reserve "C" Coy.	
	22		2/Lt H.W. CATTLE rejoined from employment with 258 T. Coy RE.	
			In the line. Quiet day.	
	23		In the line - Quiet day. Lt C.A. PERRY proceeded to attend a course of	
			instruction at G.H.Q. Small Arms School, LE TOUQUET.	
			Battalion Lt F.C. ANDERSON rejoined from 5th Army Scouting, Observation &	
	24		Sniping School, General Instruction.	
			In the line.	
	25		"B" Coy relieved "D" Coy in the line.	
	26		In the line	
	27		In the line	
	28		"	
	29		Capt M.S. McGAHEY granted leave t U.K 28.1.18 to 26.2.18.	
	30.		Battalion relieved in the line by 9th East Surrey Regt (72nd Brigade) & moved	
			to Brigade in Support at HERVILLY. At the beginning of this tour the trenches	

Place	Date	Hour	Summary of Events and Information	Remarks and references to Appendices
	31		were in a very muddy + wet condition. Excellent work done by whole battalion in cleaning, ordering + revetting trenches. Bright cold weather throughout. 2/Lt F.H.N. WOOD proceeded to report to AIR BOARD Office, LONDON for employment with R.F.C. + struck off strength accordingly. 2/Lt B.M. BEATER proceeded battalion with 12th SHERWOOD FORESTERS. Battalion engaged in cleaning up + working on camp. Battalion now full officers included. Draft of 37 ORs arrived from 3rd Div Depot Batt. 29.1.18 Lt W.H.D. de PASS proceeded to attend Course at 7 Corps Gas School.	

Army Form C. 2118.

WAR DIARY
or
INTELLIGENCE SUMMARY.

(Erase heading not required.)

Instructions regarding War Diaries and Intelligence Summaries are contained in F. S. Regs., Part II. and the Staff Manual respectively. Title pages will be prepared in manuscript.

Place	Date	Hour	Summary of Events and Information	Remarks and references to Appendices

Summary of Casualties during the Month.

KILLED		DIED		MISSING		WOUNDED		WOUNDED AT DUTY		TOTAL	
OFF	ORS	OFF	ORS	OFF	ORS	OFF	ORS	OFF	ORS	OFF	ORS
—	—	—	1	—	—	1	2	—	—	1	3

Drafts during Month.

OFFICERS	O.RANKS
3	48

A. N. Hingley, Major.
Commanding 13th Middlesex Regiment.

2353 Wt. W2544/1454 700,000 5/15 D. D. & L. A.D.S.S. Forms/C. 2118.

Army Form C. 2118.

WAR DIARY
INTELLIGENCE SUMMARY.
(Erase heading not required.)

Vol 28

13th Bn Middlesex Regiment

for the month of

February 1918

Place	Date	Hour	Summary of Events and Information	Remarks and references to Appendices
Confidential				

Army Form C. 2118.

13th Bn. MIDDLESEX REGT
No. MX93
Date. 1.3.18.
ORDERLY ROOM

13th Middlesex Regt.

February 1918

WAR DIARY
or
INTELLIGENCE SUMMARY.
(Erase heading not required.)

Place	Date	Hour	Summary of Events and Information	references to Appendices
Feby	1st		Battn. was in Bns. Support at HERVIN. Coy Lewis Gunnery was possible owing to large working parties. Capt R.A.H. FURTON R.A.M.C. awarded the CROIX de GUERRE also 2nd Lt Col A. TIDD D'Coy and 4898 Pte E.J. LEWIS "A" Coy. Lt C.A. PERRY given authority to wear badges of rank of CAPTAIN.	
HERVIN	2nd		Lt S. LIVINGSTONE proceeded to England for a six months tour of duty. Lt C.A. GOWERS proceeded for duty with 24th Div Bn. Lt C.A. PERRY reported from course of instruction at G.H.Q. L.G. School. Church parades for all available men at 9.15 am.	
do.	3rd		Lt S. LIVINGSTONE no struck off the strength of the BN. Lt D.A. ROSHER proceeded to attend a course of instruction at the L.G. Branch G.H.Q. S.A. School.	
do.	4th		Working Parties. 2nd Lt A.R.E. MUSK proceeded to attend a course of instruction in W.T & P.B under A.D Sigs CAV. CORPS.	
do.	5th		Working Parties 2nd Lt R. KEENE given authority to wear badges of the rank of LIEUTENANT.	
	6/8		Working Parties	

WAR DIARY
or
INTELLIGENCE SUMMARY.
(Erase heading not required.)

Army Form C. 2118.

13th Middlesex Regt.

February 1918

Place	Date	Hour	Summary of Events and Information	Remarks and references to Appendices
HERMIES/ Le.	9		Working Parties	
	10		Working Parties. Voluntary service 11.30 am. 2nd Lt H.W. CATTLE proceeded for attachment to 258th Tunnelling Coy. Lt A. HORSFORD reported from attachment to 258th Tunnelling Coy.	
do.	11		Working Parties. 2nd Lt J.E. RAFFLE reported from course of instruction at 5th Army Musketry School.	
do.	12		Working Parties. 14 Officers + 266 O.R. having arrived from 17th (S) Bn. Middx Regt. are taken on the strength of this Bn. accordingly. 1 Officer 33 O.R. (not yet joined) posted from 17(S) Bn Middx Regt are taken on the strength accordingly. 2nd Lt A.G. REDSTON reported from course of instruction at 5th Army Musketry Camp.	
d.	13		Lt Col J. GREENE D.S.O. granted leave to U.K. from 14/2/18 to 13/3/18. Lt D.A. ROSHER reported from a course of instruction at GHQ L.G. School.	
do.	14		2nd Lt W.A. MALLORD proceeded to attend a course of instruction at 5th Army Musketry Camp	

WAR DIARY or INTELLIGENCE SUMMARY

Army Form C. 2118.

13th Middlesex.
February 1918.

Place	Date	Hour	Summary of Events and Information	Remarks and references to Appendices
	15th		Bn relieved 1st Bn Royal Fusiliers on the lines N.E. of HARICOURT. Companies disposed as follows:— A Coy. Front Line. B Coy. Support on HUSSAR ROAD and ARTAXERXES POST. C Coy. reserve on HARDY BANKS — TOINE POST — ORCHARD POST — MILL POST. D Coy (at disposal of B.G.C.) ROISEL.	
In the line	16			
do.	17		Lt. R. TAYLOR transferred to England sick	
do.	18		2nd Lt. B.M. BEATER rejoined from attachment to 17 Bn Sherwood Foresters	
do.	19		2nd Lt. S.TH. PIKE M.C. proceeded to England for transfer to the R.F.C. and in strike off the strength accordingly	
do.	20		Lt. D.A. RISHER proceeded for attachment to H.Q. 73rd I.B. as I.S.O. Capt. F.L. WIGINTON proceeded for duty as "A" Zone Comdr. 2 Lt. C.H. WILTSHIRE M.M. rejoined from course of instruction at 3rd Corps School.	
do.	21		2/Lt J. BRYCE having reported for duty from the 7th Dragoon Gds on the 19th and no attached on the strength and posted to D Coy.	

Army Form C. 2118.

WAR DIARY
or
INTELLIGENCE SUMMARY.

(Erase heading not required.)

13 Middx Regt.

February 1918.

Instructions regarding War Diaries and Intelligence Summaries are contained in F.S. Regs., Part II. and the Staff Manual respectively. Title pages will be prepared in manuscript.

Place	Date	Hour	Summary of Events and Information	Remarks and references to Appendices
In the line	21		L/R KEENE proceeded to England for a two months' tour of duty and is struck off the strength. L/H TATTERSALL proceeded to attend a course of instruction at the L.G. Barracks of the GHQ S.A. School. 2/Lieut A.R.E. MUSK rejoined from course under A.D. Sigs 6th Corps.	
do.	22		9th Royal Sussex relieved the 13 Bn Middx in the line. 13 Bn Middx moved to Bde. Support in TEMPLEUX QUARRIES. Working Parties. 2/Lt R.H. PHILLIPS rejoined from course of instruction at Army Sig School DUNSTABLE ENGLAND.	
do.	23		Working Parties.	
do.	24			
do.	25		13th Bn Middx relieved 9th Royal Sussex in the line. The Bn front was extended from CARBINE TRENCH to ENFILADE TRENCH on the right thereby changing the front from a two to a three company front. Companies disposed as follows:— Left Coy "B" Centre Coy "C" Right Coy "D" Support Coy "A"	

Army Form C. 2118.

WAR DIARY
or
INTELLIGENCE SUMMARY.
(Erase heading not required.)

13th Bn Middx

February 1918

Place	Date	Hour	Summary of Events and Information	Remarks and references to Appendices
In the Field	26		2nd Lt S R Goulborn was tried by G.C.M. on the 11th Feby, 1918 and was sentenced to be reduced. The sentence was commuted to that of dismissal by the Field Marshal Comdy-in-Chief. 2nd Lt H J Hazard reported from course of instruction at 3rd Army Musketry Camp	
do	27			
do	28		Note:— In the two towns during this month the enemy's artillery was slightly more active than usual, there being a marked increase in H V guns. In other respects the line was very quiet.	

73rd Brigade.

24th Division.

13th BATTALION

MIDDLESEX REGIMENT

MARCH 1918

WAR DIARY

INTELLIGENCE SUMMARY.

Army Form C. 2118.

Vol 29

13th

War Diary
13th Bn Middlesex Regiment
for the month of
March 1918

Army Form C. 2118.

WAR DIARY
or
INTELLIGENCE SUMMARY.

13 m/Bn. Middx

(Erase heading not required.)

Place	Date	Hour	Summary of Events and Information	Remarks and references to Appendices
BERNES	2/3/18		Battn. orders were not published on 7 sby. 28th and March 1st 1918	
"	3/3/18		Training. Lt H.A.S. Shemonds reported from employment at 24 Div. Bomb Store on 2nd inst. Capt J.L. Wigginton reported from employment with 73rd Inf. Bde on 2nd inst. 2nd Lt N. Colvin granted leave to U.K. from 4.3.18 — 18.3.18	
"	4/3/18		Training.	
"	5/3/18		Training. 2nd Lt W. COUSINS M.M. and 2nd Lt G. HAYNES granted leave to U.K. for period 6/3/18 — 20/3/18	
"	6/3/18		Training. The award of the Military Medal to G.43981 Pte (a/cpl) C. BROWN "A" Coy F/1291 Pte (L/cpl) A.G. CROUCH "C" Coy in consideration of the having been reviewed the Commander-in-Chief has, in consideration of the exceptional gallantry shown by these N.C.O's, cancelled the award of the Military Medal in each case and has awarded the Distinguished Conduct Medal in its place	

Army Form C. 2118.

WAR DIARY
or
INTELLIGENCE SUMMARY.   13th Bn. Middx.
(Erase heading not required.)

Instructions regarding War Diaries and Intelligence Summaries are contained in F.S. Regs., Part II. and the Staff Manual respectively. Title pages will be prepared in manuscript.

Place	Date	Hour	Summary of Events and Information	Remarks and references to Appendices
BERNES	7/3/18		Training. A lecture on "Economy in Government Stores" by Lt Col J. HOARE D.S.O. was given to the CAVALRY CORPS HQ. CATELET. One officer & "D" Coy attended. LT H.A. SHEMMONDS & 2nd/Lt J. RAHHE granted leave to U.K. for period 8/3/18 – 22/3/18	
do.	8/3/18		Training. 2nd/Lt B.M. BEATER proceeded for a tour of duty at DIV. DEPOT BN. CURLU. 2nd/Lt E.T. SEVENOAKS proceeded for attachment to 93rd Light Trench Mortar Battery. 2nd/Lt E.R. BALL granted leave to UK for period 9/3/18 – 23/3/18	
do	9/3/18		Training.	
do	10/3/18		do	
do	11/3/18		do	
do	12/3/18		do. 1st/Lt SHERRARD EWING U.S.R. and Capt N.S. ALEXANDER 103 Inf. U.S.N.G. attached to the Battn.	
do	13/3/18		Training. 2nd/Lt E.J. FRANCIS M.C. & 2nd/Lt F.H. DENIS proceeded for attachment to 2nd Bn. Depot Bn. CURLU	

Army Form C. 2118.

WAR DIARY
or
INTELLIGENCE SUMMARY.
(Erase heading not required.)

13th Bn. 17DDX.

Place	Date	Hour	Summary of Events and Information	Remarks and references to Appendices
BERNES	13/3/18		2nd/Lt H. TATTERSALL rejoined from course of instruction at GHQ S.A. School LE TOUQUET. CAPT L.I. HORNIMAN admitted to hospital. Training.	
do	14/3/18		Lt C.A. GOWERS proceeded to England for a six months tour of duty and is struck off the strength of the Bn. Training.	
do	15/3/18		2nd/Lt C. SEAMER granted leave to U.K. for period 16/3/18 - 30/3/18. Training.	
do	16/3/18		Training.	
do	17/3/18		Training.	
do	18/3/18		2nd/Lt E.C. ANDERSON proceeded to attend a course of instruction at IVth Army Scouting Observation Sniping School VADENCOURT. Capt R. HARRISON rejoined from course of instruction at IVth Army Inf. School. Training. Lieut-Col. J. GREENE, D.S.O. & Capt. C.K. ALLEN rejoined from leave to U.K. 2nd/Lt W. CHAPLIN MM. proceeded to Machine Gun Training Centre GRANTHAM and is struck off the strength accordingly. Major A.N. HINGLEY M.C. granted leave to U.K. for period 19/3/18 - 2/4/18.	
do	19/3/18		Training.	

WAR DIARY
or
INTELLIGENCE SUMMARY
(Erase heading not required.)

Army Form C. 2118.

Place	Date	Hour	Summary of Events and Information	Remarks and references to Appendices
CERNES	Mar. 20		Orders were received that in the event of enemy attack the Bn. was to form an obligatory garrison under Div. Comdr. orders in the line of Redoubts M.E. of VERMAND. Dmn positions were reconnoitred during the morning. In the afternoon positions were reconnoitred for a Brigade Tactical Scheme which was to take place the following day.	
"	21st		About 10 p.m., Enemy bombardment at slow rate of fire began on front line & continued throughout the night. About 4.30 a.m., bombardment increased to drum-fire. At 6.45 a.m. enemy were receiving heavy casualties (with parties reconnoitring our positions). By 7.30 a.m. the Bn. was in position as under. Day. A Coy. — YARD REDOUBT (BIHECOURT) A Coy. — WOODY REDOUBT C. Coy. — WOLECUK B Coy. — WORN B. Headquarters — VERMAND CHATEAU YARD REDOUBT and Bn. Headquarters were intermittently shelled throughout the day. D Coy. suffered some casualties. Enemy offensive was shown on the Redoubts. Many of situation in front was uncertain but	

WAR DIARY
or
INTELLIGENCE SUMMARY
(Erase heading not required.)

Army Form C. 2118.

Place	Date	Hour	Summary of Events and Information	Remarks and references to Appendices
	21st (cont)		unstable throughout the day but by about 9 p.m. the 17th R were	
		7.30	had been very heavily hit, had rallied on the line of Reinforcements. Enemy following up were driven back.	
		At dawn	the enemy renewed his attacks but was several times driven back	
VERMAND	22nd		by the R.D. Coys. Posts on the right having withdrawn, orders were received	
		at about 2.30 p.m.	to withdraw towards the "Brown Line", which was then held	
		by the 50th Divn.	B Coy took an unusually heavy artillery & m.g. fire,	
			holding extended. In this action 2/Lieut. B.B. TEDMAN & 2/Lieut. M.S. MALLOND	
			were killed, 2/Lt A.R. HAYFORD wounded & missing. Capt. M.S. McCAHEY	
			though wounded three times, continued to lead his company with the greatest	
			gallantry. The Bn. was ordered to assemble at the CRATER on the ESTREES -	
			BRIE Road. This was done by about 5 p.m. The Bn. moved to camp	
			at VERMANDCOURT for the night. Emergency little trenches N. of Camp	
			were occupied during the night, owing to enemy shell-fire.	
	23rd		Orders were received early the morning to occupy positions	
			on the Green Line E. of Rivier OMIGNON. The Bn. moved at	

WAR DIARY or INTELLIGENCE SUMMARY.

(Erase heading not required.)

Army Form C. 2118.

Place	Date	Hour	Summary of Events and Information	Remarks and references to Appendices
	23rd (cont)		5 a.m. Positions were occupied by 7 a.m. No enemy with the infantry. About 9 a.m. orders recd. to withdraw to positions N. of the SOMME via Bridge at FALVY. Withdrawal carried out, assisted by a thick mist. The withdrawal was successfully carried out, assisted by a thick mist. The River having been crossed orders were recd to concentrate at MARCHELEPOT. Bn. on arrival there the Bn. marched back to HOUVRT Wood in support to 24th Inf Bde, 8th Div. During the night A & B Coys were sent forward in close support to the 2nd Northamptonshire Regt. to arm at that unit in holding the wireless crossway.	
	24th		Orders recd. early to withdraw + concentrate at CHAULNES Wood at 7 a.m. + on arrival at CHAULNES bivouacked E. of the town. About 1 p.m. orders were sent forward. Skirmish position on the PUZEAU – PONCHY line in support to the 7th Northamptonshire Regt. 9th R. Sussex Regt. Coys were disposed as follows: B. C & D Coys in the line, A Coy in immediate support. Bn. Headquarters in PUZEAU. The night passed quietly.	

Army Form C. 2118.

WAR DIARY
or
INTELLIGENCE SUMMARY.
(Erase heading not required.)

Instructions regarding War Diaries and Intelligence Summaries are contained in F. S. Regs., Part II. and the Staff Manual respectively. Title pages will be prepared in manuscript.

Place	Date	Hour	Summary of Events and Information	Remarks and references to Appendices
	Mar. 25th		7 am. orders recd. to move forward to positions for counter-attack on line CUROHU - DRESLINCOURT in co-operation with the French. Bn. was in support to O. in C. Sussex + 7th Northamptonshire Regt. Our French Counter-attack — others did not materialize. The other two Bns. of the Bde. had been heavily engaged. The Bde. was ordered to withdraw to its overnight positions. The enemy following up vigorously drove back the Sussex, Northamptons + about 6 am. E Coy was overrun east of PUZEAUX by powerful attack supported by heavy artillery fire. In this action Lieut. W.H.D. LePASS was missing (believed killed). In the ensuing engagement of the 8th Rest. W.R.T. SKINNER ? was wounded — the Bn. withdrew during line covering the E. side of PUNCHY by PUNCHY - CRAWLINGS Road. Before daylight again withdraw in many suitable positions on the line HALLU - CRAWINES. The withdrawal was covered by Lt. Trimmer ? Coy's Reinforcement Coat Trimmer Bn.	
	26.		About 7 a.m. the Bde. on the right having went forward.	

WAR DIARY or INTELLIGENCE SUMMARY

Army Form C. 2118.

Place	Date	Hour	Summary of Events and Information	Remarks and references to Appendices
	Mar 26 (cont'd)		Enemy still continuous fighting we only [?] of MEHARICOURT. B Coy. in cooperation with details of the 104- Fd Coy R.E. under Major PRIOR, Form [?] by Rifle covered the retirement, which was eventually carried out under the most adverse circumstances at about [?] the 3rd [?] Bde. having been broken, the enemy attacked in flank forcing us to form a defensive flank. This was successfully done by Lewis gun & rifle fire. The enemy were driven back under Henry artillery [?] fire. B.C. & D Coys. My retirement to MEHARICOURT accomplished, concentrated at WARVILLERS when joined by A Coy, about 3 p.m. The WILTS Regt. with HQ. Details had taken up a line at ARTILLERY DUGOUTS & we were ordered to support in WARVILLERS when the few Dugouts which were needed to shelter the few [?] of men & magazines were chosen here. About 10 p.m. Bn moved forward in support Gr R. Surry A & B	
	27th		Coys in line at ARTILLERY DUGOUTS, C & D Coys. H.Q. Details in support in WARVILLERS wood. They were heavily shelled. [?] details arriving [?] forward from time to time in support to 15th Entrenching Bn.	

WAR DIARY or INTELLIGENCE SUMMARY

Army Form C. 2118.

Place	Date	Hour	Summary of Events and Information	Remarks and references to Appendices
	27th (cont)		A Coy successfully carried out a counter attack under orders of O.C. 8th R. Sussex Regt who was hit during the operations. The support Coys moved up to ARTILLERY DUGOUTS about 2 pm. During the night Bde withdrew to rear positions, standing WARVILLERS Nth Bn. holding the line WARVILLERS WOOD to VRELY; B, C, D Coys in line, A Coy in reserve. The Sussex Northumberland were withdrawn to authorities The night passed quietly.	
	28th		About 8 am the enemy continued his advance, between well held rifle and severe casualties until [north?] of the 17th Inf Bde on the left were forced to withdraw. The Bde we ordered to retire on any [WINDMILL?] FARM. The withdrawal was carried out under very [heavy?] [MG?] fire Somewhat severe casualties were suffered. Retiring in the rearguard [action?] was continued to Divisional trenches known as the CAIX Line Ringenkirim was carried out & Coy disposed for defensive action. A line East in was [held?] by [Firewell?] [troops?] At 4.30 pm Firewell troops withdrew. The Bn was ordered to withdraw via BEAUCOURT & MEZIERES	

WAR DIARY or INTELLIGENCE SUMMARY

Army Form C. 2118.

Place	Date	Hour	Summary of Events and Information	Remarks and references to Appendices
	28th (cont)		to VILLERS – AUX – ERABLES to concentrate. The operation was carried out under great difficulties, A B & D Coys retiring in excellent order & in formation, covering the retirement of the Bde., with flanks of which were exposed. Flaming found through the French Cav E. of BERTEUCOURT. The Bn. concentrated at VILLERS–AUX–ERABLES & marches with the Bde., crossing the R. AVRE at CASTEL about midnight, & bivouacs in the BOIS DE SENECAT.	
	29th		About 1 p.m. Bn. ordered to hold S.W. of CASTEL, in support to B. R. Sussex 7– Northamptons who were holding high ground commanding Avre crossings. About 6 pm orders recd. to concentrate at HAILLES & move to THEZY – GUIMONT.	
	30th		About 4 am. Bn. C Coy. took up positions in a line of posts between BERTEAUCOURT – LONGEAU & BERTEAUCOURT – THEZY Roads. Remainder of Bn. in billets in THEZY. About 8 am, orders to take positions. Enemy attack at dusk — Second Bn. returned to billets. Intercompany reliefs at dusk.	
	31st		At THEZY, Intercompany reliefs carried out.	

Army Form C. 2118.

WAR DIARY
OR
INTELLIGENCE SUMMARY.
(Erase heading not required.)

Summary of Events and Information

Summary of Casualties during the Month.

	KILLED		DIED OF WOUNDS		MISSING		MISSING believed KILLED		DIED		WOUNDED		TOTAL	
	OFFS	ORs	OFF	ORs	OFF	ORs	OFF	ORs	OFF	ORs	OFF	ORs	OFF	ORs
	2	11	–	3	1	9	1	–	–	1	5	129	9	153

Drafts during Month.

OFFICERS	ORANKS
1	28

A.N. Hughey. Major.
Commanding 13th Middlesex Regt.

73rd Inf.Bde.
24th Div.

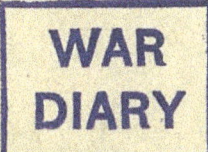

13th BATTN. THE MIDDLESEX REGIMENT.

A P R I L

1 9 1 8

WAR DIARY

INTELLIGENCE SUMMARY

Army Form C. 2118.

Vol 30
73/24

Confidential

2nd Bn. Middlesex Regiment

for the month of

April 1918

WAR DIARY or INTELLIGENCE SUMMARY

Army Form C. 2118.

13th Bn. MIDDLESEX REGT.
No. M.F. 137
Date 4/5/18
ORDERLY ROOM
13th Bn. Middlesex Regt.

Place	Date	Hour	Summary of Events and Information	Remarks and references to Appendices
THÉZY GLIMONT	April 1st		Inter-company reliefs were carried out. No events of importance.	
"	2nd		B Coy. was ordered to BERTEAUCOURT to relieve 7th Northamptons who were holding the Bridge-head. C Coy. in support in a line of trenches. A & D Coy. in billets in THEZY.	
"	3rd		The Bn. also was relieved of responsibility for the BERTEAUCOURT Bridge-head. B Coy. was relieved by regiment of the 133rd French Division. B Coy. returned to billets in THEZY. A Coy. relieved C Coy. in the line.	
BUS DE GENTELLES	4th		At 4 a.m. in accordance with orders received the previous night the Bn. moved to the BOIS DE GENTELLES, when the 73rd Inf. Bde. 18th Corps concentrated in support to the 17th Ind. Bde. Details of Coys. were withdrawn to their which had been started to the Bn. — Positions S.E. of the BOIS DE GENTELLES reconnoitred allotted to Companies. Stream & continuous rain throughout day & night. The troops suffered severely from exposure.	
"	5th		After various orders & counter-orders regarding relief, orders were finally received to withdraw to LONGEAU after dusk without waiting for relief. Bn. moved from the BOIS DE GENTELLES about 9.30 p.m.; arriving at LONGEAU about 3 a.m.	

Army Form 2118.

WAR DIARY
or
INTELLIGENCE SUMMARY.
(Erase heading not required.)

13th Bn MDDX REGT.

Place	Date	Hour	Summary of Events and Information	Remarks and references to Appendices
LONGEAU SALEUX	April 6		At 6 a.m. the Bn. entrained from LONGEAU for SALEUX, where it arrived about 7 a.m. Bivouaced all forenoon in field adjoining SALEUX Station, & at 2 p.m. entrained for S. VALERY, arriving there about 7 p.m. Capt L.L. HORNIMAN admitted to hospital sick.	
S. VALERY	7m		Billeted for the night in the casino S. VALERY. At 10 a.m. Bn. paraded which were to billets at FRESSENNEVILLE, arriving at 4 p.m. No killed and casualties.	
FRESS-ENNEVILLE	8m		Everybody, which had proceeded from SALEUX by march route, arrived. The Bn. spent the day in inspections and reorganisation. 2/Lt F. HAGSHOSH admitted to hospital. Lt D.A. ROSSER admitted to hospital.	
do.	9m		Training.	
do.	10m		The Bn. paraded at 11.15am for inspection by Brig-Gen. W. GENERAL DUGAN, C.M.G., D.S.O. Brigadier Training.	
do	11m		Lt H.A.S. SHEMMONDS proceeded for attachment to 73rd L.T.M. Battery. The Bn. paraded at 8am and marched to AULT and returned at 3pm. 2/Lt A.H. BAKER proceeded to England on 22/3/18 for a 6 months tour of duty and was struck off the strength.	

Army Form C. 2118.

WAR DIARY
or
INTELLIGENCE SUMMARY.

13"BN. M'DDX REGT

Instructions regarding War Diaries and Intelligence Summaries are contained in F. S. Regs., Part II. and the Staff Manual respectively. Title pages will be prepared in manuscript.

Place	Date	Hour	Summary of Events and Information	Remarks and references to Appendices
FRESSENNE-VILLE	April 12"		Training.	
do	13"		Training.	
do	14"		Training. MAJOR B.M. HINGLEY M.C. assumed command of the Bn today vice Lt Col T GREENE D.S.O. to command 10th Inf. Bde. Lt COL T GREENE D.S.O. proceeded today to assume command of the 10th Inf. Bde with the temporary rank of Brigadier General.	
do	15"		Training	
do	16"		Training	
do	17"		The Bn entrained at WOINCOURT the night of 17"/18" for PERNES, marched from the latter to HOUDAIN where it was stationed. Bn Orders Part I were not issued for the 17" inst	
HOUDAIN	18"		Training	
do	19"		do (52.2.18) 2nd/Lt F.W. DEWS & 2nd/Lt B.M. BEATER admitted to hospital, 22.3.18. 2nd/Lt F.A. WADSWORTH discharged from hospital	

Army Form C. 2118.

13th Bn MDDX REGT

WAR DIARY
or
INTELLIGENCE SUMMARY.

(Erase heading not required.)

Place	Date	Hour	Summary of Events and Information	Remarks and references to Appendices
HOUDAIN	April 20th		Training	
do	21st		A brigade sheel exercise was held at LE BRA SAT THEATRE HOUDAIN at 11.15am	
			Strength diminu:- Lt. ROSHER transferred to England sick. D.A.	
do	22nd		Training	
			2nd Lt N. COLVIN transferred to England sick.	
do	23rd		Training.	
			2nd Lt J. RAWLE admitted to hospital	
do	24th		Training.	
			Lt. S.J. STAVISS admitted to hospital	
do	25th		Training	
			2/Lt R.J. MCMILLAN admitted to hospital	
do	26th		Training	
			Bn. Comds + Coy Comds carried out a tactical exercise on ground between HOUDAIN and LA COMTÉ LA COMTÉ.	
do	27th		Training	
			Lt F. TROLLOPE was appointed Assistant Adjutant with effect from this date.	

Army Form C.-2118

WAR DIARY
or
INTELLIGENCE SUMMARY.

13th Mddx Regt.

(Erase heading not required.)

Instructions regarding War Diaries and Intelligence Summaries are contained in F. S. Regs., Part II. and the Staff Manual respectively. Title pages will be prepared in manuscript.

Place	Date	Hour	Summary of Events and Information	Remarks and references to Appendices
HOUDAIN	April 28th		Training.	
do	29th		Bn. moved to BULLY GRENAY was stopped on road, the move was cancelled and Bn. returned to billets in HOUDAIN.	
do	30th		Bn. moved to BULLY GRENAY and was billeted there. Cmdy Offrs. Coy Cmdrs + Sec. on Commanders reconnoitred the trenches at Hill 70 preparatory to taking over the line.	

Army Form 2118.

WAR DIARY
or
INTELLIGENCE SUMMARY.
(Erase heading not required.)

Place	Date	Hour	Summary of Events and Information	Remarks and references to Appendices
Kasasatho during April 1918			Supplementary Casualty list found 1918 ?	
			Killed in Action — Nil	
			Wounded	10 O.R.
			Wounded in Action	2 O.R.
			Wounded in Action	12 O.R.
			Previously Reported Wounded in Action, Now Reported Wounded	6 O.R.
			Previously Reported Missing, now Reported Wounded in Action	6 O.R.
			Wounded at Duty	1 O.R.
			Drafts during April 1918	

OFFICERS	O. RANKS
8	144

A. N. Hingley, Lieut Col.
Commdg 13 Manitoba Regt

WAR DIARY

~~INTELLIGENCE SUMMARY~~

Vol 31

1st/4th Bn. The Middlesex Regiment

For the month of

May 1918

Army Form C. 2118.

WAR DIARY
or
INTELLIGENCE SUMMARY.
(Erase heading not required.)

13th Bn Middlesex Regt.

Instructions regarding War Diaries and Intelligence Summaries are contained in F.S. Regs., Part II. and the Staff Manual respectively. Title pages will be prepared in manuscript.

Place	Date	Hour	Summary of Events and Information	Remarks and references to Appendices
BULLY GRENAY	May 1st		The Bn relieved the 1st C.M.R. in the Hill 70 Sector on the night of the 1/2nd May.	
In the line	2nd			
do	3rd		Lt J. Darlow proceeded to Course of Instruction at IV"Army School. Part I Bn Orders were not published.	
do	4th		Lt C.S. Smith reported for attachment for instructional purposes from XVIII Corps School 4th inst.	
do	5th			
do	6th		Lt E.A. Fuller admitted to hospital 2nd/Lt J.E. Goodchild discharged from hospital to unit 2nd/Lt H.R. Foster despatched to the BASE for re-posting	
do	7th		Part I & II Bn Orders were not published.	
do	8th		Capt J.C. Clark proceeded this day to attend a Special Course of Instruction at First Army Infantry School.	
do	9th		2nd/Lt H Tattersall proceeded on the 9th inst for duty at CORPS REINFORCEMENT CAMP	
do	10th		Strength decreases: Lt S.J. Squibbs wounded in action 3rd inst.	

Army Form C. 2118.

WAR DIARY
or
INTELLIGENCE SUMMARY.
(Erase heading not required)

13th Bn Middlesex Regt.

Instructions regarding War Diaries and Intelligence Summaries are contained in F. S. Regs., Part II. and the Staff Manual respectively. Title pages will be prepared in manuscript.

Place	Date	Hour	Summary of Events and Information	Remarks and references to Appendices
In the line	May 11		During the afternoon C Coy extended to the left and relieved the Right Front Coy of the 9th Sussex Regt. During the night the A C & D Coy were relieved by the 7th Northamptonshire Regt and A & B Coys by the 8th Queens. On completion of relief the Bn moved back to billets in LES BREBIS. 2nd Lt R.J. McMILLAN discharged from hospital. Major R.S. DOVE M.C. having reported this day from six months tour of duty at home no taken on the strength.	
LES BREBIS	12th		Training. 2nd Lt G.T. ASHMAN proceeded this day for a period of rest at the Officers' Rest House PARIS-PLAGE	
do	13th		Training. Extract from Adjournments Commission of List No. 186. 2nd May 1918. — Temp. Major A.N. HINGLEY M.C. to command Bn and to be Temp. Lieut. Col. whilst so commanding. Captain (Temp. Lieut. Col.) T. GREENE D.S.O. 7/Dragoon Gds. (to command 10th Infy. (B.W.) 16th April 1918. T/Capt. R.S. DOVE M.C. to be T/Major (January 1st) Authy: London Gaz Mr 14/5/18	

Army Form C. 2118.

WAR DIARY
or
INTELLIGENCE=SUMMARY.

(Erase heading not required.)

13th Bn. Middlesex Regt.

Instructions regarding War Diaries and Intelligence Summaries are contained in F. S. Regs., Part II. and the Staff Manual respectively. Title pages will be prepared in manuscript.

Place	Date	Hour	Summary of Events and Information	Remarks and references to Appendices
LES BREBIS	May 14		Training	
do	15th		Major R.S. DOVE M.C. assumes the duties of Second in Command with effect from this date.	
do	16th		Training	
do			Training	
			1876 Sgt (a/CSM) D. JUDD "C" Coy awarded the Distinguished Conduct Medal (Auth): A/2S. Third Army M.R. 1218 of 10/4/18.)	
do	17th		Training	
			Strength decrease: 2nd Lt J. PAYNE transferred to England. Sick 1/5/18. (Auth: XIII Corps A/4/1187/37 d/11/5/18.)	
do	18th		The Bn. relieved the 9th Bn Royal Sussex Regt in the line the night of 18th/19th inst.	
			Lt J.T. BEER, 2nd Lt G.J. HAYNES, 2nd Lt M.O. TICKLE, 2nd Lt H.P. STEWART, 2nd Lt W. COUSINS proceeded this day for training at the Advanced Divisional Hqrs. MAISNIL-BOUCHÉ	

Army Form C. 2118.

WAR DIARY
or
INTELLIGENCE SUMMARY.
(Erase heading not required.)

13 Bn Middlesex Regt.

Place	Date	Hour	Summary of Events and Information	Remarks and references to Appendices
6th the LINE	May 19		2nd/Lt N. OFFORD discharged from hospital 16/5/18.	
do	20"		Lt P.G. HUTSON } proceeded this day to England to report at the AIR MINISTRY for 2nd/Lt N. OFFORD } transfer to R.A.F. and are struck off the strength	
			R.A.M.S. R. PRINGLE having been selected for appointment as temporary Quartermaster General (1st) Infantry proceeded this day to report to the BASE COMMANDANT CALAIS to join the 3rd P. Quartermasters and is struck off the strength accordingly. (Auth) AG 2058/2743 (o) 2/13/5/18.	
			Extract from Appointments etc from List No 187 dated 12 May 1918 Temp Lieut E.G. BAKER to be acty Capt whilst commanding a company 16/4/18.	
do	21st		2nd/Lt S.J. ASHMAN reported this day from the Officers' Rest House PARIS-PLAGE	
do	22nd		2nd/Lt S.J. ASHMAN proceeded this day to 24 Divisional Wing MAISTER-BOUCHE	
do	23rd			
do	24"		CAPT E.G. BAKER proceeded this day to attend the 20th Course of Instruction at the Army Musketry Camp	
			Lt T. BEER, 2nd/Lt G.J. HAYNES, 2nd/Lt H.G. TICKLE, 2nd/Lt H.P. STEWART, 2nd/Lt H. COUSINS M.M. reported from 24 Divisional Reinforcement Camp	

Army Form C. 2118.

WAR DIARY
or
INTELLIGENCE SUMMARY.   3'Bn. Middlesex Regt.
(Erase heading not required.)

Place	Date	Hour	Summary of Events and Information	Remarks and references to Appendices
In the LINE	May 25		—	
do.	26		Permission has been given for Lt. E.G. BAKER to wear the badges of rank of CAPTAIN (A/Capt additional) pending the appearance of his promotion in the London Gazette. (Auth: 2nd Bde. No. A 90/284 d. 23/5/18)	
			2nd Lt. E.T. SEVENOAKS admitted to hospital.	
do	27			
do	28		The Corps Commander has awarded decorations to the undermentioned N.C.O's + men for gallantry and devotion to duty in actions:—	
			15470 A/Cpl. C. SOOBY "A" Coy	
			18607 A/Cpl. A.H. LANGLEY do.	
			203177 Pte. C. BIRCH do.	
			42740 " F. SANDFORD do. (att. 7/2 L.T.M.B.)	
			4819 L/Sgt. G. SMITH B Coy	The Military
			43176 Pte. S.G. BRADHAM do.	Medal.
			8199 " R. DEAN C Coy	
			34854 " A.S. PARKER do.	
			2039 " A. POWERS do.	
			42877 " T.W. ROADS D Coy	
			41887 A/Cpl. G. DUNNE do.	
			(Auth: XIX Corps R.O. No.1177 25/5/18)	

Army Form C. 2118.

WAR DIARY
or
INTELLIGENCE SUMMARY.

13th Bn Middlesex Regt.

(Erase heading not required.)

Place	Date	Hour	Summary of Events and Information	Remarks and references to Appendices
In the LINE	May 29		Bn Orders were not published.	
do	30		The Bn. was relieved this night by the 7th Bn NORTHAMPTONSHIRE REGT and proceeded to billets in LES BREBIS.	
LES BREBIS	31		Training. 2nd Lt E.T. SENEVIRAS was transferred from hospital to No1 Can. C.C.S. 26/5/18 2nd Lt R.J. McMILLAN admitted to hospital 30/5/18	

WAR DIARY
or
INTELLIGENCE SUMMARY.

(Erase heading not required.)

Army Form C. 2118.

War Diary

for month of June.

13th Battalion Middlesex Regt.

Army Form C. 2118.

WAR DIARY
or
INTELLIGENCE SUMMARY.
(Erase heading not required.)

Place	Date	Hour	Summary of Events and Information	Remarks and references to Appendices
LES BREBIS	June 1		Training. The following decorations were awarded by the Jul's marshal Commanding in Chief. Bar to distinguished service order. Capt (T/Major) J Greene D.S.O. Military Cross. T/Capt R.K. Allen. T/Lieut (A/Capt) W. Mears T/Lieut (T/Capt) Monaghan. T/Lieut S.J. Ashman T/2nd Lieut Conder Meeke. The Distinguished Conduct Medal 42156 R.S.M. A.P. Andrews RSM. 42156 R.S.M. E.G. Baker relinquished the acting rank of Capt.	
	2		on ceasing to command a Coy (15 May 1918). Capt J Greene DSO dragon granted from tent duty as Co Indian Regt to be Temp. Brig. Gen.	

Army Form C. 2118.

WAR DIARY
or
INTELLIGENCE SUMMARY.
(Erase heading not required.)

Place	Date	Hour	Summary of Events and Information	Remarks and references to Appendices
In the LINE	June 5		The Battalion relieved the 9th ROYAL SUSSEX on the line on the night of the 5/6 June.	
	6		1st Lieut J. Rothman M.O.R.C. U.S.A. was attached to the Battn for duty as Medi: Offr. (effect from 4.6.18). Capt R.A.H. Dutton R.A.M.C. proceeded for duty with 3rd Field Ambulance.	
	8		No 2057 Regt Sr Mr Sergt R.Rimple to be Temp: 2nm and Hon. Lieut. (20.5.18)	
	12		2/Lieut E.J. Francis M.C. was admitted to Hospital.	
	13		Sec Lieut. (A/Capt) W.O'Meara MC to be Lieut. (London Gazette Supplement) 10.6.15).	
	14		Temp Major H.N.Stroughly M.C. to Command a Battn until to Temp. Lieut Colonel. (London Gazette Supplement June 1918).	
	15		Lieut J.T. Beer was granted leave to United Kingdom 16-6-18 to 30.6.18.	
	17		The Battn carried out a raid on the enemy trenches (H 26 d 0 30:30) Lieut D.C.L. MURRAY mchgs — other officers 2Lieuts E.C.ANDERSON	

WAR DIARY
or
INTELLIGENCE SUMMARY.
(Erase heading not required.)

Army Form C. 2118.

Place	Date	Hour	Summary of Events and Information	Remarks and references to Appendices
Inchyfield June			2/Lieut G.J. Haynes. 2/Lieut Ely Hale. 57 O'Rourke.	
			The raid was entirely successful. One unwounded prisoner was taken.	
			A number of casualties were inflicted on the enemy - number of machine gun emplacements destroyed - dugouts blown up & material were destroyed. The Battn was relieved with the line on the night 17/18 June by the 7th presentation determined over great success	
	17		Northamptonshire Regt. and proceeded E. Billets at LES BRE BIS. 2/Lieut G.J.Stayner was killed in action — (17.6.18)	
ES BREBIS	18.		Training.	
	19		2/Lieut P. ACKSEY was admitted to hospital.	
	21.		2/Lieuts B.M.BEATER was granted 21 days sick leave to England. Capt. Parker A. Buxton C.F. and 1 Lieut J. Rahman M.O.R.C. U.S.A. were admitted to hospital.	
	22		Capt. R.A PERRY was admitted to hospital.	
	23		Capt CK ALLEN M.C. was granted leave to United Kingdom 23.6.18 to 7.7.16.	
	24		Capt. Li. HORNIMAN admitted to hospital.	
	26		2/Lieut H.W. CATTLE admitted to hospital.	

Army Form C. 2118.

WAR DIARY
or
INTELLIGENCE SUMMARY.
(Erase heading not required.)

Instructions regarding War Diaries and Intelligence Summaries are contained in F. S. Regs., Part II. and the Staff Manual respectively. Title pages will be prepared in manuscript.

Place	Date	Hour	Summary of Events and Information	Remarks and references to Appendices
LES ORELIS			Awards:- Meritorious Service Medal. 13022 Sgt. ———— west D Coy.	

Army Form C. 2118.

WAR DIARY
or
INTELLIGENCE SUMMARY.

(Erase heading not required.)

Summary of Events and Information

Summary of Casualties during the Month.

KILLED		DIED OF WOUNDS		MISSING		MISSING BELIEVED KILLED		DIED		WOUNDED		WOUNDED AT DUTY		TOTAL	
Offs.	O.R's	Offs.	O.R's	Offs.	O.R's	Offs.	O.R's	Offs.	O.R's	Offs.	O.R's	Offs.	O.R's	Offs.	O.R's
1	6	—	5	—	3	—	—	—	1	2	32	—	8	2	55

Drafts during Month.

Officers	Other Ranks.
3	86

H Bingley. Lieut-Col.,
13th Middlesex Regt.

Place	Date	Hour		Remarks and references to Appendices

Instructions regarding War Diaries and Intelligence Summaries are contained in F. S. Regs., Part II. and the Staff Manual respectively. Title pages will be prepared in manuscript.

WAR DIARY

INTELLIGENCE SUMMARY.

(Erase heading not required.)

Army Form C. 2118.

Vol 33

1/4th Bn The Middlesex Regiment

For the month of

July 1918

R/M* 2442 / Army Form C. 2118.

WAR DIARY
of
INTELLIGENCE SUMMARY.
(Erase heading not required.)

13th Batt: Middx Regt.

Place	Date	Hour	Summary of Events and Information	Remarks and references to Appendices
Inthefield	July 1		PASTFIELD Lieut J.W. ~~Pastfield~~ and 2/Lieut W. EARLEY having arrived at 21st Bn. Recp Camp were taken on the strength.	
	2		2/Lieut HATTERSALL taken on the strength on return from duty at 21st Bn. Reception camp	
	3		The Band proceeded this day to the Irish Army Infantry School for duty Revd A BUXTON discharged from hospital (30.6.18) C.E.	

	4		Honours and awards — Under authority delegated by the Field Marshall
			Commanding in Chief the Corps commander has awarded decorations
			to the undermentioned NCO's and men for gallantry and devotion to duty
			in action.—
			    THE MILITARY MEDAL
			  1922 Sgt W GIBBONS D Coy
			  89268 - S.G. WHITCHER C "
			  4577 - E DRURY D "
			  G5775 Pte T PARMENTER A "
			    [Auth. 18th Corps R.O. N° 1117 of 1-7-18]	

Army Form C. 2118.

WAR DIARY
or
INTELLIGENCE SUMMARY.
(Erase heading not required.)

Place	Date	Hour	Summary of Events and Information	Remarks and references to Appendices
Inthefield	July 5		2/Lieut P.A. CASEY was struck off the strength. Transferred to England sick.	
			(Army XVIII Corps A/1187/SU dt 1-7-18)	
			The Battalion was relieved in the line on the night of 5/6 July by the 7th Bn.	
			Northamptonshire Regt. and proceeded to LES BREBIS	
LES BREBIS	6		Training	
			The undermentioned officers arrived 5.7.18 and were taken on strength	
			Capt R. HARRISON	
			— C.P. HAYWARD	
			Lieut E. FOXON	
			CAPT E MOORE arrived 6.7.18 and was taken on the strength	
			Capt L.I. HORNIMAN Lieut E.A. FULLER and 2/Lieut F.W. DEVIS rejoined from	
			Hospital (5.7.18).	
		8	Major R.S. DOVE M.C. assumed temp Command of the Battn since 21/6 of RN	
			HINGLEY M.C. granted leave to England for 14 days.	
			2/Lieut C.J. KNIGHT rejoined from Corps School at FRESSIN	

WAR DIARY
or
INTELLIGENCE SUMMARY.
(Erase heading not required.)

Army Form C. 2118.

Place	Date	Hour	Summary of Events and Information	Remarks and references to Appendices
Inchy	July 10		The Battn relieved the 9th Royal Sussex Regt in the line on the night of the 11/12 July.	
	12		Lieut A HORSFORD proceeded to a course of instruction at GHQ Lewis Gun School at LE TOUQUET.	
			M.G. 2/Lieut S.J. ASHMAN, rejoined from leave of instruction at First Army Musketry School.	
	13		Lieut E.A. FULLER admitted from to hospital (16-7-18)	
			Honours and awards. Under authority delegated by the Majesty the King the Field Marshal Commanding-in-Chief awarded the following decorations for gallantry in the field.	
			The Military Cross.	
			Lieut D.C.L. MURRAY.	
			2/Lieut E.C. ANDERSON.	
			2/Lieut A. WADSWORTH proceeded to attend a course of instruction at First Army Musketry School.	
	14		2/Lieut F.W. DEWS proceeded for duty as Town Major, HYTHE TUNNEL	

WAR DIARY
INTELLIGENCE SUMMARY
(Erase heading not required.)

Army Form C. 2118.

Place	Date	Hour	Summary of Events and Information	Remarks and references to Appendices
Ytres	July 15		Honours and awards. Under authority delegated by His Majesty the King, the Field Marshall Commanding in Chief has awarded the following decoration for gallantry in the field. The Distinguished Conduct Medal. 37.153 Corpl W. BEAN A Coy (acting Sergt A.R.O. 2858 d/12-7-18).	
	16		The Band reported from duty with 73rd Army Infantry School (15-7-18). On handing over command of 73rd I. Bde. Brigadier-General W. DUGAN addressed a letter to his late command thanking them for the assistance given him in the past and wishing them good luck in the future. Gen DUGAN concluded his letter by an exhortation to "STICK IT".	
	17		2/Lieut W.G. COUSINS M.M. was granted leave to U.K. 17-7-18 to 31-7-18. The 4 named officers were removed from establishment and transferred regulars attached. 2/Lieut S.J. PILE M.C., 2/Lieut E.G. GODDARD, 2/Lieut F.H.V. WOOD, 2/Lieut H.O. DAVIES.	

WAR DIARY
or
INTELLIGENCE SUMMARY.

(Erase heading not required.)

Army Form C. 2118.

Instructions regarding War Diaries and Intelligence Summaries are contained in F. S. Regs., Part II. and the Staff Manual respectively. Title pages will be prepared in manuscript.

Place	Date	Hour	Summary of Events and Information	Remarks and references to Appendices
Ardrefield	July 19		2/Lieut H.G. TICKLE was wounded in action while making a very gallant attempt to secure identification from the enemy	
			Honours and awards	
			G1151 C.S.M. I.W. JOHNSON (late of 6 Bn) awarded meritorious service medal (London Gazette 4/17.6.18).	
			B' Lieut Col (T/Brig. Gen.) R.T. COLLINS CMG, D.S.O. Royal Berkshire Regiment assumed command of 92nd Inf Bde. (15.7.18).	
			Lieut & 2/Lt M.P. S.H. HENDERSON was granted leave to U.K. for 14 days.	
	20		22.7.18 to 3.8.18.	
			Lieut R. HORSFORD rejoined from course of Instruction at G.H.Q. Lewis gun School at LE TOUQUET	
	21		Capt H.R. MALLETT arrived at 24th Divl Reception Camp and was taken on the Strength.	
	22/23		The Battalion were relieved in the line by the 7th Northamptonshire Regt in night 22/23rd July	

WAR DIARY
or
INTELLIGENCE SUMMARY.
(Erase heading not required.)

Army Form C. 2118.

Place	Date	Hour	Summary of Events and Information	Remarks and references to Appendices
LES BREBIS	July 24		Training.- Lieut Col AN. HINGLEY. M.C. assumed command of the Battn. on return from leave.	
			2/Lieut J.E. GOODCHILD rejoined from course of instruction at XVIII Corps Infantry School.	
			2/Lieut R.J. McMILLAN discharged from hospital.	
	26		The Battn also marched to the range at MAZINGARBE, where a demonstration in musketry was carried out.	
			2/Lieut B.M. BEATER found unfit by medical Board was struck off strength.	
	28		2/Lieut Anderson M.C. proceeded to 3rd Supple for duty.	
	29		The Battn relieved the 9th Royal Sussex Regt in the line on the night of the 29/30 July.	
	30 & 31st			

Army Form C. 2118.

WAR DIARY
or
INTELLIGENCE SUMMARY.
(Erase heading not required.)

Instructions regarding War Diaries and Intelligence Summaries are contained in F. S. Regs., Part II. and the Staff Manual respectively. Title pages will be prepared in manuscript.

Place	Date	Hour	Summary of Events and Information	Remarks and references to Appendices
			Summary of Operations during the Month.	
			Killed in Action / Wounded in Action / Wounded at duty / Shot.	
			Off. OR / Off. OR / Off. OR / Off. OR	
			1 6 1 12 . 3 . 1	
			Drafts	
			Officers / Other Ranks	
			4 / 51	

A. D. Dingley, Lieut Col.
Commdg 13th Middlesex Regt.

Army Form C. 2118.

WAR DIARY
INTELLIGENCE SUMMARY.
(Erase heading not required.)

Confidential

13th Bn Middlesex Regiment

for the month of

August 1916

Page 1.

Army Form C. 2118.

WAR DIARY
INTELLIGENCE SUMMARY

(Erase heading not required.)

13th B. Middlesex Regt.

August 1918

Place	Date	Hour	Summary of Events and Information	Remarks and references to Appendices
In the Field	August 3.		Capt. E.A. Moore and Capt. E.P. Howard proceeded for attachment to 1st Bn. Royal Fusiliers and 8th Bn. the Queens, respectively.	
	4.		2/Lieut. Alsadworth rejoined from Course at the 1st Army Musketry School. 11 N.C.Os and 5 O.Rs were present at a Special Service & Intercession held at the 1st Army H.Q.s	
	5.		A Special Order of the Day was issued by Field Marshal Sir Douglas Haig, K.T. G.C.B. G.C.V.O. K.C.I.E. C. in C., bringing out all the features of the present war and emphasing the wonderful behaviour of British troops.	
			2/Lieut. Ths. Dews rejoined from duty as Town Major Hythe Tunnel.	
	6.		Capt. J.C. Clark proceeded on leave to the U.K. for 14 days.	
	7.		2/Lieut. E.R. Ball proceeded to 2nd Army Rest Camp.	
			2/Lieut. E.H. Wietshins and 10 O.Rs went to take part in the 1st Army Rifle Meeting	
			2/Lieut. Ths. Dews proceeded to the 24th Div. Reception Camp.	
	8.		Honours & Awards. 2/Lt H.C. Tickler – The Military Cross – for very gallant and at great personal risk, attempting to secure an identification on 19 July.	
	9.		2/Lieut. G.T. Pastfield proceeded to the U.K. on 14 days leave.	

Page 2.
Army Form C. 2118.

13th Bn. MIDDLESEX REGT.
No............
Date............
ORDERLY ROOM.

WAR DIARY or INTELLIGENCE SUMMARY.

13th Bn. Middlesex Regt.

August 18

Place	Date	Hour	Summary of Events and Information	Remarks and references to Appendices
Lillers	August 9		Lieut. E.N. Fuller was granted 21 days Sick leave to the U.K. from 22.7.18.	
	10		Capt. R.P. Haward — attached to the 8th B. The Queens — was reported "Missing". 2/Lieut. E.J. Francis M.C. was granted 21 days Sick leave to the U.K. from 23.7.18. 2/Lieut. W.C. Cousins M.M. rejoined from 2nd Div. Reception Camp.	
	11.		2/Lieut. Alsadworth left to attend a course in Antigas measures at the Corps School.	
	12		The Bn. was relieved in the line by the 7th Bn. Northamptonshire Regt. on the night of 11/12. Lieut. J.J. Been was granted an extension of leave from 30th July to 4th August. The Battn. marched to Marguffles Rifle Range, returning after tea. Capt. Rothermine proceeded to attend a Course of Instruction for Coy. Commanders under Major W.H. Cornall M.C. at the 2nd Div. Reception Camp.	
	13		2/Lieut. Herbatte was discharged from Hospital. Capt. L.L. Horniman left to attend the Instructors Course at the Senior Officers School at Aldershot.	
	15.		2/Lieut. E.A. Wiltshire rejoined from the 1st Army Rest Camp for a term of duty. The Band proceeded to the 1st Army Rifle Meeting (Flexicoq. 75th).	
	16		Major R.S. Dove M.C., Capt. E.A. Perry and Lieut. B.C.L. Murray M.C. proceeded to the 2nd Div. Reception Camp.	
	17		2/Lieut. Alwadworth rejoined from Course of Instruction at the Corps Gas School.	

Page 3.
Army Form C. 2118.

WAR DIARY

INTELLIGENCE SUMMARY
13th B. Middlesex Regt.
(Erase heading not required.)

August 1918

Place	Date	Hour	Summary of Events and Information	Remarks and references to Appendices
Lillers	August 17.		R.S.M. ———— returned the 9th Batt. Royal Sussex Regt on the night of 17/8th.	
	18.		2/Lieut. F.W. Dew rejoined from the 24th Div. Reception Camp and left again for the Hythe Tunnel, on duty, as the Town Major.	
	19.		Capt. B.K. Allen M.C. proceeded to 73rd I.B. for duty, having been with this Batt. as Adjutant for some considerable time. Capt. C. Perry rejoined from 24th Div. Reception Camp and took over the duties of Adjutant.	
	21.		2/Lieut. J.C. Goucher proceeded on 14 days leave to the U.K. 2/Lieut. E.R. Ball rejoined from the 1st Army Rest Camp. Lieut. D.C.L. Murray M.C. rejoined from the 24th Div. Rest Camp and proceeded to the 73. I.B. as Brigade Works Officer.	
	22.		Capt. J.C. Edwards left for the 24th Div. Reception Camp. Capt. R. Harrison rejoined from the 24th Div. Reception Camp after having finished the Course for Coy. Commanders. 2/Lieut. F.W. Dew rejoined from duty in the Hythe Tunnel and was succeeded as Town Major by Lieut. J.D. Barr.	
	23.		Capt. E.A. Perry proceeded to Paris on leave until 1st September.	
	24.		2/Lieut. H. Tattersall being granted leave until 7th Sept. proceeded to the U.K.	

Page 4
Army Form C. 2118.

WAR DIARY
INTELLIGENCE SUMMARY.

13th Bn HIDDLESEX REGT.
ORDERLY ROOM.

1/3rd Middlesex Regt.

August 1918.

Place	Date	Hour	Summary of Events and Information	Remarks and references to Appendices
In the Field	August 24		Extract from Appointments. Temp. Major R.S. Dove M.C. to be 2nd in Command to full establishment. 14 May 1918.	
	27.		On the night of 27/28th the Battn. was relieved in the line by the 7/8th K.O.S.B's.	
	28		Capt. A.J. O'Meara M.C. proceeded to the U.K. on 14 days leave until 11th September.	
	29/8.		I.O. 13 Been rejoined from duty in Hythe Tunnel.	
	29/8.		R.J. McMillan proceeded to U.K. on leave until 13th September.	
			Lt. A. Honotora rejoined from Course of Instruction at 2nd Div. Reception Camp.	
	30.		The Battalion moved to Marquefer and billeted there.	
			At the Sports & Horse Shows held during the Course of the Month, the Battn. obtained the following places:-	
			Brigade Divisional Corps.	
			1st Tug of War (Catchweights) 1st Tug of War 2nd Tug of War (light).	
			(light) Final was reached.	
			1st Officers Chargers.	
			2nd Light Draft. 3rd Officers Chargers.	
			3rd Turnout.	

Page 5

Army Form C. 2118.

13th Bn. MIDDLESEX REGT.
ORDERLY ROOM

WAR DIARY
or
INTELLIGENCE SUMMARY.
(Erase heading not required.)

Instructions regarding War Diaries and Intelligence Summaries are contained in F. S. Regs., Part II. and the Staff Manual respectively. Title pages will be prepared in manuscript.

Place	Date	Hour	Summary of Events and Information	Remarks and references to Appendices
			Summary of Casualties during the month.	

Killed in Action		Missing		Wounded in Action		Wounded (Gas)		Died of Wounds		Wounded at Duty	
O.	O.R.	O.	O.R.	O.	O.R.	O.	O.R.	O.	O.R.	O.	O.R.
-	1	1	1	-	5	-	6	-	1	1	3

Drafts.

Officers	O. Ranks
-	169

R S Gore Major
for Lieut - Col.,
Commanding 13th Bn. Middlesex Regt

D. D. & L., London, E.C.
(A8011) Wt. W1771/M2031 750,000 5/17 Sch. 52 Forms.C2118/14

13th Machine Gun Regiment

WAR DIARY.

WAR DIARY

INTELLIGENCE SUMMARY. 13th Bn. Middlesex Regt.

Page 1.

September 1918

Place	Date	Hour	Summary of Events and Information	Remarks and references to Appendices
In the field.	September. 1.		Capt. H.R. Mallett M.C. proceeded to the 2nd Dvil. Reception Camp, Vendroil, to attend a course of instruction for Coy. Commanders	
	2.		2nd Lieut. H.L. Pearce, having joined the Battalion, was posted to 'C' Coy.	
	3.		2nd Lieut. E.L. Neale proceeded on a Physical & Bayonet Training Course.	
	4.		2nd Lieut. S. Ockman M.C. proceeded on leave to United Kingdom.	
	6.		2nd Lieut. H. Reid proceeded to Canadian I.M.B.D. for 3 days attachment to the 16 Sq. R.A.F. The Battalion relieved the 9th Royal Sussex on the line on the night of 6/7th	
	7.		Major R.S. Bone M.C. and Lieut. F. Trollope proceeded to the 24th Dvil. Reception Camp	
	8.		2nd Lieut. H. Reid rejoined from attachment to the 16th Squadron R.A.F.	
	9.		2nd Lieut. W. Scotfield was killed while walking round his posts in the outskirts of Lens.	
	10.		2nd Lieut. E.J. Ball and 30 O.R's left for the 1st Army Rest Camp. 2nd Lieut. E.J. Francis, having been marked unfit by Medical Board, was struck off Strength.	
	11.		Lieut. Rev. Phillips and 1st Lieut. J. Rothman M.O.R.C. left for 10 days leave to Tranville.	
	10.		1st Lieut. H.H. Peck M.O.R.C. was attached for temporary duty as Medical Officer. Capt. H.R. Mallett M.C. rejoined from the Coy Cdrs Course.	
	11.		Lieut. E. Eason proceeded to the 24th Dvil. Reception Camp to attend a course for Coy. Commanders.	
	12.		2/Lt. E.C. Anderson M.C. left for 14 days leave to the United Kingdom.	

WAR DIARY

INTELLIGENCE SUMMARY — 13th Bn. Middlesex Regt.

Page 2. Army Form C. 2118.

September 1918.

Place	Date	Hour	Summary of Events and Information	Remarks and references to Appendices
I.R.Sur September	13.		The transfer of Capt. R.A. Moore M.C. to the 1st Bn. Royal Fusiliers having been approved, he was struck off the strength of this Battalion.	
	14.		The Battalion was relieved in the line by the 7th Northamptonshire Regt, and became Bn. in 1st Support.	
			Lieut. S. Bampather M.C. rejoined from the 1st Army Musketry Camp.	
			Major R.S. Bone M.C. and Lieut. F. Trollope rejoined from the 24th Div. Reception Camp.	
			Lieut. J.J. Beer proceeded to attend a course of Instruction at the 1st Army Musketry Camp.	
			"Special Order of the Day" was issued by Field Marshal Sir Douglas Haig, K.T. G.C.B. G.C.V.O. K.C.I.E. C. in C. British Armies in France, in which he gave a resumé of the happenings of the past month, and in which he expressed his thanks to all the troops under his command for their excellent behaviour.	
	16.		Lieut. E.C. Baker proceeded on 14 days leave to the United Kingdom.	
	18.		2nd Lieut. Aliadworth left for the United Kingdom on 14 days leave.	
			Major J.J. Stattero M.C. proceeded to England on Duty, and was struck off strength.	
			Capt. W.J. O'Mara M.C. was granted an extension of leave from 11th to 12th Sept.	
			The Bn. was relieved by the 7th Northamptonshire Regt. in 1st Support, and proceeded to Marquettes Farm.	
	22.		Lieut. R. Foxen rejoined from the Coy. Commanders Course at the 24th Div. Reception Camp.	
			Lieut. S. Bampather M.C. proceeded to the 24th Div. Reception Camp to attend a course for Coy. Commanding.	
	23.		Lieut. Rev. Phillips and 1st Lieut. Rothman M.O.R.C. rejoined from leave to Fronville. 1st Lieut. McPech M.O.R.C. proceeded to the 72nd Field Ambulance, having terminated his temporary attachment as Medical Officer.	

Page 3. Army Form C. 2118.

WAR DIARY

of

13th Bn. Middlesex Regt.   September 1918.

(Erase heading not required.)

Place	Date	Hour	Summary of Events and Information	Remarks and references to Appendices
In the field	September 26		2nd Lieut. E.G. Hale rejoined from the Course of Physical and Bayonet Training.	
	27		2nd Lieut A.E. Roberton, 2nd Lieut A.K.E. Hurst and Lieut Allerton having joined this Battalion were posted to C, C, and A. Coys respectively.	
	28.		Lieut. E.A. Fuller proceeded to England, Sick, 8th September.	
	30.		The Battalion moved to Obhain Camp and stopped there the night prior to moving to Doullens.	
			Appointments.	
			Temp. Capt. F.J. Stratton M.C. to be Temp. Major, 16th April.	
			Temp. Lieut. ———— E.A. Perry to be Temp. Captain, 16th April.	
			Temp. 2nd Lieut. R.w. Phillips to be Temp. Lieut. 1st September.	

Army Form C. 2118.

WAR DIARY
or
INTELLIGENCE SUMMARY.
(Erase heading not required.)

Summary of Events and Information

Summary of Casualties
during the Month.

Killed in Action		Wounded in Action		Wounded at Duty		Injured S.I.	
O.	OR	O	OR	O	OR	O	OR
1	1	-	4	-	2	-	1

Drafts.

Officers	o Ranks
4	32

A.N. Dingley. Lieut-Col.
Commanding 13TH Middlesex Regt.

Instructions regarding War Diaries and Intelligence Summaries are contained in F. S. Regs., Part II. and the Staff Manual respectively. Title pages will be prepared in manuscript.

Place	Date	Hour		

73rd

Part No. 36

WAR DIARY
INTELLIGENCE SUMMARY

Army Form C. 2118.

13th Bn Middlesex Regiment
for the month of
October 1918

M 280. 12.11.18.
Army Form C. 2118.

Page. 1.

WAR DIARY
or
INTELLIGENCE SUMMARY.
(Erase heading not required.)

13th Bn. Middlesex Regt.

Oct. 1918.

Instructions regarding War Diaries and Intelligence Summaries are contained in F. S. Regs., Part II. and the Staff Manual respectively. Title pages will be prepared in manuscript.

Place	Date	Hour	Summary of Events and Information	Remarks and references to Appendices
In the field	October 1		The Battn. entrained at HERSIN and entrained for MONTECOURT, moving on arrival to POMMERA where it went into billets.	
	2		Lieut P. BARNFATHER. M.C. rejoined from company commanders course at 2nd Divisional Reception Camp. Training.	
	3		2nd Lieut E.C. Anderson M.C. was transferred to the General List and struck off the strength of the Battn. A letter from Lt.Gen. Sir AYLMER HUNTER-WESTON K.C.B., D.S.O. commanding VIII Corps to the Divisional Commander was published in Batt Orders. The Corps Commander expressed his appreciation of the work done by the Division and his regret at its departure from his Corps. Training. Lieut F. TROLLOPE granted 14 days leave to United Kingdom. Capt L.T. HORNIMAN rejoined from course of Instruction at Senior Officers School, ALDERSHOT.	
	4			
	5		The Battalion entrained at POMMERA and arrived at HERMIES in the evening about 1900 hours, marched to a point East of MOEVRES and bivouaced for the night.	
	6			
	7		The Battn. marched to GRAINCOURT and relieved the 1st Artists_ taking over their camp_ owing to the weather and lack of ⎯	

WAR DIARY
or
INTELLIGENCE SUMMARY
(Erase heading not required.)

Place	Date	Hour	Summary of Events and Information	Remarks and references to Appendices
In the field Oct"	8		accommodation. great discomfort was experienced on each of these nights. Remained in camp completing equipment and ammunition – Several Casualties were caused by shell fire. At 1700 hours marched to RUMILLY area, and remained in old trenches during the night.	
	9		The 24th Division relieved the 63rd. in the line about NIERGNIES. and in the morning of the 9th followed up the enemy as far as AWOINGT. which was occupied. the 73rd Brigade then took up a line in advance of the town, and advancing got into touch with the enemy about midday, on the line CAGNONCLES – CAUROIR. The 8th Middx were in support during this operation. the other two Batt'ns of the Brigade. The night 9/10 was spent with nothing exciting in front of AWOINGT.	
	10		The enemy having retired as far as RIEUX. The 9th Royal Sussex followed. The 13th Middx passed through and pushed on – cyclists and cavalry reported enemy holding line beyond RIEUX and AVESNES. The Batt" was ordered to advance and succeeded in gaining the high ground NE of RIEUX, the	

WAR DIARY
or
INTELLIGENCE SUMMARY.

(Erase heading not required.)

Army Form C. 2118.

Page 3.

Place	Date	Hour	Summary of Events and Information	Remarks and references to Appendices
Inthepide	Oct 10		Objective ordered. The order of advance was A.C.D. Coys in line and B.Coy in close support, this Bay was subsequently pushed into line. Heavy shelling and machine gun fire were met with, the total casualties being 6 officers and 100 men killed wounded and missing. The line gained was held during the night and in the morning B. Coy in the right centre attempted to extend the line along a sunken road. Considerable opposition was met with Capt Clark being wounded and 2nd Lieut EARLY killed. During the morning however the line was established. Lt Col AN HINGLEY D.S.O. was this day wounded by a machine gun bullet while visiting the C.Os, and Maj R.S. DOVE NC was about to assume command of the Battn at about 600 hours the 17th Brigade passed through the line to continue the attack, and the Batn came under heavy shell fire all night and the following morning. During the evening the Batn was withdrawn to billets at RIEUX arriving during the afternoon.	

Army Form C. 2118.

WAR DIARY
or
INTELLIGENCE SUMMARY.
(Erase heading not required)

Page 4.

Instructions regarding War Diaries and Intelligence Summaries are contained in F. S. Regs., Part II. and the Staff Manual respectively. Title pages will be prepared in manuscript.

Place	Date	Hour	Summary of Events and Information	Remarks and references to Appendices
Julignies	Oct 11/13		The Battalion remained in billets at RIEUX until 13th Oct. when it moved to AVEINES-LES-AUBERT, arriving in the evening about 1730 hours and	
	13			
	13/16		remained there until the 16th. Cleaning up and reorganising.	
	17		moved to CAUDRY arriving about 1620 hours.	
	17/25		The Battn. remained at CAUDRY until 25th Oct. & during its stay was engaged in Battalion and Brigade training. Spent its	
	26.		The Battn. marched to billets in HAUSSY. and remained until the	
	27/31.		of the month.	

(A5092). Wt. W12839/M1293. 75 10 0. 1/17. D. D. & L., Ld. Forms/C.2118/14.

Army Form C. 2118.

WAR DIARY
or
INTELLIGENCE SUMMARY.
(Erase heading not required.)

Page 5

Instructions regarding War Diaries and Intelligence Summaries are contained in F. S. Regs., Part II. and the Staff Manual respectively. Title pages will be prepared in manuscript.

Place	Date	Hour	Summary of Events and Information	Remarks and references to Appendices
	Oct 11		Major J.T. STRATTEN. M.C. assumed duties as 2nd in Command vice MAJ. R.S. DOVE appointed to command the Batt.	
	13		Capt. L.I. HORNIMAN. proceeded to VIII Corps School for duty as Instructor.	
	19		Lieut W.F. JONES. M.C. arrived and was taken on the strength, being posted to C. Coy.	
	20		Lieut. A.H. Baker struck off establishment. (M.S.E.C.in.C. M.S/D/2021 of 18-10-18). Lieut R.W. PHILLIPS. and 2/Lieut. E.R. BALL granted leave to United Kingdom 21/10/18 - 4/11/18.	
	21		Military Medals were awarded.	
			T2904 Pte J. COLEMAN. B. Coy.	
			43206 - Lt PARKER A -	
			G.41474 Sgt. A.E.H. REYNOLDS C -	
			292505 Pte E.J. MOXHAM. late D -	
	23		Capt LOCKETT M.C. joined and was posted to A Coy. Capt and adjt C.K. ALLEN M.C. resumed duties as adjutant.	
			Military Medals were awarded.	
			T955 L/Cpl P. MOULD. D Coy.	
			43605 Pte J.C. CLIFFORD. C -	
	25		2/Lt J.W. REID granted leave to United Kingdom 27/10/18 - 10-11-18	

WAR DIARY or INTELLIGENCE SUMMARY

Army Form C. 2118. Page 6.

Place	Date	Hour	Summary of Events and Information	Remarks and references to Appendices
Schafen	Oct 25		Capt CAPERRY. Proceeded to England to attend 2nd Course at the Adjutants school CAMBRIDGE, and was struck off the Strength according.	
	26		2/Lieut C. SEAMER. granted leave to United Kingdom. 25-10-18 = 11-11-18.	
	27		2/Lieut E.G. HALE rejoined from hospital. 2/Lieut C.T. KNIGHT granted leave to United Kingdom 30-10-18 - 13-11-18	
	30		T/Maj R.S. DOVE M.C. granted permission to wear the badges of acting rank of Lieut Col. pending appearance of his promotion in the London Gazette.	

Army Form C. 2118.

WAR DIARY
or
INTELLIGENCE SUMMARY.
(Erase heading not required.)

Summary of Casualties during October, 1918

Killed in Action		Wounded in Action		Wounded (Gas)		Missing		Died of Wounds		Injured Acc.d	
O	OR	O	OR	O	OR	O	OR	O	OR	O	OR
0	0	0	3	1	15	—	1	—	0	0	2
2	14		100								

Drafts

Officers	O. Ranks
1	98

R.S. Jons
Lieut - Col.,
Commanding 13th Middlesex Regt.

WAR DIARY

INTELLIGENCE SUMMARY

9837

73/24

Army Form C. 2118.

Confidential

Bk/B Middlesex Regiment

for the month of

November 1918

WAR DIARY
INTELLIGENCE SUMMARY

Page 1.

13th Batt. Middlesex Regt.

Nov 1918

Place	Date	Hour	Summary of Events and Information	Remarks and references to Appendices
In the field	Nov 1		The Batt. moved by route march from HAUSSY to BERMERAIN, where it remained in billets during the night of the 1/2 Nov.	
	2		The Batt. relieved units in the line as follows. A.B. and D Coy moved to high ground in rear of MARAISCHES during the afternoon and at dusk relieved the 2/5th GLOSTERS on a line in front of MARAISCHES from near FONT DESVEAUX to the River RHONELLE. C Coy relieving 1 Coy ROY. BERKS. continued the line S. of the river. Being in touch and the GUARDS on the right. The positions were maintained until early afternoon of the 3rd.	
	3		During the afternoon patrol having found that the enemy had retired the line was advanced and at dusk was established on the line JENLAIN (exclusive) VILLERS POL (exclusive). A and D Coy in front line. C and B in support. C Coy having crossed from S of the LA RHONELLE river.	
	4		The remaining Battns of the brigade passed through the Batt. at 06.30	

Army Form C. 2118.

Page 2.

WAR DIARY
or
INTELLIGENCE SUMMARY. 13th Batt Middlesex Regt. Nov 18

(Erase heading not required.)

Place	Date	Hour	Summary of Events and Information	Remarks and references to Appendices
In the field	Nov 4		and drove the enemy over the AUNELLE River. This being effected the 12th M.x. concentrated towards the left near LE CORON and advanced through WARGNIES LE GRAND, during the afternoon. A line was established E of that village, considerable opposition being experienced from machine guns. Capt H.R. Mallett M.C. was wounded.	
	5		Early in the morning the line was further advanced - and the 17th Brigade then moved through - taking up pursuit of the enemy. The Batt then moved into billets at WARGNIES LE PETIT, remaining there until 7th when it to an advance to BAVAI was made by route march.	
	7		The Batt was billeted in BAVAI during the night 7/8 Nov and on 8th moved to LE LOUVION being billeted there during the night 8/9 Nov.	
	8			
	9		On the morning of the 9th the Batt. moved out to what proved the last fight before signing of the armistice	

Army Form C. 2118.

Page 5

WAR DIARY
or
INTELLIGENCE SUMMARY. 13th Batt Middx Regt.   No. 76

(Erase heading not required.)

Place	Date	Hour	Summary of Events and Information	Remarks and references to Appendices
Indre futur	Nov 9		Move was made (the Battn being in Support during the early part of the day & the rest of the Brigade). by LABERLIÈRE and LES BAS VENTS. at this point the Battn went into front line the 9th ROYAL SUSSEX being on the left, and the 7th N'HAMPTONS on the right. The line was advanced to about 1000 yards. E of the MONS - MAUBERGE road and about 1600. the Battn received orders to return to billets at LES BAS VENTS. little opposition was experienced during two days operations.	
	10		The Battn moved to billets in LABERLIÈRE. Military medal was awarded to N° 43863. Pte STONE C Coy. Major H.H. Hebden M.C. 1st Roy. Fusiliers assumed command of the Battn.	
	11		The Battn moved to billets in LE LOUVION.	

Army Form C. 2118.

Page 3.

13th Batt. Midd'x Regt.   Nov 18

WAR DIARY
or
INTELLIGENCE SUMMARY
(Erase heading not required.)

Place	Date	Hour	Summary of Events and Information	Remarks and references to Appendices
LE LOUVION	Nov 11		The Lieut P Bampfather MC is granted permission to wear badge of rank of Capt. (additional).	
	16		The Field Marshal Commanding-in-Chief under authority granted by His Majesty the King, awards the following:-	
			The Distinguished Service order - Lt(a/Lt.Col) A.N.Hingley. M.C.	
			The Military Cross 2/Lt. Ju.Reid.	
			2/Lt. E.R.Rose.	
			Bar to Dist. Conduct Medal. 627. C.S.M. L/t.Sandoe DCM. MM	
			Dist. Conduct MEDAL 24768. P/G S. Ruddle.	
			290805 Cpl D Clarke.	
			9196 Sgt W.Wicks.	
	17		The Batt. moved billets at WARGNIES LE GRAND. under 18th to ROUVIGNIES.	
	18			
	19		move was made to billets at AUBERCHICOURT.	
	25		The Batt moved to LECELLE's by route march and to LA	
	26		GLANERIES on 26th. remaining here until the ending themselves	

Army Form C. 2118.

Page 4

WAR DIARY
or
INTELLIGENCE SUMMARY. 13th Br Middx Regt.

No 18

(Erase heading not required.)

Instructions regarding War Diaries and Intelligence Summaries are contained in F. S. Regs., Part II. and the Staff Manual respectively. Title pages will be prepared in manuscript.

Place	Date	Hour	Summary of Events and Information	Remarks and references to Appendices
	Nov. 30.		From 16th Nov onwards the Battn. was engaged in reorganisation and training whenever possible.	

Army Form C. 2118.

WAR DIARY
or
INTELLIGENCE SUMMARY.

(Erase heading not required.)

Summary of Events and Information

Summary of Casualties during November, 1918.

Killed in Action		Wounded in Action		Wounded (Gas)		Wounded at Duty		Missing		Died of Wounds	
O	OR	O	OR	O	OR	O	OR	O	OR	O	OR
-	11	1	50	-	3	-	2	-	2	-	6

Drafts.

Officers	O Ranks
5	47

4/12/18

Y. Stratten
Major
for Lieut-Col.,
Commanding 13TH Middlesex Regt.

Army Form C. 2118.

VII 3 8

WAR DIARY
or
INTELLIGENCE SUMMARY.
(Erase heading not required.)

War Diary

13 Middlesex Regt

WAR DIARY
or
INTELLIGENCE SUMMARY.

Army Form C. 2118.

18th Bn. MIDDLESEX Regt.
Date: 1.1.19
ORDERLY ROOM

Page 1
18th Bn Middx Regt

Place	Date	Hour	Summary of Events and Information	Remarks and references to Appendices
LA GLANERIE	Sep 1		The Battalion continued to be engaged in training. Special attention being given to organised recreation.	
	3		The 2nd Battn of the regiment being billetted nearby, the Battn marched over to meet them TAINTIGNIES equipt. A match of Football being played and won by 6 goals to 2.	
	9		T/Capt T.L. WIGINTON removed from establishment of the Battn (effect from 30-9-18). Transferred E.T. SEVENOAKS relinquishes his commission on account of ill-health. (MS/D/2021 d/4-12-18).	
	13		The Battn moved to billets in RUMES.	
	17		T/Lt. Col A.M. Hingley D.S.O, M.C. rejoined Battn. and assumed command vice a/Lt. Col J.H. Judden M.C.	
	21		T/Capt CA PERRY returned for demobilization in England and struck off establishment of the Bn. AG 21158/8411 (0) d/25-12-18).	
	27		Lieut E.D. GODDARD posted from V/10 H.T.M. Battery reported for duty.	

WAR DIARY or INTELLIGENCE SUMMARY

Army Form C. 2118.

Place	Date	Hour	Summary of Events and Information	Remarks and references to Appendices
	Dec 3		**Appointments and Promotions**	
			T/Lieut A. REDFORD granted permission to wear badge of rank of Capt (acting Capt while comdg. Coy).	
	6		T/Lieut P. BARNFATHER M.C. to be acting Capt (additional) 26.10.18 (Div N° 2154 24-11-18).	
	14		T/Lieut W.F. JONES M.C. to granted permission to wear badge of rank of Capt. (2d Div. A 1219 of 12-12-18)	
	23		T/Lieut W.T. JONES M.C. to be acting Capt while Comdg. Coy (Div N° 217 of 8.12.18)	
	26		T/Lieut A. REDFORD to be acting Capt while Comdg Coy. (Div N° 218 of 15.12.18)	
	28		2/Lieut A. WADSWORTH } granted permission to wear badge of acting Lieut 2/Lieut E.C. ANDERSON M.C. } (2d Div N° A/1348 of 26.12.18)	

WAR DIARY
or
INTELLIGENCE SUMMARY.

(Erase heading not required.)

Army Form C. 2118.

Summary of Events and Information

Summary of Casualties during December 1918.

Nil.

Drafts.

Officers	Other Ranks.
2	38

A H Dingley. Lieut. Col.
Commanding 13th Middlesex Regt.

4.1.19.

WAR DIARY
INTELLIGENCE SUMMARY

Army Form C. 2118.

Contentment
13th Bn Middlesex Regiment (D.C.O)
for the month of
January 1919

WAR DIARY
or
INTELLIGENCE SUMMARY.
(Erase heading not required.)

January 1919

Place	Date	Hour	Summary of Events and Information	Remarks and references to Appendices
RUMES, Belgium	Jan 1st		The Battalion continued movements billets in RUMES, & was engaged in training & recreation.	
	6.		A very interesting lecture on "Rudyard Kipling" was delivered by Capt. Peebles.	
	7.		Lieut. E. SEAMER relinquished appointment of Transport Officer, & was succeeded by Lieut. H.S. WHITLOCK.	
	14.		Lieut. S.E.L. MURRAY was evacuated to England sick (13.i.19)	
	15.		The Bn. team drew football match against the D.A.C. in the Divisional League.	
	18.		Lieut. F. THILLIPS proceeded to 73rd Inf. Bde. for duty as A/Staff Capt. Lieut. E.A. TOWERS proceeded to I Corps Concentration Camp for duty.	
	21st		Lieut. H.A.S. SYMMONDS evacuated to England sick (8.i.19) Notification appeared in C.R.O. that Capt. H.R. MALLETT had been awarded Bar to the M.C.	
	23rd		B Coy. proceeded to TOURNAI for 2 days. Bn. won at football against 107th Bde. R.F.A. Coy. R.Q.M.S. M. ASHFORD awarded M.S. Medal (R.G. Suppt. 20.i.19)	
	25th		C Coy. proceeded to TOURNAI. The Bn. won the semi-final in the Div'l	

Army Form C. 2118.

WAR DIARY
or
INTELLIGENCE SUMMARY.
(Erase heading not required.)

Instructions regarding War Diaries and Intelligence Summaries are contained in F. S. Regs., Part II. and the Staff Manual respectively. Title pages will be prepared in manuscript.

Place	Date	Hour	Summary of Events and Information	Remarks and references to Appendices
	25.		Football fixture against the 7. Northamptonshire Regt. by 5 goals to 1. Snow & hard frost set in this day & lasted to the end of the month.	
	26. — 31st.		Training. Education classes were carried on throughout the month. Ranks remained in the same condition as when the Almighty made it among the last works of creation. During the month the following numbers were demobilized:— Officers — Nil. O.R. 135.	
			Casualties. Nil.	
			Drafts. O. Nil. O.R. 4.	
			A. N. Kingley. Lieut. Col. Commanding 13th Middlesex Regt.	

Army Form C. 2118.

WAR DIARY
or
INTELLIGENCE SUMMARY.
(Erase heading not required.)

Vol 4

War Diary

13th Bn Middlesex Regt

Place	Date	Hour	Summary of Events and Information	Remarks and references to Appendices

WAR DIARY
INTELLIGENCE SUMMARY.
(Erase heading not required.)

February 1919.

Place	Date	Hour	Summary of Events and Information	Remarks and references to Appendices
RUMES. Belgium	Feb 1.		The Battalion continues to occupy billets in RUMES and were engaged in training "recreation. Amusements of open air were devised. the remainder struggle all through of the month (Feb) being.	
	4		No. F.287 C.S.M. GIBSON. T. was appointed acting Regimental Sergeant Major and promoted Warrant Officer Class I. The following were granted promotion & were temp 7 rank 7 Lieut. 2nd Lt. R.J. MACMILLAN 2nd Lt. G.M. DAWKINS.	
	6		Lieut. J.T. BEER being retained in England for demobilisation was Struck off the Strength of the Batt 6/Feb-3-1-19 (WO/21537/6925 (0) a/28-1-19).	
	7		Lieut J.J. Bishop admitted to hospital 10-1-19 was granted sick leave to England 24-1-19 to 15-2-19.	
	10		The following honours were made.	

Military Cross Capt. J.C. CLARK

WAR DIARY
or
INTELLIGENCE SUMMARY.

(Erase heading not required.)

Army Form C. 2118.

Place	Date	Hour	Summary of Events and Information	Remarks and references to Appendices
RUINES Belgium	Feb 1918		Major R.S. Dove M.C. proceeded to England for demobilisation. Lieut J.J. Pastore being returned to England for Medical Boards. Struck off Strength. (1st Corps No. A 55/42:3 of 21.2.19). During the month the following numbers were demobilised: Officers 5 O.R. 348. Drafts. NIL. Casualties. NIL.	

G.N. Ingoldby.
Lieut. Colonel,
Commanding 13th Middlesex Regt.

24 Division
73 Infantry Brigade
13 Battalion Middlesex Regiment
March 1919 Missing

13 Middlesex
No 42

Army Form C. 2118.

WAR DIARY
or
INTELLIGENCE SUMMARY.
(Erase heading not required.)

Instructions regarding War Diaries and Intelligence Summaries are contained in F.S. Regs., Part II. and the Staff Manual respectively. Title pages will be prepared in manuscript.

Place	Date	Hour	Summary of Events and Information	Remarks and references to Appendices
No 2 Reception Camp.	1/4/19		The Battalion paraded at 10.30 Hrs. for inspection by G.O.C. 98" Inf. Bde.	E193
HARFLEUR	2/4/19		The ordinary Routine Parades were held	E193
	3/4/19		At midnight 2.3/4/19 the 1st Battalion, two each were absorbed into 1st 13" Battalion, Officers & Others to the Ranks being in all cases posted to their original companies.	E193
	4/4/19		On this date the command of the camp was assumed by Lt.Cl AN. HINGLEY D.S.O, M.C, 1DW H.Cl LL. Fargites D.S.O. 1st Bn	E193
	5/4/19		Whilmsl. L.2 Re-caird. Capt. G. Feathweston M.C. was admitted to the hospital	E193
	6/4/19		Lieut. W. BRINE proceeded on special leave to U.K. Lieut. P.P. BURMAN assumed the duty of Camp Adjutant during his absence.	E193
	7/4/19		Lieut. P.P. Lloyd proceeded on leave to the U.K.	E193
	8/4/19		2/Lt. G.R. Ellis proceeded to U.K. for demobilisation. 2/Lt. Gavin rejoined from leave to U.K.	E193
	9/4/19		Capt. V.E. Stark M.C. & Lieut. R.P. Choat rejoined from leave to U.K. Capt. M.T. Young & 2/Lt. S.W. Linnell proceeded on leave to U.K.	E193
	10/4/19		4 Officers +20 OR rejoined the 13TH Bn. The Officers were Capt. W.J. O'Mara M.C. Lieut. C.H. Wilkshaw M.M.T. Lieut. H.S. Whitlock, Lieut. C.E. Seaman.	E193

Army Form C. 2118

WAR DIARY
or
INTELLIGENCE SUMMARY
(Erase heading not required.)

Place	Date	Hour	Summary of Events and Information	Remarks and references to Appendices
No 2 Reception Camp, HARFLEUR.	11/4/19		The following Officers proceeded to the Concentration Camp for Demobilisation. Capt. A. SHEELL M.C. 2/Lt A.S. MERRETT. 2/Lt S.F. BROOKER.	8/13.
"	12/4/19		2/Lt H.S. WHITLOCK. 2/Lt W. Blackman returned from leave & resumed the duties of Camp Adjutant via list. 2/Lt. P. Burman. Lt. H.S. Whitlock proceeded to U.K. for duty with the Regular Army.	8/13
	13/4/19		Lieutenant R.P. CHOATE (who joins the 1st Bn - Bay 915.) proceeded to concentration camp. demobilised.	8/13
	14/4/19		Major STRATTEN M.C. proceeded for demobilisation. Lt. A.S. Grey proceeded on leave to U.K. A parade service was held at 12.30 HRS. 7 all OR who could be spared from the R of E duties.	8/13
	15/4/19		2/Lt C.J.S. Thoday proceeded to Concentration Camp for Demobilisation. 2/Lt. P.A. Young proceeded on leave to U.K. Captain E Pethukton M.C. returned from hospital & resumed command of D Coy & no 3 Wing.	8/13 8/13
	16/4/19		A redistribution of duties, involving the transfer of a number of Officers & other ranks between Companies was effected. B Company assumed entire charge of the Detainees, & A Company took over no 2 wing. This arrangement was made to ensure that men employed on particular jobs should so far as possible be drawn from the same platoon. 2 Lt R.G. Bennett returned from hospital.	8/13
	17/4/19		A draft of 9 OR joined on 15/4/19 from "13/22" & "1/24" London Rgts:- The draft was conducted by 2/Lt W. List, who had orders to rejoin his unit. The 98th men gave a dance at 18.30 HRS to which some members of the W.A.A.C. and the African this Battalion were invited.	8/13
	18/4/19		2/Lt A.C. Gray returned from leave to U.K. Lt R. Butcher returned from leave to U.K.	8/13.
	19/4/19		A football match was played against Havre Base.	8/13.
	20/4/19		A church parade of all OR not actually on Camp Duty was held at 10.00 HRS.	8/13.

Army Form C. 2118

WAR DIARY
or
INTELLIGENCE SUMMARY
(Erase heading not required.)

Instructions regarding War Diaries and Intelligence Summaries are contained in F.S. Regs., Part II. and the Staff Manual respectively. Title Pages will be prepared in manuscript.

Place	Date	Hour	Summary of Events and Information	Remarks and references to Appendices
No 2 Rest Camp	21/4/19		A battalion parade of all men on P. activity on duty was held at 0915 hrs. Similar parades were held to be held daily in the future. The following officers proceeded on leave to U.K. Lieut. C. Seaman.	
HARFLEUR			Capt. & adjutant R. Dalgety proceeded on demobilisation. 2/Lt. R.S. Ross M.C.	E/13
	22/4/19		Capt. G.H. James M.C. assumed the duties of acting adjutant, vice Capt. R. Dalgety.	E/13
			Capt. S. Feathersham M.C. proceeded on leave to U.K.	
			2/Lt. C.S. Austin proceeded on leave to U.K. 2/Lt. F.H. Allnutt proceeded to Conchahi Camp for demobilisation.	E/13
	23/4/19		The following officers reported for duty on 22/4/19. 2/Lt. A.W. Bevan, 2/Lt. T.H. Ewing. Both were posted to "D" Company. Lieut. R. Lloyd returned from leave to U.K. The Cadre of the 3rd Bn Middlesex Regt arrived from the East & passed through the camp in the ordinary way.	E/13
	24/4/19		Lieut. R. Hargreaves rejoined from leave to U.K.	E/13
	25/4/19		2/Lt A.C. Gray proceeded to U.K. on 2 mths leave. 2/Lt A. Oldham proceeded on 2 mths leave. Capt. M.T. Young & 2/Lt Linnell reported back from leave to U.K.	E/13
	26/4/19		Lieut. G.C. Antram M.C. proceeded for demobilisation.	E/13
	27/4/19		A draft of 190 OR was despatched to the 17th Bn. Royal Sussex Regt. Lieut Butcher & 2/Lt Pince were in charge of the draft on its journey.	E/13
	28/4/19		Capt. M.T. Young was despatched for demobilisation. Lieut. P. Hamilton assumed command of C Coy vice Captain Young	E/13

1875 Wt. W593/826 1,000,000 4/15 J.B.C. & A. A.D.S.S./Forms/C. 2118.

Army Form C. 2118.

WAR DIARY
or
INTELLIGENCE SUMMARY.
(Erase heading not required.)

Instructions regarding War Diaries and Intelligence Summaries are contained in F. S. Regs., Part II. and the Staff Manual respectively. Title pages will be prepared in manuscript.

Place	Date	Hour	Summary of Events and Information	Remarks and references to Appendices
NO 2. Reception Camp. HARFLEUR.	29/4/19		Capt Mackenzie returned from Hospital. Lieut A.S. Jones proceed on leave to U.K.	873
	30/4/19		Lieut W. Brian returned from leave to U.K. Warning order was issued that 879. Nos. 1 Harm ale, were to proceed at of Brindi held rank as May 15th on account of the "Jour de Manifestation."	879

A.N. Hingley
Lt Col
Cmdg. 13TH Bn. Middlesex Rgt.

24

13 Middlesex Army Form C. 2118.

WAR DIARY
or
INTELLIGENCE SUMMARY
(Erase heading not required.)

Instructions regarding War Diaries and Intelligence Summaries are contained in F. S. Regs., Part II. and the Staff Manual respectively. Title pages will be prepared in manuscript.

(1) 43

A.7.1

Place	Date	Hour	Summary of Events and Information	Remarks and references to Appendices
No. 2 Reception Camp	1.5.19		Lt Captain L.L.C. Badbury & 2/Lieut. to Lt. Ed. Lothian proceeded on leave to U.K.	
Shorncliffe	2.5.19		2/Lieut. R.S. Bennett proceeded to England for demobilization.	
			Lieut. R.S. Butcher and 2/Lieut. H.S. Peers rejoined from draft conducting to Dunkirk	
			2/Lieut. T.P. Bunney assumed the duties of Assistant Adjutant vice Lt. C.R.E. Lethaby on leave	
	3.5.19		The ordinary parades were carried out.	
	4.5.19		The ordinary parades were carried out. Church Parade at 10.00 hours.	
	5.5.19		The ordinary parades were carried out.	
	6.5.19		Captain R.E. Wilson, 23rd Bn Middlesex Regt. and Lieut. S. Letchall 23rd Bn Royal Fusiliers reported for duty.	
	7.5.19		Captain F.W. Mackenzie and 2/Lieut. A.C. to Marsh proceeded to U.K. for demobilization. Lieut. L. Skinner and 2/Lieut. R.S. Wood, M.C. returned from leave to U.K.	
	8.5.19		Major Braithwaite, M.C. returned from leave to U.K. 2/Lieut. Austin returned from leave to U.K.	
	9.5.19		2/Lieut. S.C. Jones, 2/Lieut. R.S. Knight and 2/Lieut. A. Childs 23rd Bn Middlesex Regt. reported for duty. Lt. H. Bartlett and 2/Lieut. Crowe proceeded to join 17th Middlesex Regt.	

Army Form C. 2118.

WAR DIARY
~~INTELLIGENCE SUMMARY.~~
(Erase heading not required.)

Instructions regarding War Diaries and Intelligence Summaries are contained in F. S. Regs., Part II, and the Staff Manual respectively. Title pages will be prepared in manuscript.

Place	Date	Hour	Summary of Events and Information	Remarks and references to Appendices
No.2 Reception Camp, Etaples	10.5.19		Lieut. H. L. Coombs reported for duty from the 24th Royal Fusiliers. Major to Frattenheln to assume the duties of 2nd-in-Command, vice Major S. S. Stratton, M.C.	
	12.5.19		Major S. King, L. S. W. Duck, 2/Lieuts. H. S. Holbrook, L. L. Rankin, H. Matheson and J. M. Berry reported from 23rd Bn. Middlesex Regt. Reinto. to strength M.C., R. Branwell, L. S. Butler, E. E. Lloyd and 2/Lt. R. E. Coombs proceed to England for demobilisation. 2/Lt. H. W. Lewry granted extension of leave by Medical Board, was struck off strength as from 30.4.19. 2/Lt. A. Shield admitted his hospital 11.5.19.	
	13.5.19		Lieuts. C. P. Brunner and J. H. Hollins, M.C. to officers left for England on leave. Reinto. S. W. Duck, W. S. C. Mrosttner, H. Godfrey, 2/Lieuts. G. Austin and L. St. Stubbins proceed to England for demobilisation.	
	14.5.19		Capt. R. A. Elghie and Lt. S. H. Stephenson reported from the 23rd Bn. Middlesex Reegt.	
	16.5.19		Athletes Day. As many as possible of the Battalion were taken in lorries to the Battalion Sports. The weather was very fine, and the whole day a complete success. Lt-Col. L. Pringle, M.O.R., 2/Lt. L. L. Service proceed to England for demobilisation	

Ex.J.T.

Army Form C. 2118.

WAR DIARY
or
~~INTELLIGENCE SUMMARY~~

(Erase heading not required.)

Instructions regarding War Diaries and Intelligence Summaries are contained in F. S. Regs., Part II. and the Staff Manual respectively. Title pages will be prepared in manuscript.

Place	Date	Hour	Summary of Events and Information	Remarks and references to Appendices
No.2 Reception Camp, Shorncliffe.				
	17.5.19		2 Offrs. & 2o.R.'s (Orderly room) & 2 linc C.'s & 2 S.B.'s attached from leave in England.	
	18.5.19		A parade service was held at 10.30 hours.	
	19.5.19		Reinforts. finishing furlough on leave to N.K.	
	20.5.19		A parade of 186 men was held at 9.00 hours.	
	21.5.19		Orders were received for this company to be ready to move to No. 24 Wimereux ("Cie.B")	
	22.5.19		Reinc. Dr. K.S. Baile proceeded to England for Repatriation to South Africa. Reinc. Q.E.H. Stratham & Reinc. J.S. Reid M.C. proceeded to England for demobilisation.	
	23.5.19		Reinc. A.S. Jones assumed duties of Asst. Adjt., vice Reinc. E.E. Strathern.	
	24.5.19		Men of "A" & "B" Coys. did not take place.	
	25.5.19		A parade service was held at 10.30 hours.	
	26.5.19		Reint. J.C. Collins M.C. + Reint. E.P. Burman returned from leave in England.	
	27.5.19		Orders were received that No. 2 Reception Camp would be taken over by 253. Reserve.	
			Regt. on Friday 30.5.19	
	28.5.19		A parade of 115 other ranks was held at 9.00 hours. Re Buckingham St. 15" B" Coy.	
			re-enlisted for 4 years.	
	29.5.19		2 Offrs. Lt. J. O'Mearn, M.C. signed forms leave.	

Army Form C. 2118.

WAR DIARY
or
INTELLIGENCE SUMMARY.
(Erase heading not required.)

Instructions regarding War Diaries and Intelligence Summaries are contained in F. S. Regs., Part II. and the Staff Manual respectively. Title pages will be prepared in manuscript.

Place	Date	Hour	Summary of Events and Information	Remarks and references to Appendices
No.2 Reception Camp, Shorncliffe	30.5.19		A visit S.G. balling M.O. to to the amdith M.O. proceeded to England for demobilisation. A visit Lt. S. Bradbeer proceeded to England for service in the Regular Army. Lieut. Col. Martin D.S.O. took over command of No.2 Reception Camp Shorncliffe vice Lieut. Col. A. N. Shingley D.S.O., M.C.	
	31.5.19		Lieut. Col. D.S.D. the same M.O., proceeded to England for service in the Regular Army.	

A.N. Shingley.
LIEUT. COL.
COMMANDING 13th BN. MIDDLESEX REGT.

Headquarters,
　98th. Infantry Brigade.

Herewith copy of WAR DIARY for JUNE 1919.

1-7-19.　　H.H.Catchpole　Lieut-Colonel,
　　　　　　　　Commanding 15th. (S) Bn. Middlesex Regt.

13 Middlesex Regt
Army Form C. 2118/24

WAR DIARY
INTELLIGENCE SUMMARY
(Erase heading not required)

Instructions regarding War Diaries and Intelligence Summaries are contained in F.S. Regs., Part II. and the Staff Manual respectively. Title pages will be prepared in manuscript.

Place	Date	Hour	Summary of Events and Information	Remarks and references to Appendices
No 2 Rest Camp Harfleur	1-6-19		Ordinary service was held at 1030 hours	
	2-6-19		2nd Lt E. Hopridge opened this day from Duty with R.T.O. Toquerra	
	3-6-19		2nd Lt W.C.E. Howard proceeded on leave to England	
	4-6-19		Battalion Rail Head to Rouville Took place 18 Offrs and 403 other ranks, women ranks. 2/Lieut W.H. Farrington proceed from leave to UK	
	5-6-19		Captain E. Sutherland M.C. and 2nd Lt E. Hopridge proceed to England for demobilization	
	6-6-19		Major J. King assumed the duties of 2/i/c and Captain Featherstone M.C.	
			11 Sgt Champion re-enlisted for 3 years	
			Extract from Battalion Orders. Honors awarded. Military Cross: Lieut F. Roberts, Lieut at Wadsworth and 2nd Lt J. Reeve. D.C.O. Distinguished Conduct Medal — 4708 Sgt Pratt J. F 586 Sgt Peter N° 7864 Sgt Bean N° 3981 Sgt Jackson P — Chatty. Extract from Genl dated 3-6-19.	
	9-6-19		Entrained at Soquence at 1330 hours and commenced Proc. Moved H. Qet, 13 May. Boquette Marboeuf arrived Turdighem at 0001 hours 11-6-19. B & C Coy remained in Train and proceeded to Touseent. A & D Coy and Bn Hqrs detained at Turdighem and marched via St Sylvester Cappel to Turdighem	
TER DEGHEM	12-6-19		All available men were employed in cleaning up the camp, clearing quarters etc etc	
	13-6-19		11 & c of the Extra cruited to Battalion. Lieut Col H. Batchy Joined the Battalion	
	14-6-19		This was carried on improving and cleaning up camp. The O.C. Regiment ordered that once the Battalion	
	15-6-19		Lieut E.P. Bazeman reported the 13 Mxx with near party from Harfleur	
	16-6-19		Party of 20 O.R. left for new command by D Coy	
	17-6-19		Arrivals at Bernaucht & Bourdogues was handled by D Coy	
	18-6-19		Time was occupied on Sundry special drills	
	19-6-19		Three guards and route March Lesson was not of the Battalion	
	20-6-19		2nd Lt. F.A.T. Batchard assumed command of the Battalion and Lt Col J.A. King D.S.O. M.C.	
	21-6-19		Wearing of distinguishing bands was and resumed C.C. Yellow triangle	
	22-6-19		at parade. Usual world held at 1045 hours	
	23-6-19		Ordinary parades were carried out	

Army Form C. 2118.

WAR DIARY
or
INTELLIGENCE SUMMARY.
(Erase heading not required.)

Instructions regarding War Diaries and Intelligence Summaries are contained in F. S. Regs., Part II. and the Staff Manual respectively. Title pages will be prepared in manuscript.

Place	Date	Hour	Summary of Events and Information	Remarks and references to Appendices
TERDEGHEM	24-6-19		Information received that Germans had accepted peace terms and that Treaty was signed last night.	
	25-6-19		To-day was observed as a general holiday in celebration of Peace	
	26-6-19		2/Lieut Barton N.H. proceeded on leave to U.K. Lieut J.B. Hunterlock rejoined the Battalion	
	27-6-19		Sent T.E. JONES and 2/Lieut A.H.R. Blagg and A Bean proceeded on leave to U.K. Lieuts J.D. Hamilton & J.N.E. Noel proceeded on leave to U.K.	
	28-6-19		Capt J.R. James M.C. proceeded on leave to U.K. Lieut A.J. Jones assumed the duties of N/Adjt vice Capt J.N. James M.C.	
	29-6-19		A Parade service was held at 1030 hours	
	30-6-19		A party of 1 Off. & 26 other ranks were sent to Dunkirk for a days outing	

TERDEGHEM
1-7-19.

H H Catchpole LIEUT. COL.
COMMANDING 13th BN. MIDDLESEX REGT.

24 DIVISION
73 INFANTRY BRIGADE
13 BATTALION MIDDLESEX REGIMENT
JULY 1919 MISSING.

WAR DIARY
or
INTELLIGENCE SUMMARY.
(Erase heading not required.)

Army Form C. 2118.

Place	Date	Hour	Summary of Events and Information	Remarks and references to Appendices
TER DEGHEM	1/8/19	—	Major S. King proceeded on leave to U.K. Lieut C.H. Wilkie M.M. returned from leave.	
	4/8/19		2 Officers & 80 O.R. proceeded by lorry to Lille to No 5 Rest Stn.	
	6/8/19		Y.O. Bloggs returned from hospital.	
	7/8/19		Li. S.I. Denton returned from leave.	
	8/8/19		Lt. J.C.I. Hall proceeded to U.K. for demobilisation.	
	10/8/19		Li. H.G. Heles returned from leave. Capt. R. Boughton M.C. & 50 O.R. were inspected by Brigadier Generals at HAZEBROUCK.	
	11/8/19		2/Li. R.K. Linnell returned from leave.	
	13-8-19		2 Lt. J. Jones returned from leave.	
	16-8-19		Lieut. N.B. Morton proceeded on 3 days leave in France	
	18-8-19		Lieut G.H. Ewing was admitted to Hospital	
	21-8-19		Major S. King returned from leave to U.K.	
	22-8-19		Capt. R. Boughton M.C. Lieut. N.J. Brown Lieut. E.R. Burroughs & 2/Lt. H.R. Baxter proceeded for demobilization	
	23-8-19		Lieut. E. Hooper proceeded for demobilization	

WAR DIARY
or
INTELLIGENCE SUMMARY.
(Erase heading not required.)

Army Form C. 2118.

Place	Date	Hour	Summary of Events and Information	Remarks and references to Appendices
TERDEGHEM	26/8/19	—	2/Lieut. H.L. Pearce proceeded for demobilization.	
	27/8/19		G.O.C. 95th Brigade visited the Battalion	
	29/8/19		Four German prisoners were captured by 1/5th Middlesex	
	31/8/19	—	Lieut. L.P. Burman proceeded on leave to U.K. 2/Lieut J.R. Ewing proceeded for demobilization	[signature]
TERDEGHEM 1-9-9				

[signature]
LIEUT. COL.
COMMANDING 13th BN. MIDDLESEX REGT.

M.X. 586

Secretary,
　　War Office (S.D.2),
　　　　London. S.W. 1.

　　　　Herewith copy of WAR DIARY for month of SEPTEMBER, 1919, forwarded to you vide G.R.O. 7263 please.

TERDEGHEM.
3-10-19.
　　　　　　　　　　　　　　　Major.
　　　　　　　　Commanding 13th (S) Bn. Middlesex Regt.

Army Form C. 2118.

WAR DIARY
INTELLIGENCE SUMMARY
(Erase heading not required.)

Instructions regarding War Diaries and Intelligence Summaries are contained in F. S. Regs., Part II. and the Staff Manual respectively. Title pages will be prepared in manuscript.

Place	Date	Hour	Summary of Events and Information	Remarks and references to Appendices
TERDEGHEM	3/9/19		Capt. E. H. Hoghton rejoined the Battalion from duty with 59th Div. School.	
	3/9/19 to 5/9/19		The Commanding Officer made a tour of & inspection of the guards & posts found by the Battalion	
	6/9/19		The release of "Derby" men in progress	
	7/9/19		G.O.C. 98th Infantry Brigade visited the Battalion	
	9/9/19		Lieut. H. Coombes rejoined the Battalion from leave to Germany.	
	11/9/19		B & C Companies rejoined Battn. Headquarters from TOURCOING & H. Coombes proceeded for duty under A.P.M. No. 5 AREA	
	15/9/19		Lieut. W.H. Levingston proceeded on leave to U.K.	
	16/9/19		Lieut. E.P. Burman rejoined from leave to U.K.	
	20/9/19		Capt. B.H. Alliston rejoined from leave to U.K.	
	21/9/19		Capt. E.H. Hoghton proceeded to England on duty	
			The release of "Derby" and voluntarily enlisted men in progress. 12 g/r about to this date.	
	24/9/19		Lieut. Col. H. Gathorpe proceeded on 7 days special leave to U.K.	
	27/9/19		Demobilization cased temporarily owing to Railway strike in England	
	30/9/19		Capt. E.H. Hoghton returned from duty at No.1 Record Office HANWELL	

TERDEGHEM
3-10-19

COMMANDING 13th BN. MIDDLESEX REGT.

M.X.565

Secretary,
　War Office (S.D.2),
　　LONDON. S.W.1.

　　　　　　Herewith War Diary for month of OCTOBER, 1919

forwarded to you vide G.R.O. 7263.

TERDEGHEM.　　　*M.H.Catchpole*　　Lieut-Colonel.
1.11.19.　　　　　　　　　Commanding 13th (S) Bn. Middlesex Regiment.

WAR DIARY
or
INTELLIGENCE SUMMARY.

(Erase heading not required.)

Army Form C. 2118.

Instructions regarding War Diaries and Intelligence Summaries are contained in F. S. Regs., Part II. and the Staff Manual respectively. Title pages will be prepared in manuscript.

Place	Date	Hour	Summary of Events and Information	Remarks and references to Appendices
TERDEGHEM FRANCE	2-10-19		R.S.M. Tollin rejoined the Battalion from Hospital.	
	5-10-19		A Church of England Parade Service was held at 1030 hours. 105 other ranks were present.	
	6-10-19		A small fire which occurred in the Officers' quarters was extinguished by 5 Sept. out slight.	
	7-10-19		The C.O. visited District Major Lille, also the guard at MARQUILLES.	
	11-10-19		The Rev. V.F.B. Norton joined the Battalion. Demobilization recommenced.	
	12-10-19		A Church of England service was held at 0930 hours by the Rev. V.F.B. Norton C.F. Thirty one other ranks proceeded to concentration camp for demobilization.	
	13-10-19		Thirty other ranks proceeded to concentration camp for demobilization.	
	14-10-19		Eleven other ranks proceeded to England for demobilization.	
	16-10-19		Lieut. N. Coombs left the Battalion for demobilization.	
	19-10-19		Fifty other ranks under Capt. B.V. Knight & Lieut. E.P. Perry took part in celebrations at LILLE on the occasion of the first anniversary of the deliverance of the town. The troops were afterwards entertained to luncheon by the Maire of LILLE.	
	20-10-19		Lieut. Col. A.H. Batchpool returned from leave, also Lieut. Livingstone.	
	21-10-19		Major S. King proceeded on Special Leave to U.K. & Capt. J.H. James M.C. proceeded on leave to U.K.	
	22-10-19		Lieut. A.W.A. INNELL proceeded for demobilization.	
	23-10-19		Brig. Gen. Maxse, D.S.O. visited the Battalion.	
	25-10-19		Lieut. L. Giles rejoined the Battn. from leave to U.K.	
	26-10-19		Lieut. L. Giles proceeded for demobilization	
	29-10-19		Lieut. A.R. Bevan proceeded on leave to U.K.	
	31-10-19		Capt. J.R. Hamilton proceeded on leave to U.K.	

A.H. Batchpool
LIEUT. COL.
COMMANDING 13th BN. MIDDLESEX REGT.

Army Form C. 2118.

WAR DIARY
or
INTELLIGENCE SUMMARY.
(Erase heading not required.)

Instructions regarding War Diaries and Intelligence Summaries are contained in F. S. Regs. Part II. and the Staff Manual respectively. Title pages will be prepared in manuscript.

Place	Date	Hour	Summary of Events and Information	Remarks and references to Appendices
TARDEGHEM	1-11-19		The S.O. visited different Headquarters with reference to the forthcoming move of the Battalion to Boulogne. Instructions of embarkation issued, all Officers were warned from leave.	
	2-11-19		Telegrams sent recalling men from leave	
	3-11-19		Lieut. J. M. James M.C. Lieut. E. B. Hopkinson and Capt. J.W. L. Hamilton M.C. returned from leave.	
	4-11-19		Major S. King returned from leave	
	5-11-19		Lieut. T. E. Jones proceeded for demobilization	
	10-11-19		Orders received for proceeding to BOULOGNE for making up Batts. moved to BAVINCHOVE and entrained their for BOULOGNE	
	11-11-19		Battalion arrived at TURLINGTON SIDINGS detrained and marched via BOULOGNE to No. 4 REST CAMP, HENRIVILLE where the Battalion is accommodated	
	14-11-19		The W.O. and Sergts. gave a dinner to the officers.	
No. 4 REST	15-11-19		Capt. J.W.L. Hamilton proceeded for demobilisation. Forty seven other ranks proceeded for demobilisation	
CAMP BOULOGNE	16-11-19		Lieut. E. B. Hopkinson M.C., Lieut. J.W.L. Brown and 50 other ranks proceeded for demobilization	
	17-11-19		Lieut. G. Hopkinson, 2/Lieut. E. H. Blagg and 123 other ranks proceeded for demobilization	
	18-11-19		Lieut. J. M. James M.C. Lieut. E. A. Terry and 6 other ranks proceeded for demobilization	
	19-11-19		Twenty other ranks proceeded for demobilization the 13th Bn. Middlesex Regt. was disbanded	

[signature] LIEUT. COL.
COMMANDING 13th Bn. MIDDLESEX REGT.

www.ingramcontent.com/pod-product-compliance
Lightning Source LLC
Chambersburg PA
CBHW080922230426

43668CB00014B/2180